YOUR TEENAGER

YOUR TEENAGER

Thinking About Your Child
During the Secondary School Years

Martha Harris

Published for
The Harris Meltzer Trust
by

KARNAC

Published in 2007 by
Karnac Books Ltd
118 Finchley Road
London NW3 5HT

British Library Cataloguing in Publication Data

A C.I.P. for this book is available from the British Library

ISBN: 978-1-85575-408-9

Edited, designed, and produced by The Studio Publishing Services Ltd
www.publishingservicesuk.co.uk
e-mail: studio@publishingservicesuk.co.uk

Printed in Great Britain

www.harris-meltzer-trust.org.uk

www.karnacbooks.com

CONTENTS

films and TV. Unresolved feelings in parents. Protection against sex crimes and sexual promiscuity.

ABOUT THE AUTHOR

Martha Harris (1919–1987) read English at University College London, and then Psychology at Oxford. She taught in a Froebel Teacher Training College and was trained as a psychologist at Guy's Hospital, as a child psychotherapist at the Tavistock Clinic, where she was for many years responsible for the child psychotherapy training in the Department of Children and Families, and as a psychoanalyst at the British Institute of Psychoanalysis. Together with her husband, Roland Harris (a teacher), she started a pioneering schools' counselling service. With Donald Meltzer, whom she married after Harris died, she wrote *A Psychoanalytical Model of The Child-in-the-Family-in-the-Community* (1976, 1994) for multidisciplinary use in schools and therapeutic units, and taught widely in Europe, North and South America and India. Her books have been published in many languages and include *Thinking about Infants and Young Children* (1975) and *Your Eleven-year-old, Your Twelve-to-fourteen year old*, and *Your Teenager* (1969, reprinted in this volume). her papers are collected in *Collected Papers of Martha Harris and Esther Bick* (1987).

For a biography of Martha Harris see www.harris-meltzer-trust.org.uk.

The three books here collected in one volume were first published in 1969 as part of a complete year-by-year series on child development written by therapists from the Tavistock Clinic.[1] The purpose of the series was to describe for parents the normal features and problems encountered in bringing up children from birth onwards. Martha Harris was unusually well qualified to write the books on the secondary school years, owing to her experience and training as teacher, teacher-trainer, psychoanalyst, and her position as head of the training of child psychotherapists in the Child and Family unit at the Tavistock for many years. She also co-operated with her husband Roland Harris—head of an inner-city comprehensive school—in pioneering a schools' counselling service; and in addition to her direct professional experience she had teenage children at the time of writing these books.[2]

Martha Harris's specialist professional knowledge from the therapeutic and educational fields is applied with a light touch to particularize her description of the emotional stresses undergone by children and parents in these adolescent years. These stresses, with their mingled joy and pain, are given a local habitation and a name. Clinical jargon is absent; instead, the language of everyday life is delivered with an elegance of style that bears witness to her literary education and well-honed communication skills. This language is deceptively simple in appearance, yet, as in all classical literature, each successive reading reveals a new profundity. The author was one of those who could "tell the truth but tell it slant":[3] the truth penetrates all the more effectively for being delivered at a slight angle.

The books offer practical guidance in all the compartments of school and family life—friends, brothers and sisters, studies, leisure interests, together with the problem areas of harmful or antisocial behaviour. These are set in the context of the mental and physical development of children in these growth-spurt years. In particular, parents are helped to consider imaginatively the impact of the teenager's life at school, where most of their time is spent, yet which can frequently be a closed book to parents once their child has moved on from primary education.

Despite the inevitable social changes that have occurred since these books were written (in particular those deriving from the electronic revolution), it is noteworthy how little the fundamental preoccupations have changed from those of forty years ago—including the problem areas of teenage promiscuity, drugs, or smoking and drink, "dropping out", etc. Also, the 1960s were, in many ways, an enlightened and innovative era in educational terms—extending the years in education, bringing in more parent–school and community involvement—mirroring the implicit changes in principles of child-rearing. The dual function of education as encouraging personality development and equipping the next generation with life-skills and qualifications became officially acknowledged. The struggle to provide such an education over the spectrum of a socially and culturally diverse society is far from achieving resolution.

The general picture is illustrated by examples of particular children with particular problems and individual characters. The author points out, however, that the function of such examples is less for parents to compare their own child (who may appear completely different) than for them to find a way of *thinking about* their own child's conflicts and difficulties. Her method of exegesis reinforces this point. It puts the spotlight on the self-education of parents during these turbulent years, and suggests how an active *interest* In their child has its own therapeutic value for both children and parents. Rather than fall victim to dismay or complacency, parents can make use of the contradictory feelings and anxieties aroused by their child who is growing out of childhood and into adulthood, in order to enrich their own lives and experience—to enliven their own perceptions and perhaps also their own relationships. She writes, "If we as parents think of rescuing our teenager from his sea of troubles [*Hamlet*] we have to get wet ourselves' (Book Three, p. 166). For the single most effective tool in helping a child to pull through adolescence is his or her identification with parental figures who are themselves still developing—whose minds are not closed in the various forms of premature stability.

Martha Harris reminds us that the distinction between work and play is one invented by adults; it would be incomprehensible to the small child, and remains incomprehensible to the developing inner self of adult or teenager. Parents, however grinding their daily routine may be, have the opportunity to renew contact with their own inner spirit of growth and development, thereby at the same time fostering that of their child. For the parental function, she writes, is "not so much to be reasonable or rational; it is to engender or discover a situation where reason can operate" (Book Three, p. 166).

Meg Harris Williams
March 2007

Editorial note: Some endnotes have been added, with minor emendations in square brackets, where social changes seem to impinge. In terms of style, the traditional use of "he" as shorthand for "he or she" has been retained throughout as more elegant and economical even if less politically correct.

Notes

1. Although out of print in this country for many years they have remained in print in foreign translations.
2. Some of the fruits of this co-operation may be seen in the psychosociological study "The child in the family in the community", which was

written with the psychoanalyst Donald Meltzer, whom she married after the death of Roland Harris. See Appendix II.

3. As cited from Emily Dickinson by Donald Meltzer in his preface to Martha Harris's *Collected Papers* (Clunie Press 1988, p. viii).

BOOK ONE
YOUR ELEVEN-YEAR-OLD

Introduction

This book does not aim to tell you how your eleven-year-old ought to be and how he should behave. It will not give a comprehensive guide to this age; for children develop very differently and at different rates in their bodies, their intellect, and their feelings. Rather, it says some general things about children around eleven that stem from observing a number of children but that will not apply to all. Because generalities are dull, and because you will be thinking about your child and his brothers and sisters and friends, I have in one or two instances talked about a few children in slightly greater detail to illustrate the way one would set about trying to get a picture of their situation and of their development.

The idea is to encourage you—if indeed you need encouraging—to value your unique experience of observing and getting to know your own child as he continues to develop. If you are *really* thinking about him there are almost certain to be times when you will be puzzled and times when you worry. Knowing a little more about how children tend to be at his age will not take away the need to puzzle and to worry a little; that is a parent's work and pleasure. But other people's thinking about other children may be of some help in the way that you think about your own.

We can seldom afford to sit back and feel that our child is growing up smoothly and satisfactorily without any heart-searching on our part. A well-known novelist, in her autobiography some years ago, said that her daughter just happened to grow up beautifully, like a flower, without needing any attention. But those of us who are gardeners know that few flowers, alas, will survive this treatment. Human growth takes place partly by process of maturation over which we have no control, but also as a result of trying, struggling, worrying, and enjoying; through hating and loving, through recognizing differences and trying to reconcile them.

Talking to others, most especially to our own children and to our marriage partner, helps us as parents to notice the special qualities and the strivings that form our own children's personalities. By noticing them we help our children to be more aware of them and to use them better; we also add to our own growth and wisdom as parents.

Some parents who read this little book may be worried about special problems with their eleven-year-old. There can be no definite solutions to these. Instead, I would suggest that you first talk together with your child, and then maybe your child's teacher, or family doctor if you have that kind of relationship, to see whether this results in your feeling a little more hopeful. But if you are still worried—and it is better to be worried if you really think there is something to be worried about than to try to pretend that everything is fine—it is a good idea to try to find your way through school or doctor to a professional specialist in problems of children and parents.

CHAPTER ONE

The eleven-year-old and school

Starting secondary school

I t will be in their eleventh year that most of our children go to secondary school for the first time. It is a very important year for them—very exciting, and perhaps rather frightening too. Generally, the local secondary school will co-operate with the junior school by inviting the new first years over to see the school while they are still safely at home in their familiar junior school environment; and sometimes the junior school will welcome some senior pupils as visitors for a day to talk with the new pupils-to-be, and to tell them all about life in the big world of the secondary school. Such early and friendly contacts are much to be desired.

But whatever the school is trying to do to help preserve some sort of continuity for the children, there is still a radical change to which the eleven-year-old has to accommodate. The new school is a big world indeed—sometimes quite literally, especially in the typical comprehensive school. It is an Alice-in-Wonderland process: in the last year of junior school the child has been the big girl or boy, cock o' the walk; and now, all of a sudden, he is a little shrimp in a big pool, and will doubtless find some severe second year pupils to tell him so if he forgets it. Of course, he went through a similar experience some years ago when he first left his mum at the school gate; but then it was quite permissible to burst into tears, or, if it was not permissible, he did not care so much; but now he is eleven this is no longer the sort of thing any self-respecting young man can do, and in any case there is a rather exciting and pleasant side about being grown up, something to be proud of. So he is very mixed up, but because he is going in the grown-up direction it is much better for him and for his status among his future pals if his mother will leave him to go to school on his own, or at least disappear at a reasonably discreet distance from the gate.

Mother and father can help the child a great deal by their attitude before the change is made. It seems to be a question of striking the right balance between assurance and anxiety. Teachers are obliged to behave a little like strict nurses and pretend there is nothing to fuss about—but then coming to school is an ordinary part of the everyday world for them; and if they gave the least encouragement to thirty new pupils in their class to become upset and temperamental they would have a lot of trouble on their hands. Underneath they probably sympathize, however, and later on, as things settle in to the new term, they get to know their pupils as individuals. Parents, while they want their child to adapt bravely to the new strain, can afford—at least in private—to be more understanding. If they seem too calm and pretend the whole occasion is just ordinary run-of-the-mill, they are in a sense robbing the child of a real experience—the experience of meeting a challenge. If they get too upset and anxious, they offload all their worries on to the child. Either way the day is spoilt from the beginning. Most parents manage very well to be excited along with their child but at the same time to carry the worrying part of the excitement themselves, so that he is free to be adventurous and to succeed.

They can help in all manner of practical ways. Usually there will be another child from the neighbourhood, perhaps several, going to the same school; going together is a great morale-booster. Assuming all the paraphernalia for the new scholarly status helps too—the new uniform in which, for a while at any rate, pride will be taken; the new books, geometry sets, and so on. For a while, after the first day, the child will still be under considerable strain, especially if he knows few or none of the other children in his class. New alliances have to be made, and tested out. One must not be too surprised, nor even for that matter too sympathetic, if the new boy comes home one day with a bloody nose, nor too angry if his new fountain pen has been trodden on; a certain matter-of-factness helps. It is only if the feeling persists that a child is being bullied, or that he is remaining isolated from other children and not forming any friendships, that serious notice has to be taken; and the clear first step is to consult the form-teacher about things. This is not a step to take, even then, with a sound of trumpets and drums—for one thing, the child may not wish attention drawn to him. Parents and teacher together, and working together, can help the child in difficulties; if they are at odds the child is at the mercy of circumstances.

First weeks

The child has other strenuous adjustments to make, as well as those to his peers. He has to suffer the fate of all first-year pupils—to be mocked by the second-year children; to be the one who does not know any more about the school than the new teachers know; to find the highly pompous sixth-formers and prefects issuing incomprehensible orders and rebukes; to feel hurt by the apparently callous way in which the teachers, instead of taking his side in some noisy quarrel, act with Olympian impartiality and punish him and his rival equally. Furthermore, whereas in the junior school he had at last learned to cope with the sharing of one adult among many children—because the one adult was with them for most of each day—he will often, in the secondary school, have to share eight or ten adults, the teachers taking various subjects. And what is more, they will sometimes seem more interested in the subjects they teach and in his skill at these subjects than they are in him personally. It is all very cold and abstract—and very demanding too. After all, he did not choose to do all these difficult tasks. And then, to cap it all, these eight or ten demanding adults behave with extraordinary predictability—one is very strict and will not let him say a word; another is annoyed if he is not always asking questions. One says "I don't mind if the answer is wrong, as long as you understand the working"; but another says "Nought out of ten again! You must learn to be accurate at your age". He works for two solid hours at a piece of homework and is given three marks; another teacher gives him ten for ten minutes' work. It is all very confusing—at times very unfair, or so he feels.

The stresses can be just as great for the clever child as for the less clever—sometimes greater, for being clever is a trait he has to keep up, and it does not necessarily endear him to his mates.

Let us consider a little the child who has done well and who is passing from primary to secondary education with a good scholastic record behind him. He may be, and we hope that he will be, a child who enjoys school, who gets some pleasure from learning, from the work that he is doing, despite all the bore and trouble of having to do it regularly when he might prefer to be doing something else. Competition with others in the class, as with others in his family at home, is likely to be part of his motivation to work; he would not be human if it were not. Capacity to work creatively, to enjoy studying, is only possible, however, when the competitive element is not too strong, and the most competitive children are not always those who show it most openly.

The strains of competition and refusal to go to school

Here is an example where these things were connected. Edward, aged eleven, had just passed out of his junior school with flying colours and was at the end of his first term at secondary school where, admittedly, he was not top of the class, but was holding his own very well. He took his homework seriously and spent much longer on it than the time prescribed, because he was determined to get it word perfect. The school thought he had settled in and was doing well, but his mother noticed that he was getting anxious and strained and did not seem to have made any new friends.

He began to have restless nights and bad dreams, as he had done when he first went to his infant school. He became particularly touchy with his parents, felt oppressed and sulky if he was asked to do the slightest little thing, and retreated into gloom. He had a violent outburst of rage one day at the tea-table when his mother served his younger sister before him. When she rebuked him he burst out bitterly that he counted for nothing in this family—either his sister got served first because she was the baby or his dad got served first because he was the boss.

During that same week he woke up from a terrible nightmare. His father, who went in to see why he was shouting, learned of the dream. Edward said he had dreamed of a writer, a conceited man who had spent years building a tall monument to celebrate himself. The town council did not approve, and decided to send the mayor along with a gang to demolish it. The writer resisted, but the mayor did not listen and broke up the monument, which upset the man very much. But still he did not give up, and during the night he went back to the place where the monument had been, in order to salvage some of the rubble and make a small one for himself. On his way there he was caught by one of the mayor's spies, bound and thrown into prison, where he could not move.

Edward then said that he knew he had been shouting in his sleep, but he could not wake up. Finally he had ed what he had been shouting: it was his own name, "Edward!", and he woke up thinking that he himself was the man in prison.

The next day he had a cold and a temperature and his parents kept him at home. The day after that he was well enough to go to school, but he did not want to. Then came the weekend, and on the Monday morning he stated that he hated school and he was not going back. He shut himself in his room. His parents conferred together and recalled the similar trouble in the first term at infant school. They wondered about the nightmare of which he had told them when he was barely half awake, and they felt that the school now seemed to him not so much a real place as the prison of the dream.

His father decided to have a talk with him and show that he sympathized with the way he was feeling and possibly find out why the child felt this way. Edward could not tell him anything, so his father said he would take him to school the next day, and his mother would meet him at the gate when school ended. Edward protested strongly, but he went, and on the following day as well— but this time he said sourly that he did not need his mum to meet him, that made him look too much of a fool. Thus, with a little sympathy and firmness, Edward managed to get back to his studies and the crisis passed.

One would need to know more of Edward to be able to sort out the complex meaning of his nightmare, but when put in context it does throw some light on his bad temper and his fear of school. One could see his "big-headed writer" as an ambitious, omnipotent aspect of himself, whose hard work and school success was used as a monument to his own vainglory—the infant school where he was teacher's pet and cock o' the walk. The new and large school, where he is no longer unchallenged and supreme, brings in the town council, mayor, and gang to demolish that monument—the Head and teachers and other threatening clever boys who put him in his place. This makes him go back to earlier baby behaviour at home— squabbling with his little sister. In the dream he attempts to take some of the bits of the shattered monument to make one on a smaller scale—as if to say that if he cannot be dad or bigger than dad, he will try to write himself a part as the special baby. But that means going back to helplessness, to the prison of not knowing anything, the fear of even forgetting your own name . . . and so the terror of feeling lost at school and deprived of identity.

His father intuitively felt the quality and seriousness of Edward's fear of school, of losing himself, and hit upon the right way to help him back to the place that had become for him a prison, peopled by forces that were antagonistic to his "big-headedness" and waiting to reduce him to nothing. Taking him firmly but kindly to face the real place—before his terror grew more established and his confidence ebbed further—prevented a more chronic school refusal setting in. This firmness and strength in his father, moreover, also served as something of a check on the "big-headed writer" in him, and showed him that the alternative to supremacy is not always complete subjection.

Learning and competition

Not all children are successful at school in the sense of being scholastically clever. But all children can be successful in competition with themselves. They are helped in this by the very fact that, as they mature, their skills and their social assets increase—they are swimming with the tide. The wise parent and school does not therefore envisage a child as engaged in a competition, but as involved in a system of growth. All normal children want this growth, even though every now and then they become little children again and seem to want to do infantile things. It is because they want to grow that the teacher can hope to manage his large class: they know, and he knows, that despite their occasional resentments, he is trying to give them knowledge and skills and that through acquiring these they acquire also the confidence to become adult. We do not, as parents, have to deceive the child about his own level of achievement; rather we need to help him raise it in his own terms and according to his real capacities.

Comparison with others

The child is rarely deceived about his own abilities in relation to other children. He can usually guess fairly shrewdly that he is better than most at maths, or worse than most, or about average. And he can usually know whether this achievement is his proper level, or whether it is artificially high, or low because he has not been trying his best. Ask your eleven-year-old "Who is going to come top at French?", or whatever, and the reply will be "Oh, Susanna will be top—everyone knows that", said in a matter-of-fact tone, just as she might say "Susanna is taller than me". If Susanna is beaten this may give special pleasure to the victor! Or she might reply to the question "Is Susanna very clever then?" with "Oh yes, she's clever all right, but she's a real twit". The sour grapes is not serious, however, and the realistic judgement is just what it seems. It is mostly if we as parents cannot accept the realism (our Gill not as clever as Susan!) that it takes on emotional overtones of stress for Gill. Then, if we are not careful, a real failure sequence can set in: failure can lead to further failure, and in extreme cases the child has to resort to the "I don't care anyway" gesture that is the expression of, or the attempt to hide, a serious depression.

Competing with oneself

To accept a realistic level of aspiration is not the same thing as giving up. The child—particularly the active, aggressive child of eleven—never wants to sit still, mentally or physically. There is a sort of leapfrog effect in the way he develops in learning: having succeeded in a task, say in solving a maths problem, he wants to try another and then a more difficult one. He does this, manages it, feels good, and so tries still more. He becomes, in short, involved in his own progress. We can help the teacher with this leapfrogging in several ways. One is by direct guidance in the actual work—going along with the child in doing the homework; this is especially encouraging to him when he is able to show *you* what to do! But this sort of guidance can be overdone and may even interfere with the child's learning, both in holding up his independent grappling with a difficulty and in cutting across a method of work the teacher may be using. It is like teaching someone to ride a bike—there comes a moment when we have to give a push and let go.

When to help

Another way is by helping only when asked to do so by the child and in accordance with what he wants to know. Tom, for example, wanted to find out what the sign x meant in a sum he was stuck with. He insisted on his mother being the one to tell him. She was busy bathing the baby, but dried her hands, came downstairs, told him that x meant, as it happened, "the unknown quantity", and went off again to her tasks. Tom's father remonstrated, "But Tom, I could have told you about x." "Yes," said Tom, "I know, but you would have started by saying 'Well, let's work through the chapter and find out for ourselves . . .'." When the child is involved in the work he wants to get on with it. When he is at a standstill, then is the time to "work through the chapter" with him.

Collecting information

A very common difficulty eleven-year-olds have is with reference books. For one thing, they are usually great collectors and enjoy the big encyclopaedia with its random assortment of facts just like the contents of their pockets; for another, their teachers often ask them to use reference books in doing their homework. But unless the school librarian has taught them (and not all schools have a librarian or an adequate library) they often have difficulty in finding their way about the index; a little practice with parents gives them this skill.[1] It is like suddenly finding out when learning to swim just how to co-ordinate legs and arms—after that you can get along faster on your own.

Being involved, which was mentioned above, really means paying attention. Acquiring skills and knowledge demands long sustained attention, but none of us can attend consistently to demanding tasks for overlong periods. We learn fast at first, then come to a block or a levelling out before we start upwards again. When a child has come to such a block, then a change of task is a help—it is not just a distraction which might hinder learning, it is a chance for what has been learnt to be digested. Most children seem to find music, radio, even television, not necessarily a distraction. Parents who keep their child's nose to the grindstone may be doing as little good as parents who yield to his every desire to be released from work.

Parents' attitudes

We attend to work best, and therefore learn, when we are interested; and our eleven-year-olds get interested basically not through external rewards and punishments but through identifying with their parents, friends, and teachers. The child's use of language, his curiosity about what is going on in the world, his ways of thinking and judging, his attitudes towards other people and groups, are strongly influenced by what he experiences all round him. His actions and interests are reflections or rejections of our own; and whatever attempts to provide "equal opportunities" the school system may try to create, the central opportunity for learning is the one provided by the home environment, and by the open-minded interests of the parents. These are things in which the growing child can increasingly participate. This indirect way of helping is, perhaps, the most important contribution that parents can make to the education of their child.

School discipline

School is an institution, and therefore has rules. Ideally, the rules are intended to help everyone benefit from the community, but to the new eleven-year-old some of them will seem to be arbitrary and bewildering. Most, in fact, will be based on sensible ideas—whether of physical safety, or convenience—of social training in courtesy. Some may be merely matters of fashion; some may be relics from a local tradition. Not much sympathy needs to be wasted on the eleven-year-old's grumbles about rule-discipline; institutions change faster than their rules, and children soon learn which rules are only paper tigers and which have a real bite. Rules also have the function, especially when they are, perhaps, a little unreasonable, of providing a justified target for resentment. Rules can sustain without harm much of the hostility that would otherwise be directed against people. Rules are also status-markers; the child who knows the rules and how to use them really belongs; and in a curious way the very illogicality of some of them offers a useful training in democratic government and exercises the natural reformist as well as conformist tendencies in children.

This non-purist attitude to rules does not of course imply that really bad rules ought not to be acknowledged as bad and changed where possible, nor that really important ones, even if resented, ought not to be supported by parent as well as child. For example, smoking is usually forbidden at school. Since the child wants to appear adult, parents unwittingly encourage children to break this rule when they smoke themselves. Children will stop smoking, one imagines, when they judge that adults are foolish for continuing to smoke, not when adults judge them foolish for starting.

There may well be much pressure on a child, especially a boy, to start to smoke—pressure from his gang. His starting is not then his own decision, and he may even welcome a strict prohibition from his parents that might at least be operative until he is ready to make a decision for himself. Children of eleven are frightened of total self-responsibility, as well as longing for it. They want to be controlled at times, to feel that their parents care enough about their welfare to protect it while they can, even at the expense of being unpopular.

Note

1.   These days, of course, this also entails internet skills.

CHAPTER TWO

Hobbies and interests

There are always differences between children—some are ready to read, for instance, much earlier than others; some mature physically much earlier than others, and so on. Every individual child has to be considered individually, and especially so by those who know him best—his parents. But generally it may still be true to say that the age of eleven or thereabouts is the end of childhood. It leads to the beginning of puberty and is the entry into adolescence.

This change, and protection against this change, is marked in all sorts of ways, not only in fundamental things such as physical development, but in childhood pastimes and hobbies also.

Collecting

Collecting is one example of these. Later on, collecting may develop into a more rational procedure—that is, it may be a way of making profits, or of organizing knowledge, or acquiring a reputation as an expert in this or that. At eleven years, however, it seems to be a process undertaken almost for its own sake. Mothers despair on finding Johnny's pockets stuffed with all sorts of "rubbish"—coloured pebbles, bus tickets, pencil stubs, a foreign coin, a sea-shell and much else. And if he has a room of his own there will probably be stamp albums, drawers with dead insects, notebooks filled with train numbers [lists and classifications of all kinds].

Before it is all swept away, however, it is worth remembering that for Johnny it may have a meaning. Perhaps it is a way of holding on to the fragments of childhood experience, tokens with which to venture forward into the next uncertain stage of growth—just as we adults "shore up our ruins" with our fragments of art, literature, science, and our other cultural tokens. The child of eleven who has been, and still is, in the process of being rigorously trained into becoming a social animal may well decide to cling on to the treasures of his own cave, which he will not give away and which nobody must touch. Nothing seems to cause more irritation to him than to have his things "tidied up". At the same time, the child is able to use the collecting habit as a way not to isolation but to making contacts—he will swap comics [football cards, friendship bangles], and find some special friends and fellow-enthusiasts through his hobby. The hobby becomes a means of making important emotional contacts, and even of earning status within the group.

The keeping of pets

The keeping of pets is a special form of game. For the child it offers the great advantage of permitting an expression of tenderness and sympathy that the school environment and rivalry may (especially in the boy) tend to exclude as unmanly and soppy. For a lonely child, too, the uncomplaining and uncritical pet rabbit, or dog, or pigeon is always a comforting listener, and a certain privacy must be allowed the child and his pet. It can, of course, be a sign of human loneliness when the child restricts himself overmuch to reliance upon his pets for his solace and companionship, but more often than not he will find in them only the temporary retreat that he needs. He will also learn—through caring for them—a great deal about responsibility, about the true and unsentimental relationship that allows an animal to be itself and not simply an extension of his own needs.

Games

All childhood games have aspects that are significant in emotional and social development. Some games allow for the working out of aggression: games such as chess, for example, which is an assassination game (the king is dead!) permit the expression of the most deliberate and planned violence in socially acceptable and emotionally safe ways. And it may even develop into a form of art. In team games of the more organized type, the safe, if more physical, component of aggression is more obvious—football and hockey render harmless the nasty aspects of aggression by adding the social insulation of team spirit and loyalty. Such games are often particularly important to the eleven-year-old, who may have found some aspects of school competition less satisfying—who does not, perhaps, always thrive on lessons and examinations in academic subjects. In organized games he is at no disadvantage, not because they require fewer brains but because they call out in him the full attention, the loss of self-consciousness, that brings success.

So, this is an age when children tend to involve themselves enthusiastically in school games, partly as a flight from the responsibility that comes, and is expected, with adolescence. Clumsy bodies can sometimes perform beautifully when concentrating upon games.

Games and character

We are all familiar with the platitude that games form your character and, like all platitudes, it contains some truth, although it can be pushed to the point of absurdity. Let us consider an example that demonstrates a little of the truth in such a maxim.

Mark is a boy who is now nearly twelve years old, and is at the end of his first year in a comprehensive school. He has two sisters who are very close to him in age. He never seemed to get over the jealousy and resentment that he felt when they were born—jealousy that he showed at first by attempting to ignore them completely rather than protesting outwardly. As they, and he, grew older, this jealousy showed itself by his continually interfering with their activities. He bossed and controlled them, and seldom allowed them to be alone with their mother. He was so occupied in seeing that they did not get anything that he did not get first that he never really made any friends of his own to bring home or to go off and play with at the weekend. He was growing up to be a strong, tall, hefty lad, and his clinging to his sisters and to his mother's apron-strings began to seem a little absurd and also a little shameful.

In his new school there is a much more organized games programme than there had been in the junior school. Mark, who is naturally good at football, found himself one of the star players of his year and was drafted very willingly into regular fixtures at the weekend. In the course of this first year at the secondary school he has become intensely involved in his team, in his games, in the same kind of fashion that he was involved earlier with his mother. One can see in him the same straining to be the star, to be acclaimed for getting the goals, as he had exhibited in straining to be the favourite child, the centre of his mother's attention. Yet, in order to be a member of a football team and to have the chance to shine, he has had to subordinate, to some extent, his desire to be always first—to hold on to the ball, as it were. He has had to learn to pass it on, to fit in with others for the good of his side. He has had to learn to control his jealousy when another member of the team shines, if he is not to be called a bad team-player by the others.

This does not mean that a total transformation has been wrought in Mark's character; human nature does not change so easily. But he has the opportunity to play out the rivalry he had with his sisters in a wider field among his equals in age, where the same rules apply to all.

Of course, many another eleven-year-old in Mark's situation might not have managed to use the games field in this way. Had he not some degree of talent, he might have been confirmed in his home-tied wrangling with the younger children. There was also an important incentive in his case. His father was very keen on following football and had been a good player in his own youth. This strengthened the bond between them and, in identifying himself with his father as a footballer, Mark had less need to cling to his mother.

Enthusiasms

Children can become involved in crazes at most ages. The form these take varies at different ages and from child to child. With adolescents the craze is most often another boy or girl—sometimes a teacher, a film star, a pop singer. These, too, can be objects of devotion to the eleven-year-old. There is a great attraction in being "crazy" about someone, in being taken out of yourself in company with others of your own generation away from the family. In the case of bands and pop groups the craze is catching, a group phenomenon. Part of the fun is losing your head, losing your identity, shouting and crying and yearning with the rest. It is similar to a crowd at an adult football match, except that with a crowd of young pop-star fans there is no enemy side to quarrel with: they are one in adoring their idols, vying only in extravagance of expression.

But a craze can also be a very individual matter, and if pursued persistently can entail a great deal of planning and thought and collecting of material. Children can develop greatly through following their enthusiasms. Take the example of Anne, who, before she was eleven years old, had developed an obsession about horses and learning to ride. One summer holiday by the seaside she had invented two imaginary horses, Mayflower and Maypole, who accompanied her everywhere—at mealtimes, bedtime, galloping along the beach. She seemed to forget about them after the holiday.

Shortly before her eleventh birthday she began to pester her mother for riding lessons as a birthday present. Her mother turned a deaf ear, thinking that riding lessons seemed an unnecessary expense and that a passion for horses in a little girl who lived in a big city was not to be encouraged. Undeterred, Anne became friendly with another girl who was having riding lessons, went with her to her riding school, and managed to get a riding lesson or two with pocket money and birthday money that she had saved. She got a few more lessons free in return for mucking out the stables and for helping take the small children on pony-rides.

In the meantime she was reading every horse book that she could lay her hands on, including every horse story written especially for little girls, and exhausting the selection in her local library. She then conceived the idea of writing a horse book of her own, sending it to a publisher and buying a horse with the proceeds. For weeks and weeks she wrote every night in a series of exercise books. Hitherto she had been sharp and quick at her schoolwork, but careless and impatient. She tended to give up if an answer did not come right at the first attempt. So her parents were astonished; and her father tried to warn her, gently, that it was not so easy to get a story accepted—such things as grammar, punctuation, and legibility mattered if you really wanted to get anyone to read what you had written. Just occasionally Anne would allow him to look at what she had written, and though she would sulk at his attempts at helpful criticism she nevertheless paid some attention and tried to modify her work. She listened more acutely to the conversation of the grown-ups and of her older sister, and would say suddenly, "That's a good word—I'll have it in my story." The story became voluminous and rambling and filled several exercise books.

Finally, she decided that it would need to be typed if a publisher was to consider it seriously. In the past she had played with her father's typewriter, but now she set about learning to type in earnest. When the story was finished her twelfth birthday had passed. She sent her manuscript to the publisher of her favourite paperback horse books—hopefully. Her parents had warned her not to be too disappointed. It was returned, of course, but with a very nice, friendly letter encouraging her to go on writing. This did very little to soften the immediate heartbreak, but after a week she took the letter out again and went to her mother with it. "You think she really means what she says—that I've got talent? She's not just trying to be nice because I wrote it when I was eleven?" And then, later on, she added, "I didn't really believe they would publish my book, but I couldn't let myself think that, or else I would never have finished it."

The pleasure of reading

In the Second World War it was found that about seven per cent of the recruits to the Army were illiterate—they could not read in any sense that mattered. In 1968 figures as high as one million were given for illiteracy [and this is an ongoing social problem]. This came as something of a shock—and not only for teachers. We some-times try to pretend that it does not matter, given the new technologies that might appear to replace reading, but as is acknowledged by all educationalists, reading is still the major technical skill we expect our children to acquire in their schooldays, and we know that without it not only will they lose many chances and choices of career, but they will probably lose self-respect, enjoyment, and independence too.

It is actually amazing that the illiteracy figures are so small. For, after speech, reading is one of the most complex achievements of the child. Yet the great majority, clever or not so clever, manage to be quite proficient at it. That this is so is a tribute not only to teachers and children, but also to public policy that provides attractive libraries and, above all, to the parents who assist the younger child through the strain of mastering a difficult skill in which success and failure are highly charged with emotion.[1]

If a child, at eleven, is still having so much difficulty with reading that he can find no enjoyment in it at all, there is need for some specialist help, possibly of a purely technical sort, which can diagnose what are the physical difficulties with which the child is trying to cope, and what are the faulty methods and habits that are hindering him. It is not unusual for parents of a child at this age to feel very anxious and guilty at their child's backwardness, and they, too, will need friendly advice on how to weather the emotional stresses that will accrue as the child is given help. For a long experience of failure is a hard pattern to break, and can lead to rejection, depression, and delinquency. This is hardly likely to be a new problem for the eleven-year-old, for it will have become visible during his time at primary school; but it can be felt again keenly with the transfer to secondary school, where the teachers will expect a certain standard of skill on which new learning can be based. Most schools do have special needs teachers to help with this, but not all are so fortunate, and it often happens that in a way the child whose skills are severely inadequate is better off than one who is a little behind but not so far that special teaching has to be found for him. He has to sink or swim for himself. There is one advantage in the change to the secondary school even in these cases. It offers an opportunity to make a new start. Parents who are too agitated or too busy to help their child themselves can try to engage someone to come along, say, once or twice a week to coach him. The teachers at school may be able to recommend someone. Where this really cannot be afforded, there is sometimes an older brother or sister or another older child who may be able to help, and whose help may be accepted, especially if it is not all one-sided: the non-reader is not necessarily unskilled in other ways and could "pay his way" by helping his friend make a go-kart or a music recording [or offer technical help with some other project or construction].

These are special cases, but children and parents in happier situations are not without worries. Many of the worries are unnecessary. The normally placed child of eleven is no longer at the stage where he wants to learn to read as such; what he wants is to get some value out of it. So, whenever we provide books that might catch his eye and interest, we can hope that at least he will try them out. These will often be books about his own hobby—building radio sets, horse riding, or art and craft work; or they may be stories. Most children find a favourite author: then they read every book by that author, and although to the adult reader all the stories seem the same, the child never tires until the whole lot have been devoured. Adults have to suspend their finicky judgement about the "goodness" or "badness" of books, and let the child have his head. Fortunately, modern libraries are very sophisticated in the likes and dislikes of children and can often cunningly recommend, for a trial, a book with the right kind of storyline to appeal to a child and a sufficiently high standard of writing to satisfy the sternest critic. Where parents use the facilities of the local library, their children usually will too.

It is the same with comics and magazines. They cater, as they always have done, for the most blatant indulgence in fantasy and the most extravagant and unrealistic powers on the part of the hero or heroine. Usually the villains are such obviously undesirable characters that it is permissible, without strong feelings of guilt, to inflict a terrible doom upon them.

Parents still have to decide for themselves whether there are some comics, or books for that matter, which they have to bar their children from reading; for that matter, there has always been plenty of unhealthy and sadistic material in children's reading and entertainment.[2] However, to have to make that decision is a happy state to be in, for it means that at least the child can read. Sooner or later he will decide for himself what he is to read, and how to use his skill. Generally, it will seem inconceivable to the child that he should ever want to abandon his favourite magazines—he just does not believe the adult who says he will "grow out of it". But he does grow out of it in the ordinary course of development, and one day the comics are not bought, although that is not usually at eleven.

Television

Television is, on the whole, a stimulus to reading. You cannot take the television under the bedclothes. Television has its own quite peculiar contribution to make to the education and experience of the child, with its pictorial nature and the immediacy of real events. Because it is such a public medium, it is relatively free from the more difficult moral and other judgements that confuse parents with regard to books. It adds to knowledge, even if it does so in a haphazard way (except in specific schools programmes), and although the impression it gives of important drama is bound to be relatively cold and lacking in ritual and theatrical atmosphere, it is nevertheless a valuable alternative.

As it becomes a mere habit, it loses its immediate impact, and then it may become simply another background to the child's live interests or learning, in the same way that radio used to be. Ideally, at this stage, watching might be restricted to a deliberate selection of programmes, a selection in which the children share. Here, as elsewhere, children tend to do what parents do; but they are seldom quite so strongly addicted as their elders, and you might find [with some encouragement] that they are in fact quite willing to do something active after a while.

Talking

Talking is one of the great pleasures of life, and around the twelfth year conversation about all sorts of things, sometimes just plain gossip with other children and with adults, comes to play a greater part in their lives.

Here is Sarah, musing on her second term at secondary school: "We don't run about in the playground nearly as much as we used to. Often we just sit and talk . . . about what we think about each other . . . and what we thought Miss D meant in the history lesson . . . and where she'd got her new shoes from . . ." The tea-table, the dinner-table (maybe not the breakfast table!) are fine occasions for talking together with the whole family, and your eleven-year-old can often appreciate that chance if he is included in the conversation and does not have to be nagged too often about his manners. Now is the time for him to share more in your thoughts about the world and your affairs, especially if you want him to be able to feel that he is living in the same world as you are and, when he becomes an adolescent, having a share in remaking it. If you let him in on your thinking when he is still a child, and take his comments seriously, he will be all the more likely to consult you and take your opinions seriously when he is old enough to do without you.

Note

1. The increasingly varied ethnicity of our culture has also led to concerted efforts to overcome adult illiteracy.
2. In terms of unsuitable content, protection since the advent of the internet is even less feasible, despite computer locks, etc.

CHAPTER THREE

Family relationships

Roles in the family

In a family there is a tendency for children to be pressured into taking up certain roles in relationship to each other. These are often set initially by the place the child has in the family and by what his parents expect as a result of this. For instance, the eldest, especially if she is a girl, is often expected to take the place of mother in looking after the younger ones. The more capable she shows herself, the more tends to be expected of her in this way, both from mother and from the little ones. Many large hard-up families have been brought up in this way, with the eldest girl often missing out on the opportunity to have much of a childhood or real adolescence of her own.

For this reason, then, if you are the eldest in your family the new school can be quite an opportunity to strike out on your own and to forget for a little the younger brothers and sisters you are supposed to be responsible for. It may even do the younger brothers and sisters no harm to do a little more of the care-taking for themselves.

But the role is not always set by the place in the family. Often it is called forth by certain qualities in the child and is very much influenced by the way that we as parents react to these qualities. Sometimes we can be so delighted by qualities of, say, warmth or of intelligence in a child, that we tend to want to see only those qualities. The child feels that he is loved for these alone, tends to overplay them, to conceal others, and hence to develop in a lopsided, too idealized fashion. On the other hand we may, in another child, be so irritated by certain qualities—for example, jealousy or timidity—that we begin to see little else in him but these qualities, and he himself begins to feel that that is all there is to him.

The qualities we want to see in this exclusive way are usually qualities that we would like to have ourselves. We see the chance of possessing them in our child and living out our ideal self through him. The qualities that irritate us most strongly are likely to be qualities in ourselves that we do not like being reminded of, because we have not managed to find a way of reconciling them in our own personalities. So, when we see them in the child, we keep nagging at him in an unhelpful way, or try to push him away so that we will not be reminded of them.

This is put over-simply, but perhaps it is enough to suggest how it comes about, for instance, that we can have in the same family— say—Mary, who is apparently a paragon of sweetness and light, and Stuart, who can be relied upon to let the side down: how the expected tends to happen with both of them. Brothers and sisters often take the cue from parents and see each other through their parents' eyes. On the other hand, some may in time get so fed up with the angel Mary, and driven by their own jealousy, identify themselves with the outcast Stuart, that they join the "against the parents" camp. The permutations and combinations are infinite.

As parents, we can hold the family together better if we are capable of seeing each child as an individual who has changing needs as he grows, but who always needs our respect. His qualities may call forth our admiration and pride, or they may evoke guilt and compassion. If our pride is overweening and our guilt too overwhelming, then we are surely not seeing the child in a realistic light, but treating him too much as our own creation. We are not granting him that spark of individuality, of uniqueness, that was in him from the day of his birth, and which sets him apart as a separate human being. We can facilitate or hinder his growth as an individual, but we cannot create it. We need to recognize our separateness from him as well as our responsibility to him if he is to have room to grow. If we, as parents, recognize this, then brothers and sisters are more likely to give each other breathing space—to treat each other with respect as individuals, needing an appropriate share of psychological living space. An appropriate share may not mean an exactly similar shape.

It is always a problem when one of the children does not fit in with the others as far as school and ability to learn from books is concerned. We, as parents, may feel strongly that we want all our children to have an equal chance in life, and therefore want them all to go to the same school. We may feel that we do not want one of them to get a better education than the others lest they feel envious and reproach us later on for giving them less. We may feel worried about one who is lagging behind the others and try to push him to keep up with the same sort of schooling as the others have had, even if it does not fit his capacity.

This way of going on will not solve the difficulty or alter the fact that children, even in the same family, may have greatly differing scholastic ability. We cannot—even if we would like—make them all the same, or give them exactly the same chance in life. The more we are able to appreciate how different they are from each other and from ourselves, the more we may help them to develop confidence in what they are and what they can reasonably hope to do. If we appreciate them for what they are, then they are also more likely to accept each other in this way, and to cast a less envious and calculating eye on what the other is getting.

The twelfth year is one during which these differences in school ability tend to become clearer. In this country, in the past, many a child suffered badly from failing to get into grammar school with his brothers and sisters. If his parents felt badly about it he would feel even more of a failure. Or he may be the only child in the family who *did* manage to pass the "eleven plus" exam. On such occasions, as on many others, it is worth looking at our own motives for feeling ambitious on a child's behalf. Did we feel that we never really had a proper chance to achieve in a particular area (academic or otherwise), by contrast with our brothers and sisters? It is hard on a child to feel that he *has* to be a success in order to soothe the chip on our shoulders.

Here is an example of a family with a contrasting pair of children, James and Claire. James was the first child. His parents were looking forward to his birth and delighted to have a boy. He was a strong baby, a greedy feeder, but restless, over-demanding, and a poor sleeper. His mother felt she could never satisfy him, and grew more weary and depressed, getting little help from her husband, who at that time was often away from home for days at a time. James began to get patches of eczema and bad bronchial colds, which increased his irritability, and his mother felt more and more of a failure. She was horrified to discover, before he was two years old, that she was again pregnant.

Claire came into the world to a lukewarm reception. She, however, turned out to be a very much easier baby—responsive and easily satisfied—and she became a child who learned quickly and could play happily by herself. She often seemed to find a way of coping with James's jealousy of her by letting him have what he wanted and accepting something else for herself as a substitute. When the third child, Alison, was born, Claire turned to her in a very motherly way, although she was not much more than two years old at the time. These two younger children are growing up very close to each other, in many ways very like each other, and a great comfort to both their parents.

James, now thirteen, continues to be a problem, rather grudging and surly, poorish at school and a disappointment to his parents, although they try to hide this from him. Claire, now eleven, is growing fast in every way—showing signs of adolescence physically, mentally, and emotionally. She has been a very happy child, but now begins to have periods of withdrawal and depression. She has not been able to tell her mother or father what is the matter, but usually shuts herself away at such times and tries to do some homework or read. Then Alison, when questioned by her mother, said, "I think she's upset about James. She thinks she isn't nice enough to him and that's why he's never really happy!"

When the parents got together to talk about this, they could see no reason for Claire feeling this way, as she has often amazed them by her tolerance of James. They are beginning to feel, however, that this tolerance may be at times at too great a cost to herself, and that she is trying to take on an over-responsibility for James that does not really belong to her. They do feel that her friendliness and solicitude for him is genuine, not a cover-up for hostile feelings against him. As they talked, her mother said "It's as if she's got his share of niceness and intelligence as well as her own, and so it's up to her to make it up to him!" They then began to wonder how much they had been contributing to her feeling that she always *had* to be nice, helpful, kind. How much had her mother's depression and tiredness when she was a baby made her feel intuitively that her mother could not stand too much? Because she seemed to be born with a great capacity for love, she could contribute more and ask for less in her relationships. This has, in fact, tended to result in her being given more love.

Now why is she having these secret fits of depression at the age of eleven, when she is apparently successful, a loved and loving child? Why does she feel so responsible for James's difficulties? This spurt of growth, this early approach to adolescence, is probably reawakening in her in a new way potential aspects of herself that have not found expression as yet and that are clamouring to be realized. Her parents' need to have a good child may have made her cut off her own grumbling, greedy, or resentful feelings without realizing them. James may have been used to express that side of herself. So, in worrying about James's difficulties, she is really also worrying about a side of herself that is asking to be recognized and given attention. The worry about James himself is probably also genuine. A child who feels for others unconsciously feels that she is treating another person badly by making him carry the blame for unpleasant, unrealized parts of herself—using him as a scapegoat. It is a relief not to always *have* to be good.

Growing up in the family

About this time many children begin to form a more realistic idea of what it is to work and earn your living: an idea formed more on the model of what their own parents, their brothers and sisters and relatives are doing than upon childhood fantasies of glorious exploits, or of the magical powers and enjoyment available to grown-ups simply because they are grown up.

By this time they have had some years of experience, trying to meet the requirements of school work in company with others of their own age and, inevitably, the opportunity to compare themselves with these others in what they can and cannot do. In many cases they feel their careers to be already very much determined or limited by the kind of school they have managed to get into for their secondary education. Urged by parents' anxieties, some begin to think what they are going to do with their grown-up lives.

It is a great help to our children if we encourage them to talk or to think about what they might like to do when they are grown up, even when they are several years away from leaving school and starting work. The little boy who at the age of six wants to be a pilot or a zookeeper just might really become one. But whatever he does, it is going to come more easily if he learns gradually to think about what the job really entails—to meet the experience in his imagination and to enlarge his acquaintance with it through reading and talking, before he has to commit himself to it in reality. Most children, of course, change their minds many times about what kind of work they want to do to earn their living. The important thing is that they should have ideas, should be given time to explore them imaginatively, be given information when necessary and when possible, and allowed to change their minds. This is the way they will be able to prepare for the later, real decision about work.

This is the way, too, that your child will feel he has some freedom to make a choice; he does not have to follow in your footsteps because he feels it is expected of him, or because he cannot think of anything else to do. On the other hand, it is a pity if he is made to feel that he *must not* follow in your footsteps—that he must not do as well as you or that he must do better.

A feeling that he must not do as well as you have done is likely to be quite unconscious on his part. It may show itself perhaps by his doing badly at, or failing in, work that might lead him to this. You may be unwittingly encouraging this feeling in him by believing too firmly that you know best, and that he ought to know that you know best. You may make him feel that he must not presume to try to do what you do, in case you get threatened if he does it well. On the other hand, it may be that he is scared of the extent of his own competitive feelings towards you and feels it better to stay out of the way so that he does not collide with you.

If he feels that he must do better than you, this may be just straight rivalry and competition that spurs him on to work hard. In that case, as a parent one hopes that the rivalry and hostility is not so strong that he will forget where he came from! It may be, however, that he perceives something of his parents' disappointment in their own unrealized ambitions, and he may feel parental pressure to make up for these failures—to realize and live for them their unlived life. Some children manage to do this; others give up under the strain; but in neither case is this a really satisfactory outcome. We can only live our own lives, and as parents we can help our child best by helping him to find out what he himself can really do and what he enjoys doing. This is most likely to be work that stretches him a little but offers the reward of some degree of success.

Need for privacy in the family

For some children around this age a diary begins to fill the role of secret confidant. It can be prefaced by some large sign such as "Keep out nosey parker"—a warning to the rest of the family, but also a temptation to look and see the fascinating secrets hidden therein. Such a diary can go on for years. Girls seem to feel the need much more often than boys, and their diaries are usually more interesting repositories for cryptic notes about hopes and disappointments and heartbreaks, to be understood usually only by the writer and the diary—her bosom friend, her alter ego.

It is a terrible mistake to be known to read your daughter's diary, and a crime to laugh at it. The writer of a diary is usually most sensitive to the slightest sign of ridicule and humour, however kindly meant. The beginning of the adolescent striving for grown-upness is, like all beginnings, rather shaky and liable to collapse suddenly without warning.

Already, at this stage, some girls are intensely involved or trying to fight off involvement in the adolescent's yearning for an ideal love relationship, the "being in love with love". Others may still be clinging very strongly to the final stages of uninhibited tomboyishness and fill their diaries with records of hockey fixtures, or runs and goals scored, or matches lost or won. Matters such as these are typical of boys' diaries. They are emotionally charged to the writer, but uninformative to the public reader.

Keeping a diary is a sign of growing up, of awareness of time passing, of the need to take account of time and use it, to plan ahead, to note happenings as part of the history of one's life.

CHAPTER FOUR

Discipline, encouragement, and protection

The actual form that discipline takes alters from year to year with the growth of the child, and, of course, varies from child to child. We must continue to bear in mind that our aim is to help our children towards disciplining themselves, and in such a way that they can find a style of life where their talents reach fullest expression and realization. This can usually be achieved only by learning to co-operate with others. If we remember these things we have some rational thread to follow when trying to decide on the difficult issues of what is and what is not permissible.

At all ages, one of the problems is to decide when a child should be curbed for his own good, when he has to be protected against himself, or when it may be advisable to let him have a little rope and learn from bitter experience. The eleven-year-old who has already had years of experience of a firm but kindly discipline from his parents is likely to be preparing for a less stormy and defiant adolescence than the child who has encountered erratic, unpredictable, and unreasonable handling. This often produces a child who expects his mum or dad to be "on to him" if they happen to find out when he is up to something he should not be, but who takes a sporting chance of not being found out, as he does not see why he should not try to get away with it if he can. We have to take our children with us if we want them willingly to endorse our standards. That means at times re-examining these standards ourselves and being willing to discuss them with the child when he is really questioning. If our rules are founded on reason they will bear examination.

Blaming other people's children

We all know that there are times when we can trust our children on their own to behave in a sensible manner, but fear that in company with others it can be a very different matter. Then we are only too ready to complain with self-righteous indignation of John or Chris or Emma to their parents. But we then have to ask ourselves what makes our blameless offspring so ready to be led into ill-doing? There is a tendency in every child—for every human being is infinitely complex—to seize, or even seek, an opportunity in company to satisfy aggressive or antisocial tendencies that he would repudiate and prefer not to take responsibility for on his own.

If our children see us, their parents, scapegoating others for faults that we do not recognize in ourselves—if we do, in fact, blame them for the very things in which we indulge—then they are not likely to think much of our discipline or standards of conduct. It is a different matter if we recognize in other people faults that we acknowledge we have also, and that we try to struggle with in ourselves.

Questioning our own attitudes

At this age children begin to question our values and behaviour, as the uncertainties of their growth make them question themselves more. It is important for their safety and security that they should feel we do have standards—of truthfulness, of caring for others— but far from necessary that they should feel us to be perfect, to be authorities that cannot be questioned. Indeed, if we are trying to be truthful, we must question ourselves and our behaviour in many instances. As children grow older and have more responsibility and opportunities to make decisions for themselves, it becomes increasingly important for them to participate in our thinking about what is the best way to act in different circumstances. Not only does this help them to make up their own minds; it may also stimulate us to take a fresh look at our reasons and maybe, on occasion, change our own minds and attitudes.

Punishment

Someone once amended the self-righteous Victorian recommendation "Never hit a child in hot blood" to "Never hit a child except in hot blood". There are probably few parents who can say that, when sorely tried, they have always managed to refrain from giving a good smack. And maybe when that was an exceptional reaction it stopped the offending behaviour on the spot, even sometimes led the child to think soberly about why such wrath descended upon him.

But as a routine method of disciplining, hitting and the use of physical force must surely be a terrible confession of failure to reach any degree of co-operation with our child's more grown-up self. If force is used to subdue the child he may obey, but he will harbour resentment and wait for the day when he is old enough and strong enough to escape from our sanctions and get his own back. He may not knowingly harbour resentment. He may take it that by suffering the pain of a good whacking he has atoned for his offences and is absolved and free to do it again, only more circumspectly, so that he should not be found out so easily. Or he may turn into one of the advocates of physical punishment himself—"a good beating never did me any harm"—and so pass on the bullying to the next generation.

If, by the time your child is eleven, you feel that he is against you persistently, and that you are frequently tempted to hit him, it is perhaps a good idea to go and talk to someone else about it. His schoolteacher would be the most immediate and obvious person to consult: together you might work out some better method of understanding and handling the child. However, it is no use using the teacher to offload your own disciplinary responsibility.

The idea of simple punishment, whether corporal or otherwise, is not a very useful one. As revenge—to make the child suffer—it encourages in him vindictiveness, or fear, or both; as atonement, it is not realistic. Simply to suffer because you have made others suffer does not help to remedy the pain that you have caused. To pretend that it does so is not honest. If a child realizes and accepts that he has behaved badly it is not necessary to punish him; if he is trying not think about the implications of what he has done, punishment will simply give him sanction to forget all about it and to learn nothing from the incident.

Criticism, encouragement, and praise

Very few children of this age are sufficiently sure of themselves to be able to take a look at their mistakes and shortcomings in a critical yet tolerant way, to keep that sense of proportion that is needed if we are going to be able to laugh at ourselves and let others laugh with us. Eleven-year-olds are often striving too hard to find their feet among rapidly expanding interests and the demands of their environment. There are too many unfamiliar stirrings of growth within themselves for them to take their feelings other than deadly seriously. Their very seriousness can make them a little funny to indulgent grown-ups, who may not realize how vulnerable they are, how easily made to feel that they are small and stupid and just pretending to be grown-up—that it is a pretence everyone can see through and laugh at.

Helen, aged eleven, was chatting to her mother after a family reunion: "I like Aunt Joan much better than Uncle James. She's not so much fun at first, but when you talk to her about something she listens and she respects your opinion. Uncle James is very nice to me, but if I tell him what I really think, I can see from the way he looks that he's laughing inside and thinking I'm just some cute little girl pretending to be grown-up." It was evidently important for Helen at that moment to be listened to in a serious way, to be treated as one trying to grapple with the problems of living, not as a child going through the motions of appearing adult. Her uncle had not responded to her need to be *understood*—rather than petted or admired. Yet Helen had her own particular reasons for feeling vulnerable to ridicule by men. In her earlier years she had a very passionate attachment to her mother. As she was the youngest of the family and the parents did not intend to have any more children, her mother was inclined to indulge her more than the others—for instance, to take her into her own bed at night when she woke up and cried. She was allowed to stay up late when visitors were there: made much of because she was a pretty, friendly, and chatty child. Her father, who was a quiet, fair-minded man, did not entirely approve of this, and felt somewhat cut out at times by the amount of time and attention that Helen managed to inveigle from her mother.

Getting away with these privileges, with more than was really her due, enabled Helen to avoid coming to terms with the normal jealousy of acknowledging the particular importance of her father to her mother, and vice versa. It encouraged a secret pretence that she really was grown up, and that her father was really rather inferior and less special to her mother than she was. As she grew older, however, she came to admire and appreciate her father very much, and wanted to be able to talk to him and to interest him in the way that she saw her mother's conversation interested him, and also to be able to learn from him. So, in confiding her thoughts to her Uncle James, she was hoping for a real conversation with him, and was hurt when she sensed that he was treating her as sweet but unimportant and comical.

She was all the more touchy about this as she was growing critical of her precocious showing-off little-girl self, the part of herself that was quite different from the eleven-year-old child who was interested in the world and wanted to learn more about it. One of the ways of learning is by formulating one's own ideas, and expressing them to someone who will take them seriously and respond by criticizing, adding to them, pointing out where there is agreement and where difference, and so on. It would seem that at this stage Helen is still uncertain when she joins in a conversation to what degree she is motivated by the desire to be informed and to learn, and to what degree she just wants approval for being a sweet little girl. So she is particularly touchy about being laughed at.

It is quite difficult for the child—as for the adult who has become dependent on regular doses of praise or flattery—to give up this heady drug in favour of some more realistic assessment of his work and of himself. In the long run we do our children no service by praising them beyond their real achievements. In so far as they wish to be understood and to relate to the world and themselves truthfully, they are made inwardly muddled and uncertain when they receive praise from people they love for behaviour or work that they know does not deserve it. That does not mean they may not try very hard to get it—and complain bitterly that they do not get enough. The only real cure for an excessive need for praise is to set about learning and trying to do something that is within your capacity.

Why children disobey

The reasons vary, and we cannot deal with the disobedience realistically until we have some idea of what is motivating the child. Sometimes we are too busy—or too annoyed if we feel that our authority is being flouted—to bother to think, and we just wade in with a lecture or a punishment. The more children we have to deal with, the more likely we are to jump on the offender without thought. But it is worth taking the trouble to find out what is causing the disobedience. It may affect our attitude and the way that we then deal with the offender.

Here is an example of the way in which a very busy headmaster dealt with disobedience in one of his most troublesome pupils. This headteacher, with some of his staff, had spent quite a lot of time talking to Steve and was hopeful that he was really settling in at school in a better way. Some of the older boys had been reported for smoking in school and just outside the school premises. This had resulted in a lecture during school assembly. That same afternoon, as the headteacher was about to go home, his heart sank when he saw Steve parading outside the school gates smoking a cigarette, apparently in direct defiance of the instructions that morning. His first impulse was to confront Steve straight away with his delinquency in no uncertain terms. Smoking at school "got the school a bad name" as he had pointed out in assembly, and he felt that Steve was repaying his attention very ill and hitting a sore spot. He had only recently been appointed head, and was keen to get local support for his school. He realized that he felt hurt and disappointed after all the trouble he had taken with Steve, and was tempted to give him up as a bad job.

He then stopped to think that this particular kind of misdemeanour was, in fact, very unlike Steve, whose crimes in the past had been on a much grander and more imaginative scale. He did not feel, either, that it was in character for Steve to "bite the hand that fed him". So he took him back into school and asked him what this was all about. "It's not like you, Steve, to have to do this sort of thing to prove what a big fellow you are—what's at the back of it all?" Then it turned out that Steve had been teased by one of the other boys at lunchtime, told that his dad was a sis because he could not get a proper job (his father was frequently out of work) and that he, too, was a sis because he had to look after his little sisters and take them to the infant school every day. So Steve got mad and said he would show the other boys that he was tough.

Knowing Steve's background, the headteacher understood that the disobedience was not really directed against him and the school, but was a mistaken attempt to keep his end up with the other boys at a time when he was feeling especially vulnerable. He realized that stern disciplinary action on his part would merely make Steve feel still more bitterly that the world was against him. What he needed most of all was someone who would take an interest in him and take the sting out of his wounds. He could then listen to the head's point of view about the smoking and feel that he, too, had a valuable part to play in protecting the image of the school.

How can we stop children from doing things that are really harmful to them?

This becomes an obvious problem as your child grows older and less easy to forbid and to oversee, especially if you have not been able to communicate with him as he has been growing up. Even if, by and large, you have been able to enlist his co-operation, there are still occasions when he is liable to be tempted by others who encourage the quick and easy way to independence by presenting themselves as superior to any rules and regulations imposed by school or parents.

To take one obvious example (the smoking touched on in the previous section), we know it is highly irresponsible to encourage our children to smoke, but how can we stop them? Horror stories about lung cancer are too far in the future to have any real deterrent effect in most cases, and to some children they could even be an incentive. To defy the danger is a proof of one's own special invulnerability: "Who's afraid of the big bad wolf?" Who's afraid of death when it is so far away!

Also, we can hardly expect our children to accept limitations or take precautions in any sphere where we do not act on our own advice. "Do as I tell you, not as I do" is just asking to be ignored. The twelfth year is one in which children are still very much looking to their parents and teachers for role-models. A few years later they may be too disillusioned to want to take a lead from us.

CHAPTER FIVE

Gratitude, courtesy, and developing consideration for others

E ach step in growing up means that a child can be entrusted with a little more responsibility for looking after himself and his belongings, for helping in the general family upkeep. Each child is an individual and has his own particular rate of development, his own particular developing capacity to assume responsibility for himself and his share of the little society in which he lives.

What can you expect of your eleven-year-old in the way of help about the house, in pulling his weight when there is extra work to be done, when there are visitors to entertain, when perhaps the visit of some elderly and not too congenial relative conflicts with plans that he has made to do things with his friends? You probably know by this time the response that you are likely to get from him when such conflicts of interest arise. It may not be all you would like; and you go on puzzling how you can lead or force or cajole him into acting with greater consideration for others—to recognize that he is not the only pebble on the beach, that there are other members of the family, and that there are other people in the world who need to be considered as well as members of his immediate family.

As with so many general questions about personality and conduct, there is no simple answer. As always, the child's way of acting and thinking is likely to be much more deeply influenced by what he sees us do than by us telling him what he ought to do. He may have imbibed a little of his parents' standards and values and begin to be able to identify with them. Or he may still do what we tell him to do because it is the line of least resistance, because he wants to please us, because he is afraid of punishment or an argument. If this is the only reason why he does it, and if he has any spirit in him and wants to find his own feet, he is all the more likely in adolescence to join the various anti-parent anti-authority groups.

We can encourage our children to strive towards standards of considerate and courteous behaviour from which we fall far short ourselves, provided we recognize that we fall short, and provided we really do value them and acknowledge that it is indeed difficult to maintain such standards. If we are aware of the difficulty as a result of our own attempts and failures, we are much less likely to be too hard on our children and hypocritical in our teaching.

It is not easy to be both considerate and honest. Many a parent who has tried to preach truthfulness at all times to her children has had difficulty in trying to reconcile the two. When your eleven-year-old son, an ardent pop fan, is given his favourite album twice over for Christmas by his grandmother and an aunt and when—moreover—he has already managed to save up and buy it for himself, do you let him write a rather disappointed letter to the donors explaining that their present would have been greatly appreciated if he did not happen to have it already? Perhaps this might be in order if the aunt and grandmother happened to be untouchy and understanding people. But if they *are* touchy then you may have to explain this to your son, who, if he is at all perceptive, may already understand only too well that it is more kindly to convey the thanks and suppress the disappointment, which after all was not the fault of the present-givers. Being truthful does not always entail telling all. It can be useful if children are able to learn, as they grow a little older, that too candid reactions can sometimes be a self-indulgence at the expense of others.

A child with some sensitivity to the feelings of others can, of course, often gauge them intuitively and hurt no one. Katie, writing to her Aunt Nancy to thank her for a Christmas present, wrote:

"Dear Aunt Nancy, thank you for the ten pounds, which was more than I had expected. You have never been so generous before." Aunt Nancy had a sense of humour and said that the receipt of this letter quite made her day. If the same letter had gone to Great Aunt Hilda, however, it would probably have met with quite a different reception and been construed as impertinent.

Should we as parents insist that our sometimes clumsy eleven-year-olds observe certain formal courtesies which they may at times find a trial, and have to be nagged to perform, even in a perfunctory manner? The already mentioned "thank you" letter for the not too welcome present, the bread-and-butter letter to a friend's mother whom he may have regarded as merely an incidental convenience when he went to stay with the friend, the formal morning and evening greeting to each member of the family, including elderly relatives, may have become more of a trouble than a pleasure. Each family has its own conventional courtesies, related often to its social milieu. If these courtesies have any meaning for us, if they really are a ritual way of expressing some consideration for others, it is worthwhile bringing up our children to observe them too.

We have to recognize and allow for the fact that they will not always be performed with enthusiasm. They are decent forms of behaviour that may express spontaneous feeling, or alternatively tide over relationships when spontaneity is lacking at that point. "Why are you getting at me so often these days? I can't like everybody", grumbled Henry to his mother. This was after being taken to task because he had scowled and munched his way all through family tea, where the presence of one of his mother's friends had hindered him from fully discussing a projected school trip and straightway getting his mother's permission to join it. "Straight away" was the operative expression for Henry, as it is so often and for so many children at this age, and at other ages when their own enthusiasm is kindled. Enthusiasms can lead to discourtesy when others are in the way, even if we do happen to like them.

The parent who is over-enthusiastic about good behaviour or about consideration for others at all times and in all ways may force the child into setting a standard for himself that he can never reach, and that stimulates in him a crippling sense of guilt. He may give up striving for it, and this could pave the way to later rebellion and idealization of freedom and self-expression—let the rest of the world go hang! This kind of reaction, however, is much more likely if what we are so insistent upon is not real courtesy out of consideration for others, but courtesy because we want to be seen to have a well-behaved child who will do us credit in the eyes of others. Real courtesy would, after all, take into account the needs and potentialities of the child himself. Children who are trying to think for themselves can spot when we merely want to bolster our own and others' opinion of ourselves as parents. They may not be able to put it into words, but they can react strongly against it.

There are, however, children who react very ungratefully against their parents' attempts to truly consider them and to do the best for them as well as for others—who seem determined that their parents should take no part of the credit for anything good they achieve. To some extent this resistance to feeling grateful to those on whom we depend operates in us all, as children and as adults. It is, perhaps, one of the most difficult traits to admit in ourselves and, equally, it is most painful to be the parent of a child who is reacting in this way towards us: for "sharper than a serpent's tooth it is to have a thankless child".

It does not, of course, help the child to feel and to behave better if we lecture him about how he ought to be grateful for all we have done for him. It can just increase his suspicions that we have not, after all, been doing it for him, but rather for our own vainglory and self-righteousness, and therefore he is quite justified in carrying on as before. "I didn't ask to be born" has been said by many a child of eleven—and of later years—when his lack of consideration has been called into question.

Religion: where does it come in?

Many children during this year begin to ask the questions "What does man live by?" and "Where did I come from?" in a serious enquiring way. The child who has implicitly taken over the values and beliefs of his parents, and to a lesser extent of his school, will— if he is thinking and experiencing in a live way—most probably question those values either openly or privately to himself or among his companions. Girls, who as a rule are more mature than boys at this stage, may tend to be a little more advanced in their questioning. It is a questioning that, once begun, continues through adolescence.

The idea of God and religion may have been a far-away, somewhat guilt-making system of sanctions and rules. It may be yoked vaguely to the picture of some stern old man up above, or the Saviour dying on the cross, not to be doubted, not really to be understood, and maintained chiefly by lip-service. It can remain equated with an authority and knowledge so supreme that it must not be questioned. Thus, as the child grows older, his unquestioning obedience tends to become that of the adult who sides with and enforces authority. But the naïve believer of early years can later become the disillusioned rebel, accepting maybe an alternative and equally rigid belief in another form of authority. The ideal of total freedom can be one of the most exhausting masters!

For the child to be able to respect the adults' belief in God and in religion, to have any security in the creed to which he has been brought up, must mean that his belief has to stand the test of questioning. He has to be able to see how beliefs operate in practice: do his parents, do his teachers, practise what they preach, or do they just use God as the supreme weapon to goad them to good behaviour by evoking fear and guilt? The use of religion is now no longer as effective in exercising conformity in young people as it used to be when, before widespread communications, the world was a smaller place, with fewer conflicting voices heard in each family.

Cheating

In a group of eleven-year-olds playing together, one of them may be tempted to cheat, either because he is losing and cannot bear it, or because he is just within reach of winning and cannot bear to "not quite make it". He has to operate very stealthily, because discovery means indignation and moral disapproval from the rest. Because *all* of them find it difficult to keep the rules, they will turn on the one who does not.

Indignation is strongest from those who have the greatest difficulty in playing fair, who maybe would cheat themselves if they were not afraid of being found out. Hence, the outcry against the cheat tends to be loudest from children of a younger age group to whom the rules of the game are less established and thus harder to keep. In younger children the transgression of the rules is usually on impulse when the competition becomes too keen. A child who cheats regularly tends to be branded as a baby: he may, in fact, often be a younger brother or sister who feels he has to keep his end up in this way.

As children grow older and more able to control the manifestations of their violent and greedy impulses, cheating becomes less frequent and less impulsive. The eleven-year-old at secondary school among his companions is definitely not supposed to cheat. In school team games the one whose cheating might help his team to victory would usually be frowned upon if he did so, for letting his side down. But it depends very much upon the individual child as well as upon the real standards of the children with whom he is playing as to whether the real crime is the cheating, or the being found out. A child who wants to keep the rules primarily because he does not wish to give way to a greedy impulse of taking advantage of his companions will feel badly when he has cheated and not earned his success. It may be that he feels so badly while doing it that he bungles it, gets caught, and stops himself from profiting by it.

Take the example of Margaret, who, in her first year of learning geometry, was not getting on very well with it. She was too busy playing with her friends in the evening to learn her geometry homework. She knew that she was going to be tested on a particular theorem the next day, and decided she would just copy it out from her geometry book hidden under her desk. This she did, but failed to notice that when the teacher wrote the problem up on the board, he had labelled a triangle XYZ, while she went on writing it as ABC according to the book. Her teacher did not see her cheating, but it was evident when she gave in her paper. When he handed back the work the next day he kept hers back, but called her up to talk to him privately at the end of the lesson. She then went away and had a private little cry.

In her case the teacher had judged very well. It was evident that she was very divided in her mind about cheating; that she was going against her better self and so was driven to give the game away. He could talk to that better self more easily in private, and so touch her conscience. Possibly, if he had hauled her out in front of the whole class, she might have felt too overwhelmed and ashamed, and defended herself against this by a "don't care" hardened attitude, becoming more defiant against the teacher and deciding to do things more cleverly next time.

Cheating in lessons when the child—or especially, when the class as a whole—feels up against or contemptuous of the teacher can be regarded as a quite permissible and even rather clever way of behaving; just as the regular criminal finds that respectable society is fair game and outwitting the police a matter of course. When the class is on good terms with the teacher, who is felt to be fair to all, then it is not considered so clever to cheat. It is more likely to be regarded as a betrayal of trust and an unfair attempt to steal a march over the others.

It is worthwhile considering what sort of example we set our children in this matter of cheating. Most of us would agree that cheating is a bad thing, and we tell our children so and regard them with varying degrees of disapproval when we catch them at it. But what do we do ourselves and what do our children see us do? As they grow older, they become more realistically critical, capable of perceiving the practices that do not fit in with our precepts. If we play fair with them, and with other people, we strengthen that side of them which recognizes and upholds justice and fair shares for all.

CHAPTER SIX

Your eleven-year-old and sex

Curiosity about sex

You probably found that a year or two back your child was more openly curious about sex than he is now: about babies, where they come from, how they get out, how they got there; about what you and your partner get up to when you are alone in the evening. If he asks less and is not so obviously curious now, it is probably not only because he has already found out enough to be going on with, but also that he feels shyer and nearer to the time when he will be involved himself.

This can simply be a natural stage in his development—nothing to do with your shyness and inhibitions about talking to him; although, of course, it is easier for children to talk easily if they feel that their parents are not embarrassed by talking about sexual intercourse, pregnancy, and birth. Perhaps you do not find it as easy to talk about sex to an eleven-year-old as you did when he was five. This may be because you are aware of more complicated and secret conflicts in him, connected with his guilty feelings about masturbation and with a more critically detailed observation of the relationship between his parents and of the relationships of other couples friendly with the family.

It is better not to force things or to force yourself into making an issue of giving sex instruction if you feel your child has not asked enough, or does not know enough to accept understanding. The facts are fairly easy to get across. He can read about them now, as he could a year or two back, and as he will be able to again in a more sophisticated way later on. But it is important for him to feel that he has your permission to go on and find out all the facts he wants to know by reading, listening, viewing, and, most especially, by listening to conversations between grown-ups and adolescents.

If your child is not curious about sex at all at this stage you should probably wonder and worry a little. Not to show his curiosity is quite usual, and it could be insensitive not to respect his desire for privacy. It is better not to ask him questions in a direct manner. He might not know what he feels, or how to formulate what he wants to ask. Questions are likely to arise as a result of listening in to conversations between others. And what sort of conversation about sexual matters should you allow to take place in front of the children—is there anything about intercourse, pregnancy, birth that we should try to keep from children of this age?

Perhaps this question is one that we do not consider often enough. It is not so easy to answer when one thinks that the facts that they might encounter through hearsay and sometimes observation may include homosexual practices, sexually transmitted diseases, and dangerous or abnormal births.[1] And we may find it difficult to sort out our own attitudes to sex: we may be afraid of being a bad example to our children and feeding unhealthy curiosity that leads to masturbatory fantasies and practices. But the reticence that belongs to a unique love relationship that cannot be shared, and the rather guilty secrecy surrounding goings-on that are unconsciously felt to be rather naughty and not a good example to the children, are very different. There can often be an unspoken collusion between parents and children that the parents do not participate in sex. For the parents it is a way of trying to preserve a pure and "wholesome" image of themselves in the children's eyes. But neither party believes in this wholeheartedly! It is best therefore to answer as truthfully as possible whenever a question is asked or implied—even when the answer is unpleasant or frightening. It is less likely to be frightening if we answer truthfully than if the child

is left with his own theories and those of other children, which are
usually more lurid than the reality.

Menstruation

It is a good idea, if you have not already done so, to talk to your
eleven-year-old daughter about menstruation, preferably at some
point when she shows that she is interested or self-conscious about
bodily changes and is aware that she is growing up to be a woman
like her elder sister and her friends. If she has an elder sister she
probably knows a great deal about it already; in any case, she will
have her theories and fantasies about it from gossip with her
companions.

When anxieties are not too strong, girls look forward—somewhat doubtfully—to their first period, as qualifying them for some
mysterious circle of femininity. There is always anxiety: the knowledge that this is bleeding that comes from inside, from the bottom,
from private passages, is bound to cause anxiety, however miti-
gated by sound information. Bleeding means hurt, means damage;
it is associated with damage to oneself, or is a sign that one has
damaged something inside oneself. It is connected, unconsciously,
with fears of harm done by masturbation in earlier and current
years.

Preparing a girl for menstruation by talking about it, and referring to it as a natural fact of life, will not entirely remove the
worries she has about it. These may be quite concealed and unfor-
mulated, even to herself: seeing it for instance as a messy, dirty
business, like wetting herself or having diarrhoea. But telling her
about it helps and is likely to lessen the shame and mitigate the
guilt and fear about damage to herself, and about damage to her
mother (for masturbation is accompanied by unconscious hostility
to "inner" parents).

It is often quite difficult for mothers to talk naturally to their
daughters about menstruation. Despite all our experience of life, of
marriage, of babies, it tends to remain for us a very emotionally
charged affair. Not without reason is it called the "curse", a burden
that women have to bear, that men unfairly manage to escape. If we
still carry a chip on our shoulder about the drudgery of women,

and feel hard done by, then we are less likely to look forward to our daughters becoming women, and thus to help them greet menstruation as a step towards maturity. This particular step, almost more than any other, does mean that we are losing the little daughter we had—the child we perhaps idealized as innocent of sexuality (an idealization that is common, though invariably erroneous). It also means that as she grows up, so do we grow older. She reminds us of our own youth and our first periods and brings home the fact that our youth is now gone. This demands—as do so many important stages in life—the task of remembering, even of mourning, for what is gone. If we manage to cope with this we are the richer for it, and our attitude of mind is a help to our daughter in facing this next important stage of growing up. Our attitude of mind is probably more important than what we actually say to her.

Relatively few girls do begin to menstruate when they are eleven, but they are mostly thinking about it or avoiding thinking about it.[2] There comes to mind one clever, but in many ways naïve little girl, who because of her ability was in a form where everyone else was at least a year older than she was. Because she was rather small and a somewhat petted, over-protected only child, she tended to be left out of little groups of girlish confidences. This was the way that some of the older girls got their own back on her for her forwardness in class. When a little knot of girls were giggling and whispering about so and so not being able to swim in the finals of the swimming trophy, Jenny innocently asked them why. She was told that if she did not know why they could not tell her; she must ask her mother. Jenny puzzled, was hurt, but instinctively felt that this was something she *could not* ask her mother, something embarrassing and connected with sex.

Some weeks later she woke up in the night feeling sticky and thinking that she had wet herself. Putting the light on, she saw a pool of blood in the bed. Saying to herself, "Now I know what those girls were talking about", she went to the toilet to urinate, then turned over and went straight back to sleep. She slept in and was late for school in the morning. When Jenny's mother woke her she saw the blood-stained bed, and felt self-reproachful and rather embarrassed. She started to try to explain menstruation to Jenny, but Jenny airily cut her short, saying that she knew all about it already—the girls at school had told her.

For Jenny, then, menstruation came as a triumph, as an initiation into a secret that older girls and her mother had been keeping from her. One might wonder why she went right back to bed and over-slept the next morning. What anxieties was she denying by taking it in this too casual way, and why did she freeze her mother's attempt to tell her more about it? Though small, she was a great games player and refused to take it easy when she had periods. It was as if she defied any fussing about it, saying, "Other girls may not swim when they have the curse, but it makes no difference to me". It was as if this mark of femininity was accepted for its pres-tige value, but denied as lessening her claim to be a boy and to follow boyish activities.

A great many girls of her age resent menstruation as confirming their femininity but limiting their freedom. This often accompanies a secret denigration of their mothers, which stirs up fears of becom-ing like the mother whom they have—in their fantasy—spoiled. Sometimes this can be a factor in delaying menstruation for a while, and also in producing periods of dysmenorrhoea after puberty has begun.

Masturbation and "wet dreams"

As mentioned in the previous section, many children of this age feel a renewal of the urge to masturbate, to take a secret interest in sexual matters, prompted by the early stages of the development of their adolescent sexuality. This masturbation is, in their uncon-scious minds, so connected with jealousy and anger about the forbidden pleasures that the parents and the grown-up world enjoy that they feel guilty about it. If their parents' attitude to sex is too inhibited and guilt-ridden this, of course, makes them feel still more ashamed. They will have some sort of impression about this long before their eleventh birthday.

This is helped a little by giving the actual facts about sexual intercourse, reproduction, menstruation, and "wet dreams", so that children are prepared for these last two. The facts help, but just as important as the facts themselves is the sharing of them—the acknowledgement that it is all right for the boys and girls to know them, that they are not going to be grudged entry into the hitherto forbidden world of adult sexuality. Sharing the facts helps, too, to sense what your child is feeling about them. It may well be, as has been suggested above, that at this age he is much shyer of talking to you and letting you see what he feels about sex and marriage and babies than he was at a much earlier age, and so it is important not to try to force his confidence—to invade the privacy he needs to keep. It is a time when he is probably beginning to be much more curious about sex in relation to older boys and girls, brothers and sisters, than wanting to feel in any way involved himself. Both boys and girls tend to seek the company of their own sex as a kind of protection from the hints they have of changes in their own condition.

Dirty jokes, much enjoyed by children of this age, are one way of lightly passing off worries about sex and masturbation, of sharing them, of belittling them, and belittling the grown-up world and the older adolescents.

Appearance

A mother explained what an awkward time she felt this twelfth year was for her daughter: "She's getting to the age when she notices her clothes more, and wants to look nice, but she doesn't want you to show that you notice her. She came rushing into my room in tears the other day, howling that her ten-year-old brother had been nasty to her. "He poked the bumps in my jersey and said, 'What are these? Blisters?'"

In the course of her twelfth year many a little girl passes from the stage of the relatively assured command of her body and her garments to uncertainty about her budding femininity. Sometimes it is a help if she has an older sister whom she has noticed growing into adolescence, especially if that sister is kindly disposed towards her and takes an interest in helping her to tidy up and care for her appearance. Anna had an older sister. She had a brother who was one year younger than herself and whom she had, in her tomboy days, managed to outrun, outclimb, and to generally be ahead of him in all her exploits. Now he was getting his own back on her, mocking her signs of girlhood because she had sometimes made him feel small in manliness and toughness.

It is harder for the little girl who has been rather a tomboy and who has tried to beat the boys at their own game to change over to being an admired young lady than it is for the one who has always been neat and pretty and noticeable for her appearance rather than her actions.

The tomboy stage is often connected with despising mother and women, who are associated with babies as being rather soft and helpless. The freedom of daddy, of boys, is glamorized at mother's expense. So, gradually beginning to feel that you would like to be a girl, and to grow into a woman after all, is rather a delicate business. You may not even be too sure that you will like being one, but nevertheless, a sense of reality convinces that the best must be made of a bad job. But if you are trying to tidy up, look a little smarter, you certainly will not want comments from the family that draw too much attention to the change before you have got used to it yourself.

Boys are less likely than girls, in this year, to feel the first adolescent stirrings, but sometimes they, too, begin to take a new interest in their appearance, in their clothes and in their hair, a foretaste of the preoccupation with the way they look which comes in early adolescence and which reflects an uncertainty and concern about the way they feel, an uncertainty which may be still, or even more, in evidence later.

Notes

1. This book was written pre-AIDS; but it is well known among educationalists that it is not facts but the way they are presented that has an impact.
2. The average age has been falling and is currently twelve years.

CHAPTER SEVEN

The need for friends and
for time to be alone

Conformity

This is, on the whole, still a time of conformity. Most eleven-year-olds are pleased to wear a school uniform, to look like the rest of their class, to possess the outward signs of belonging to the same school. It is important to be accepted as one of the crowd, the class, the group. To belong to a group and to have a group identity is one of the ways of cushioning a disturbed composure. The child of this age who is in trouble at school, in a fight, or at odds with friends, will usually try not to run home to mummy and complain, but will fight it out with his companions and come to some understanding without grown-up arbitration.

The appearance of parents can sometimes be an embarrassment. Not untypical is eleven-year-old Barbara, looking with doubtful pleasure to her mother's appearance at Sports Day to watch her run in the finals of the hundred yards. She vets critically the clothes her mother is going to wear and says, "And if I do come in first, don't make a fool of yourself shouting and clapping and drawing everybody's attention to yourself." The important thing is not to seem to be mollycoddled, not to be a baby.

Privacy

Many children in their twelfth year need opportunities for a little more privacy, a chance to be away from the grown-ups and a chance to be free of the younger brothers and sisters. Of course it is not always easy to manage this when there are several children in a small house or flat. But ways and means can be found when parents are aware of the need.

On the most obvious level, children may have a great deal of homework at this stage and be hard put to concentrate on it when the whole family is congregated in one room, maybe with one or two younger children and a television on at the same time. It is hard not to watch the TV if your younger brothers have less to do, or if dad, home from work, is watching at the same time. There are often ways of managing this situation, however. Some schools have a special homework classroom, and sometimes it is possible to use the public library. Sometimes, too, the child who has grown up in a crowd can work better with noise around him. He has learned to be private in his mind and to return with his preoccupations despite constant interruptions.

But respect for privacy is not just a matter of providing a quiet place for work. It is a time when children are beginning to think about themselves a little more rather than remaining preoccupied with what they want to *do* next, what friend they are meeting, where they are going together. They need a little indulgence to think, to dream a little, a chance to feel that they have a mind of their own. They can begin to feel very touchy if their privacy is breached (letters opened, phone conversations listened to) or if they feel that members of their family are poking into confidences they have with special friends, or secrets that they share with no one.

School and feelings about school are to many children of this age private things that they do not want to talk about at home unless they feel like it, and about which they do not want too many questions asked. It is not that they necessarily have anything to hide, but that they have experiences they want to work over on their own. School, for them, is a more grown-up world, dissociated from their junior school and from their home, where they can still very much be little children at times.

Privacy is also needed to cope with new bodily sensations, from the sudden spring of physical growth that girls especially may experience in this year, and from the reawakening of sexual feelings as discussed in Chapter Six. When they feel "different" physically they also feel "different" psychologically: hence, often, the fight to conform outwardly with others of their age, but hence, also, the need for permission to be alone with themselves and their daydreams.

Living out family conflicts with friends

At this age intense friendships between children of either sex tend to occur most particularly with children who, at an earlier age, were passionately attached to a parent. The involvement with another child or children is a means of breaking away from the emotional tie to the family. This can be hurtful to the parents at times, especially to the mother.

Elsie, the younger of two daughters, was from birth a very cuddly baby, very much petted and most affectionate to her mother, who found this little daughter a great solace in various minor family misfortunes. Elsie could always be relied on to be cheerful and helpful. In her early days at school, much to everyone's surprise, she would often become anxious and mopey and would stay away for various slight ailments. She wanted her mother to pay her a great deal of attention. She did not really begin to enjoy school wholeheartedly until she was about ten years old, and she began to be deeply involved in it, and with one or two girl friends, when she was about eleven. She then became so absorbed in secret clubs and ploys that her mother complained that home was becoming just a hotel to which she paid fleeting visits for meals and sleep. Pleased though she was that Elsie had at last "taken" greatly to school and had friends with whom she was always busy, it was a struggle not to feel unnecessary and unwanted.

At such a time it helps both parties if the mother has a life and interests of her own that sustain her and protect her from being dependent on her children. Elsie's mother fortunately realized the danger and decided to take up evening classes in dressmaking, which not only enabled her to develop a new skill but also gave an uplift to her somewhat jaded feelings about herself. This new interest was shared with her elder sixteen-year-old daughter, Kate, who was glad to get a little help in making clothes to go out with her boyfriend.

It led to a slightly different family alignment. Mother had, up to then, always had Elsie hanging round her. Father and Kate had tended to chat with each other, or even to spend an evening at the pictures together if Kate was not out with one of her own friends. They were both more easy-going, less intense characters than Elsie, and had accepted the very strong bond between the mother and Elsie that had, at times, excluded them and tended to throw them together for company. They now realized that mother was less preoccupied with the younger child and seemed to need their company, either individually or as a couple. In some ways the mother and father began to be more of a couple again and to go out together alone in the evening, which they had not done for years except on rare occasions.

This kind of emotional separation from mother, which Elsie achieved in her twelfth year, takes place in many children long before this. In others it may not take place until adolescence, and for some children it may unfortunately not take place at all. With many children it is much less marked than in Elsie's case—as it had been, for instance, between Kate and her mother.

There did seem to be, in both Elsie and her mother, factors that made their attachment such an intense, rather possessive and prolonged affair. She had been planned as the last baby after a miscarriage two years previously, and when she was a year old her mother's mother had died. A little later the family went through a period of financial worries. Elsie responded to her mother's depression with very strong affection and a protective kind of possessiveness that tended to exclude both father and sister. The mother was inclined to collude in this, as she derived such comfort from this vigorous and demonstrative child.

Elsie's difficulties in adjusting to her primary school were surprising to the parents. Although so attached to her mother, she had seemed to be quite sociable and to play happily with the other children when she went out with her mother to the park. These difficulties then indicated that all was not as well as it seemed, that when she left her mother she did not carry within her the experience of a strong protective person on whom she could rely. Had she really internalized such an experience, it would have helped her to turn to her teacher, expecting to rediscover in her another maternal figure. Her difficulty in making friends and in playing with other children at primary school suggested an inability to cope with rivals on her own level. When she then stayed at home with various colds and infections she was able to reassure herself, for the moment at any rate, that she was her mother's only baby.

Her new engagement with friends of her own age at eleven suggests that by this stage she has worked through her possessive over-dependence. In part, this success is a measure of growing up; in part, it seems to be a breakaway, a flight from the possessive dependence on mother, to substitute a similar possessive relationship with friends. She has three special friends: one or the other is usually out of favour, but there is always one to fall back on, to commiserate with about the shortcomings of the other one or two. They form a little group or family of their own, where they seem to be experiencing and acting out among their own age group some of their parent and family conflicts—and for the moment the school family seems to be more important to them than the home one.

It is immensely important for the working through of this phase in Elsie's development that her mother *can* respond by letting go of her emotionality. She responds, moreover, in a positive way by developing new interests of her own, so that her daughter does not need to feel guilty about moving away. She is then all the more likely to move back more closely from a position of greater independence gained through experience, drawn by love and appreciation, rather than by guilt.

CHAPTER EIGHT

Some eleven-year-olds in difficulty

S ome eleven-year-olds have different kinds of problems interfering with their development, not that such problems are
peculiar to children of this age. It is a time, however, when
parents are looking towards the day when their child becomes an
adolescent and is well on the way to being grown up. Difficulties that perhaps had been passed over lightly before, in the hope
that the child would grow out of them, may not be so easy to
ignore.

Persistence of childish behaviour: bedwetting

Mrs M is worried about David, aged eleven years, who is still
wetting the bed as he has done, at intervals, throughout his life.
Sometimes he will be dry for as much as three weeks at a time,
especially when he is away from home. Until this last year or two
she always thought it would clear up if she did not worry about it;
but now she suspects that David himself worries, although she
continues to make light of it. Medical examinations have revealed
nothing abnormal. David sleeps very deeply at night and is difficult

to wake; upon advice, she has given him an alarm clock to wake himself, but this does not succeed.

Mrs M's husband left her shortly after the birth of her daughter, who is three years younger than David. For nearly two years before this, however, their marriage was quietly unhappy due to her husband's infidelity: they had "no rows, no scenes" she said, "that was never my way—perhaps better if we'd been able to have it out in the open." She has resumed the work for which she was trained and is beginning to make a satisfactory life for herself. David and his sister are attractive, friendly children. Mrs M has been grateful to them for being so undemanding in earlier years when she felt very low and, but for David's bedwetting, she would feel that they were growing up nicely and that they had not suffered from the break-up of her marriage. Her former husband has not remarried. He lives nearby and sees the children every weekend, to their mutual pleasure. "He was never one to harbour a grievance," said Mrs M, "and although he was angry when I told him to go, he has forgotten all about it now. The children never talk about why we don't live together."

As physical causes are ruled out, it would seem that David's bedwetting, which happens in his sleep, is a sign of a worry that he cannot contain and express to someone. The worry leaks out when his daytime controls are relaxed. The deep sleep in itself may be a reaction against over-controlled and careful behaviour during the day. Mrs M may be right when she commented that it might have been better had she and her husband been able to have their disagreements out in the open, although of course it is understandable and right that parents should want to protect their children from the brunt of anger and bitterness with each other. Nevertheless, the children are bound to sense hidden tensions of this kind, even in infancy, and to interpret them in their own way, to feel that perhaps they are to blame. Even though the parents are on civilized terms and seem able to share the children, the children must wonder about their parents' separation and perhaps feel guilty about it. They may try to avoid the pain of the problem by cutting it out of their thoughts.

Although they may not admit it, and may resent feeling this way, children often do feel it is their fault when things in the family go wrong. David has apparently managed well by developing as a friendly and helpful child, and being a bond that unites his separated parents. It may be, however, that he felt under too great a pressure to become a good child; that his mother was too vulnerable for him to be able to be obstreperous and angry when he felt like it, so that he even had to cut out the fact that he did have these feelings. By his bedwetting he may be expressing an anger he does not know he feels.

It is not possible, of course, with the few details we have, to be sure what it does mean and to know for certain why David does wet the bed. But we could surmise that in doing this he is expressing something of himself that he is not at present able to express in any other way. It may be necessary for him to take part in detailed psychotherapeutic treatment before he is able to understand and to express, in a more acceptable and social way, these emotions and impulses that flow out unconsciously in the wetting.

But in any case, it would be helpful for Mrs M to register openly with him that she knows he is worried about it. It will be more honest and a relief to him to recognize that it is a problem that neither of them understands, rather than to continue to make light of it. Instead of trying to probe too directly and deeply into his thoughts about the wetting, which is likely to be a sore point, it may be helpful to give him opportunities to talk of his feelings in general. Not that most boys of eleven talk easily about their feelings, but as he approaches adolescence David is likely to find it difficult to avoid being aware of a turmoil in himself that he does not understand. And, of course, the fact that he is still incontinent in a baby way will intensify all the worries that a pre-adolescent commonly has about whether his penis is all right, how it compares with that of other boys and so on.

Friendship with his father at this time is especially important, as he increasingly needs a man with whom he can identify, who is willing to help him along towards becoming a man himself. It is equally important that he should feel his mother wants this—that she does not need him to take care of her; and just as she is beginning to enjoy the work she has taken up, she looks forward to David eventually finding a way in which he will be able to make a life of his own.

Laziness

Laziness begins to be rather more of a worry to parents around this time. Increasingly now they look to see how their children are going to make their way in the world, how they are going to be able to support themselves, whether they can stand up for themselves and struggle with difficulties in work. And this concern is a very real matter. It is important for us to be able to encourage our children to work and to stand on their own feet.

It is also important, however, to understand what we mean by laziness. Here, in some detail, is an account of an eleven-year-old boy in whom sheer laziness and "shirking" (as it appeared to his school) turned out, when looked at more closely, to be a more complicated matter.

In his third term at secondary school, Christopher was summoned by his headteacher, who had received so many complaints from different members of the staff about laziness, inattention in class, and homework not done, that he thought the boy needed a stern reprimand.

Christopher was a very fresh-faced healthy-looking boy, but his demeanour and expression did not fit in with his lively colour. He seemed quite contrite when lectured, but puzzled and straining, as if he found it difficult to concentrate on what the teacher was saying, although he was trying hard to do so. The teacher tried to draw him out and discover what he thought about school, about the work, the other teachers, and whether he had any friends. He was quite positive that he *did* like school, that the teachers were nice to him, could not say that he liked or disliked any of the lessons especially, but he did know he was keen on football. He did *mean* to do his work and to get to lessons on time, but he could not say why he so often failed to do this. He could not expand much in answer to any of the questions, but trailed off in a helpless, worried way, as if he felt that more was required of him, but he did not quite understand what, or how he could meet it.

After this talk the headteacher concluded that the general school view of Christopher as a well-grown, healthy lad with plenty of appetite for games and none for work (a common malady that could usually be cured by detentions and loss of privileges) was a rather superficial one. He arranged to see Christopher's parents, together with a psychological consultant to the school.

Christopher's father, Mr C, was himself a schoolteacher, and began the interview by asserting firmly how strongly he was on the side of the school in deploring Christopher's poor work, and how strict he was at home in seeing that the boy sat down to his home-work every evening for hours at a time. He himself was too busy to help, and anyway he did not believe that parents should help children with their homework, but he certainly saw that he spent more than the prescribed time on it. But Christopher's mother, he implied, was too lenient with him. Christopher was indeed a bit like his mother: a bit soft, easily discouraged, not at all like their younger son Robin, who found no trouble at all in getting down to work and who was a great help to him in many ways. Could the school advise Mr C? He was quite willing to punish Christopher if they thought it would do any good.

While her husband spoke, Mrs C sat silent, weeping from time to time, and making occasional comments that showed she paid lip-service to the views of her husband, and that the school should be much harder on Christopher. Her comments also showed that she privately shielded and protected him behind their backs. When encouraged to talk a little more about Christopher as she remembered him when a baby and a small child, she began to do so very easily. Her husband looked impatient at first, as if he felt that this harking back to childhood was quite beside the point. "We should be concentrating on the future, what sort of life he's going to make for himself if he goes on the way he's going now." However as the teacher and the consultant were clearly interested in getting a picture of Christopher's development, he joined in gradually to fill out details that he could—not unsympathetically—recall.

In the course of the discussion, Mr C began to present a much less harsh and pious side of himself. The picture of Christopher and his family that the two people from his school tentatively reached, after quite a long discussion, was as follows.

Christopher had been born shortly after his parents' marriage at a time when Mr C, in his mid-thirties, was changing from a semi-skilled artisan job to training as a teacher. The couple were not too well off: Mr C was finding his studies absorbing, but hard going, and had not much time to spend on his wife and baby. She was quiet, vulnerable, and undemanding, and very grateful that she had a quiet, undemanding, physically healthy and blooming baby. She spent a lot of time with him, but from her description it sounded as if she had been too lonely and depressed to really enjoy him. She was living in a strange town, did not make friends easily, and remained very housebound.

When the next child, Robin, was born a couple of years later, things were a little easier. Mr C was in a job again; she had come to know the wives of some of his colleagues, and so, although he was still very busy, always active at making things when he was in the house and often out on political activities, she was less lonely. Robin was a slightly more demanding baby, but more sociable and more fun than Christopher had been. As the two boys grew up, Robin began to take the lead in trying new things, and Christopher seemed quite content to follow. The father was proud of Robin and liked to show him off to friends, but was inclined to ignore the presence of the elder boy. To compensate for this, Mrs C felt a strong unspoken sympathy for her elder son, whom she said she understood because he was in many ways like herself. It seemed as if she identified with him some inadequate side of herself that she did not know how to help along—a side she tried to keep hidden, secretly and guiltily.

The fact that she was indulging him secretly—implying, rather than saying, "Poor boy, you're hard pressed, never mind your homework for tonight . . .", or "You're so tired, take the morning off and stay in bed", while at the same time feeling that she ought to be more strict with him and encourage him to do what his father ordered, was resulting in a confusing situation for the boy. This made it all too easy for him to slip out of any regular commitment to work. Her unconscious sabotaging of her husband's efforts, plus his difficulty in getting really close to Christopher in a helpful way, seemed to increase Mr C's exasperated harshness.

These interpretations of the situation were suggested tentatively to the parents in the course of discussion. It was also suggested that one could not look at his problem as one of simple laziness, but that, on the other hand, it would not help just to feel sorry for him, to make him an exception and allow him to slide out of doing the work that he was meant to do. There was common agreement, as a result of intelligence tests he had been given at the beginning of his year in school, and because of the quality of work that he had produced from time to time, that he was in a class and in a group where he was by no means out of his depth. Falling behind the others, and far below the level of his potential, was not going to help his self-confidence and his ability to face frustration. It was agreed that the emphasis should be on trying to encourage, rather than to enforce, on some firmness to support the side of him that wanted to try and work, and to strengthen, through some experience of success, his belief that he could produce work that was of value and of interest.

It was also suggested that the family might like to try to arrange individual treatment for Christopher with a children's therapist, where he could explore matters further and help him to a better understanding of the ways in which he turned away from frustration and get a better grasp of himself. This would enable him to confront and surmount difficult tasks. Mr C, however, was most averse to this idea. He evidently considered that it would be a reflection on himself as a parent to seek such help. So it was thought better not to press the point for the time being, but to see what could be done by mobilizing resources at home and at school in the light of what had emerged so far in the discussion.

The headteacher conferred with Christopher's class teacher, and with one or two of the other teachers who had been most in conflict with him about his work. This all seemed to bring about a more promising situation over the next few months, a general improvement in Christopher's work, reliability, and general involvement in school. The basis for this was already there in his participation in games. Games can be an activity that, if you have any talent, you can sometimes use in order to run away from reflection, from other things that you find hard to live with. All physical activity, for that matter, however successful, can be a means of avoiding thinking about more indefinable fears. But sometimes, with encouragement and support, children can be helped to use and extend the experience of success in one field to enable them to struggle towards overcoming obstacles in another which presents greater difficulty to them.

Trying to understand a child's behaviour difficulties

Understanding is the first step in helping a child overcome his difficulties. This final example is of a boy who presented a real problem to his school in the first year of his secondary education. We will tell this story from the point of view of the school, and show how the attitude of his teacher changed when he came to know a little more about the troubles of the boy's parents and his home background.

Robert came to his secondary school with a reputation for being troublesome and defiant: not backward, but a very intermittent worker, and then only when interested. For instance, given a subject for composition that captured his imagination, he would write at length in a way that showed he had really thought about it. His troublesomeness was also intermittent and difficult to foresee, as were the ways in which it would express itself. His sins were always committed alone. They included truanting, very occasionally bashing up some other boy for no special reason, ringing up the local fire brigade to give false alarms, writing anonymous notes to a teacher or the local police station, giving false information about some other boy's supposedly criminal activities. These acts varied from sudden violent impulses to planned strategies that were calculated to cause trouble to the authorities.

His headteacher and form teacher were determined not just to write him off as a hopeless case, which his previous school had done. They tried, instead, to spend time talking to him and trying to find out his interests. They tried to get some idea of why he seemed to be going along all right for a week or two, and then would get involved again in some fresh and unforeseen trouble. The Head sent for Robert's parents two or three times before meeting with any response from them. Finally, he had a long letter from Robert's mother, saying that her husband was ill and that she was much too busy working long hours to come to school. In any case, Robert was no trouble at all at home! He was a great help to her in the house and with the younger children. If he was in trouble it was the fault of the other boys, especially M (and here she gave a long, incoherent account about the badness of one "M", with whom she would not allow her children to associate).

The headteacher had the uneasy feeling that this letter sounded rather more strange and persecuted than that of the usual angry mother rushing to the defence of her offspring. Following another of Robert's outbreaks, the third occasion on which he had had to protect him from police action, he made a further attempt to reach Robert's family. This time his father came—a pleasant-spoken, mild, ingratiating man, not apparently ill at all, but still out of a job and quite helpless to suggest what to do with Robert. He pleaded ignorance about the boy's outbreaks, but was quite willing to believe that they had occurred. He handed the whole problem back to the school.

A few weeks later Robert was away again, truanting once more from school. One of the boys who lived nearby, however, came in with a story about seeing an ambulance outside Robert's house, taking Robert's mother away because she had "gone mental". Following this up, the school found out that she had in fact had a breakdown. It seemed she had been living under considerable strain for some time, possibly years. Her husband had had to give up his job some four or five years back as a result of illness that was now supposed to be cured. Having given up work, however, he had seemed to become more infantile and apathetic, increasingly unemployable. She had continued to work, but with increasing resentment and contempt for her husband. The burden of this was evidently felt by Robert, who was indeed a good boy at home and helped her a great deal with the three younger children.

The strain of all this was clearly too much at times, and resulted in these sudden unaccountable outbreaks against the establishment—both a cry for help, one would think, and an expression of resentment against a world of grown-ups that was asking far too much of him.

The headteacher and his class teacher had intuitively felt something of this, before they knew any of the facts, but they did take the trouble to find them out as far as they could, instead of just punishing the boy out of hand. The school is now conferring with various welfare agencies involved to try to work out the best way to help the whole family while the mother is away in hospital.

If our children are in trouble, it usually means that we as parents are in trouble too, for our lives are intimately inter-related. Surmounting obstacles and difficulties in personal relationships is an essential part of growing and developing. Sometimes, however, the difficulties seem too great for us to struggle with. In that case it is a good idea for us as parents to try to find someone whom we respect and with whom we can discuss matters: someone less involved than we are ourselves—maybe the child's teacher, or the family doctor, or simply a friend. Such a discussion may help us to see when it is necessary to try to find some more substantial professional help, but much more commonly it may be enough in itself to help us view things more clearly and continue more hopefully.

BOOK TWO
YOUR TWELVE–FOURTEEN-YEAR-OLD

Introduction

This book, like the others in the series, is not meant to tell you how your child ought to look and to behave in these years. Children develop at very different rates in body, in mind, and in feelings. Each child has his own rate of growth and his own possible pattern of growth, and our job as parents and as educators is to do the best we can to provide the right conditions to let that take place.

Some of the things talked about here may well seem to fit your eleven-year-old, some may not apply to your child until he is well over fourteen, and some may not seem to apply at all, but that need not necessarily worry you. The aim of this book is to help you in thinking about your own unique experience and opportunity to observe your own child, and hence to be in a better position to decide for yourself whether you need to worry about him or not, and when it is useful to do so. For it is not in the nature of children or of ourselves not to worry at times; if we never do, then surely we are missing out on something. The important thing is to worry usefully in a creative way that helps you to understand yourself and your child a little better.

Growing up for your child also means growing up alongside for you as a parent. This twelve- to fourteen-year-old period of early adolescence is the second most rapid period of physical growth in the life of most children. This entails comparably rapid mental and emotional adjustment, both for the child and for the parents. If it is your first child who is entering this stage, you are going to meet for the first time the challenge of adapting from being the parent of a child to being the parent of a young person who is straining towards greater independence, is touchy about being treated as an equal, and yet may be experiencing states of mind secretly bordering on panic when he needs extra protection and comfort without feeling free to say so easily. If it is your last child who is now at this stage, you may have had some experience in adapting to budding adolescents, but be yourself in the novel situation of adapting to the fact that soon you will have no more children depending upon you. You may wonder, most especially perhaps if you have been a nonworking mother, what you are now going to do with your life.

This is a stage when your child tends to become particularly sensitive again to the way you are feeling about him, but also to your own state of mind. He is trying to understand himself and is puzzled by the contradictions in his own feelings and behaviour. This may make him all the more appreciative of your attempt to understand him, and he is more tolerant of your imperfections if he is convinced that you are trying and do not come out too often with the retorts that we are often tempted to use in moments of exasperation: "I just don't understand you—when I was your age . . .!"

In these two years the majority of boys and girls begin to mature sexually.[1] Many girls begin to have their periods, to develop breasts; many boys discover that they are capable of producing semen and have to struggle for a while with the uncertain register of a voice that is breaking to a deeper tone. Physically, the difference between boys and girls becomes more marked; the pressure to find an identity for themselves and a place in the world as a member of their own sex becomes stronger. And we see how this is resisted in these days of interchangeable garments and hair-styles.

This book will talk of your twelve- to fourteen-year-olds under some general headings, but will also talk in a little more detail about a few young people of this age to illustrate some of the points that are being made. Some of these young people may remind you of your own child, some may seem to have no point of resemblance. However, we can learn as much by observing and expressing differences as by noting similarities. The examples of children and families given here are disguised in order to be unidentifiable, but they have their origin in the observation of real life.

Note

1. As mentioned in a note to the previous book, the age of onset of puberty has been gradually lowering.

CHAPTER ONE

Relationships between parents and teachers

As already suggested in the previous book, it is likely to be a help to both you and the teachers of your child if you are able to meet now and then to talk about him together. It is most important if he can feel that home and school are both working in much the same direction to help him—that they are not at odds with one another. This means that parents and teachers need to have some respect for each other.

If the teachers are very critical of his home and his parents, if the parents blame the school for his difficulties or his failures, your child may react to this in a worried, guilty way. He feels a divided loyalty—that he is letting down one or the other. On the other hand, he may exploit the situation to set them even more at odds with each other, and thus slide out of taking any blame himself. The school and home that do not get on together are, in his experience, like two parents who do not get on together. He is likely to act the same way as he would react to divided parents. It is a time when children entering adolescence most particularly need a supportive kind of government that speaks as far as possible with one voice, because they are becoming more aware of very contradictory voices and impulses within themselves, and they are not sure which one is likely to prevail.

Here is an example of the way a young adolescent girl's troubles came to a head finally over a conflict between parents and school.

Rachel was the only child of parents who had both been married before. Their present marriage was not a happy one either, and many of the quarrels were about Rachel in a contest for her affection. She grew up an anxious, easily upset child who was over-indulged by both parents and constantly greedy for presents and for signs of affection.

If she was crossed by one of her parents she would tend to weep and then go to the other to complain, learning from experience that with their rivalry for her affection she could usually expect a sympathetic hearing from the one who had already said no. Thus she usually gained her point.

This way of going on led to her missing a great deal of her schooling through many imaginary little ailments that were apt to crop up when anything unpleasant, such as a test, was on the programme. She went on to her secondary school with a poor record for attendance. Her parents had a still worse one for constantly complaining and being quite unco-operative with the school.

When she was thirteen she had a class teacher who took a great deal of trouble with the pupils, was ambitious for them to succeed and thought that she was capable of getting good results where others had failed—which was indeed the case in many instances. She succeeded in capturing Rachel's interest, and for the first term things went better. Rachel attended regularly and produced better work. In the second term she had a quarrel with one of the girls in her class, who then omitted to ask her to her birthday party, but asked all the others and most of the boys, including one whom Rachel considered to be her own particular boyfriend.

Rachel then threw a tantrum at home and said she would not go back to school until her teacher talked to the girls and got the main sinner to apologize to her. Both her parents took her part, and descended on the school to complain and to request an apology. Rachel's class teacher, disappointed at this backsliding on the part of the pupil with whom she had taken so much trouble, and furious with the parents who were endorsing her childish behaviour, told them what she thought in terms that were more direct than diplomatic. This was a head-on collision that led to a long wrangle with the headteacher, who took his teacher's part, and eventually resulted in Rachel's withdrawal from the school.

Encouraging your young adolescent's grown-up self: "taking sides"

Things need not always be so dramatic and final in their outcome. In most adolescents, along with the part of them that wants to remain a child and to cling to the mother's protective care, there is always a part that hates being pampered and overprotected. When teachers and parents have met and talked about a child they will—unless they are abnormally touchy—have a shrewd idea of the true weight they should give to a child's demands and complaints. They will be able to judge better when action is called for to change a stressful situation—when a child really is being bullied by a classmate; or when sympathetic listening can safely be followed by telling the child he must stand up for himself. For if he does that he may, it is true, get a punch in the playground, but he will earn his own and the other children's respect. This is, fortunately or unfortunately, a common form of initiation ceremony among boys as late as twelve years of age when a newcomer is not yet an accepted member of the group. Girls, perhaps, have other types of initiation—for example, they may have to learn to put up with being at first welcomed, then snubbed; and to put on a fine show of indifference at this stage.

Children have to go through this social hoop more than once in their school career: clearly, at the change of school from primary to secondary, but also within the secondary school if, for example, they change forms or sets, or sometimes if a teacher leaves to whom they have been attached. But once the child has been accepted in the group, most of the defensive anxieties diminish rapidly. Feelings about friends, about teachers, about school, generally oscillate in early adolescence. It is only if they remain negative and distressed over a long period that extra care has to be taken in inquiring into the cause.

When parents and teachers do not talk together—and they very often do not—it is easy to forget that the child's behaviour at home may be very different from his behaviour at school. Both aspects need to be known before "taking sides", even as a last resort, can ever be contemplated, and teachers as well as parents need to keep this in mind. Furthermore, the degree of support a child needs at twelve may change considerably during the twelve- to-fourteen-year-old period, during which the majority of children enter puberty, becoming by the end of their fourteenth year sexually adult—though not mature. They are then much more likely to resent than to welcome any side-taking. But only parents can know how far their particular child has grown up, or how he or she is reacting to the changes taking place as growing up proceeds. A child does not usually want coddling, but, equally, he does not want to be abandoned. Few schools welcome the abdication of parental concern.

Should we, then, never take seriously our child's criticism of school? In fact, we should always do so, for to do so is not the same thing as "taking sides". After all, we would always take seriously something the teacher said to us about the child. Both critics tell us something about themselves and about the school. It would be ridiculous to pretend that schools and teachers are perfect, any more than parents or children are perfect. If you know your child well enough, you can probably get a fair idea of when he has justifiable complaints to make. In most cases it is probably enough to hear him out, to make clear that you do sympathize and maybe, for instance, might agree that it does seem as if he has not had a fair deal from his teacher this time. But then it might seem reasonable to indicate to him that this is all in the nature of life; injustices do occur, we have at times to learn to tolerate them, to understand when they are the result of accident or frailty rather than malevolence, and to try to act next time perhaps in such a way as to avoid a repetition.

There may be instances when you feel that your child has been too badly treated and that you must go and talk about it, either to the particular teacher concerned or to the headteacher. Even in that event, it is better to keep cool, and to contain your protests until you meet the teacher himself. Your point of view might change when you talk to him, but even if it does not, and the child has been badly treated, there will be more chance of the situation improving if you have not fanned the flames too much first. The child has to know he can, in the end, trust in your support, but he has to trust your judgement, too.

CHAPTER TWO

Enjoying school, expanding interests, and coping with competition

T hese can be years of great excitement and involvement at school, of enjoying lessons and also of talking with companions for those boys and girls who are fitting reasonably well into both their programme of studies and the society of their age group. They are beginning to see themselves as part of a much larger world, a world which has a history, which is much nearer and more real to them as they become more aware of having a personal history. A growing ability to look at themselves, a need to be aware of their own identity and place in their family and at their school, comes as they look back on their own past and begin to think of their future. It is the approach to real adolescence and grown-up independence. In the words of thirteen-year-old Nicola: "When I think back to the time I was eleven—I thought I was having a good time but it was because I didn't know any better . . . I just didn't realize about all the other people in the world, about the bombing in Vietnam and all that, and how lucky I am to be living here . . . sometimes it makes me feel miserable, but all the same life is more interesting now. I feel more alive than I used to— I look forward to doing things." This young girl had a more than usual zest for life, but she speaks for many others.

Schools offer a wonderful opportunity for the expanding interests of the young adolescent. They have occasions for discussion when they can get to know their own opinions and the opinions of each other. At this stage the views of their teachers and of their parents are usually still eagerly sought, even if only to be argued against. The girl mentioned above came home from school one day full of a discussion in history lesson about the French revolution, its causes, and whether it might have been prevented. Her father led the conversation on to the students' revolution of May 1969 and ventured a few ideas of his own. After some fierce arguing his daughter suddenly decided that some of what he had to say might be worth considering: "You know, Daddy, you're really quite intelligent—I never thought you knew anything about history. Of course, we are living in history now—I never thought about that before."

Help with homework: pressures at school

The beginning of this twelve to fourteen period can be a difficult one for the child at school. When he first transferred to secondary school at eleven he was probably anxious but full of enthusiasm about going to a "real school" and doing "serious work". Regular homework was a privilege that marked him out from the more playful atmosphere of the junior school, and as it did not generally take too much time each evening, it was a privilege fairly lightly earned. Furthermore, teachers are used to adapting their teaching to a level within reach—at first—of the average or below-average member of the class, so that all the new children have a fair chance of getting off to an equal start. Parents, too, at this stage often show obvious interest in what their children are learning, and sometimes remember enough of their own schooldays to be able to help with a problem, especially as methods of teaching in secondary schools tend to be more reminiscent of parental days at school than are primary school methods.

But in the second year the pressure is on. Gaps begin to appear between the performance of the brighter and harder-working children and that of the slower and indifferent ones. The anxieties of success—how to continue to do better than the next child—are not less than the anxieties of relative failure—how to keep up with him or not fall too far behind. Exams and tests, streaming, promotions, and demotions, reinforce these anxieties not only in the children but in the teachers, for whom it is a point of pride that "their" classes perform efficiently, and in the parents, too. Homework time is stepped up, and will always be longer for the conscientious and slow worker, whose proper pride will leave nothing unfinished. We may not wish to endorse this type of pressured learning, but in most schools we have little choice but to accept it, or to opt out.

The effect of parents' attitudes to success

In this sort of situation, how can we help the child? Some writers, in the past, have suggested that the way for a parent to help their child to academic success is to be ruthless, excessive in the demand for achievement, critical, ambitious, and domineering. Parents who have these characteristics are unlikely to change, anyway. Parents who do not depend on their children to achieve the ambitions in which they themselves have failed, or to emulate achievements which, if rejected, would negate the parental values, may fortunately find a more humane way of helping their children.

To develop at school, a child has need of stress and anxiety, but it must not be so intense as to cripple his sense of adventure, his trust in his parents and his own self-respect. He needs to be able to put off immediate satisfactions in order to encompass long-term ends, and he needs an appropriate mixture of succouring and of independent responsibility. We need to learn to satisfy our own needs as parents in helping to satisfy the needs of the child. It is the same task—though longer and more deeply important—as that of the good teacher. If we rely on our child to succeed for us, we impose a quite unfair strain. This is why children of this age may hate being "shown off" by their doting parents. The child needs to be praised but not to be used as a boast. He needs the encouragement of a reward, and if this is to be a present of some sort, it is best given before examination—for his effort—rather than after, as if dependent only on his success. He does not want to be caught in a commercial transaction in which, if he delivers the goods (success) he will be loved, but if he does not deliver, he will be despised.

Excessive anxiety about his relationship with his parents on this score *may* result in achievement, but only at a high price, and it is far more likely to destroy both the relationship and the achievement.

Facing up to failure

If a child is secure in his trust and knows that his parents hope for his success but do not demand it as a condition of their love, he is the more likely to be able to put his heart into his work. Doing that, he is more likely to succeed, and so to earn his own self-respect. Sometimes, however, he will not succeed. The experience of failure has then to be lived through, and cannot simply be ignored as if it did not matter. The child will not be reassured or encouraged to try again if his failure is dismissed as of no consequence. He will know there is a deceit in this response for, if it were genuine, then equally his success would be of no value. It is better to help him to face up to the failure, to prepare to try again, or to realign his sights in accord with a realistic estimate of his abilities, and so to make the best of what he can in fact achieve. Here the advice of a sympathetic teacher can be helpful to parent and child.

Ups and downs in feelings about school

We must remember from our own schooldays that a child's attitude to school is not always the same. One week he will come home full of excitement about his teacher or his friends and the events at school. Another time he may be full of disgruntlement and sourness. It is not always easy to discover what has led to this reversal: perhaps the teacher has lost a piece of homework on which the child had spent much time and effort, or perhaps there has been a quarrel with a best friend. Whatever it is, the child may not tell and indeed may not know. What is probable is that the sudden dislike of school—"it's so *boring*"—will make the parent anxious. It is important not to offload this anxiety on to the child, but instead to accept the parental role and help to relieve the child of his anxiety. This may sometimes be done simply by not arguing against his judgement on school and its boredom, while not colluding with it.

After a while, as with so many growing pains, the disgruntlement will pass. If it persists for long and seems to be interfering with work progress, it would be worth inquiring into the matter with the teacher. Is the child in the right stream, doing the right subjects, attacking the learning problems in the most constructive way? There may be many points to consider. There are many children in a classroom, and a teacher may not always manage to note each child's special difficulties; but he is usually anxious to help, especially when he knows that a parent is also keen to help and is not there simply to grumble.

Atmosphere at home

Work will be too much for the child when his friends make other claims on his time, or when he genuinely finds the work too difficult. Again, he will not be able to cope when, owing to other family situations, he cannot get the facilities to do his homework well—when he has no quiet space and there are distractions all round. It is a curious thing that it is not the noise of a radio as such that distracts the ordinary child from managing his homework—it is the noise of someone else's radio. Children will often have a radio [or music player] going while they study. Up to a certain level at least, it does not seem to intrude on their learning; like the traffic, it is simply a familiar background noise. Voices arguing or simply talking distract much more. This is the chief reason why a child studying needs a room of his own, if possible.

The environment provided by the home has a direct effect on the child's learning. Where there are no books, books are not usually valued, and the skills of reading and writing and numeracy are essentially bookish skills central to education. A child whose family has no respect for, or interest in, the arts and sciences is unlikely to study them, save to escape from his family, and then he will have to overcome considerable emotional strain to do so. A child whose family does not discuss, question, and examine what is going on in the world will himself tend to be dull in response, limited in argument, and incapable of extending his thoughts or tolerating new experiences. Where books and talk are usual, and where reason is given along with orders, a child has a framework into which his efforts to study will fit naturally. By keeping ourselves alive as parents we help also to keep our children's interests growing, as Nicola's father helped her to relate her history lesson to her current life.

Parental help with homework

Homework itself may present particular problems. The answer is, I think, that it depends on how we set about it. It is no help just to do all his sums for him, for he needs to learn how to tackle them himself. If, by any chance, we are able to do them easily, this only proves to him how stupid he is. If we cannot do them and shrug them aside, saying that it is his job, he remains baffled. A useful approach is to try to discover with him what the method is for working out a given problem. Turn back a few pages in his textbook to find this out (even if you already know). This encourages him to learn the important technique of revision, and to use the tools—the books—that are provided. To do this is much more important in the long run than getting a particular answer right.

On other occasions it is not the pure difficulty of a piece of homework that stymies the child, it is that he cannot work up any enthusiasm for a subject—it does not seem to have any point, any relevance to life. "Who wants to know about the French Revolution anyway?" The point becomes clearer when, in discussion, he sees that he is a bit of a revolutionary himself—that revolution is a continuous aspect of life, that we are always trying to change things or to fight against their being changed, and that out of this tension comes most of our progress—and also most of our catastrophes. History is not only in the textbook but in the here and now, and the child is history also. But you will never convince him of this if you say it in order to get him to do his homework. As far as he is concerned, that is not a real point at all. Your reason for saying it must be a genuine one—because you are interested and because it matters. Of course, not everything a child is taught at school does matter. The worse enemy to any genuine learning is pretence. But if he wants to make a good sound argument against the French Revolution being important he will still need to know the facts and to put them in order. He must learn how to get evidence and then how to use it. It is your willingness to discuss this with him, to ask for the evidence, that helps him with his homework.

Work and competition

This age group is past the age of collecting "stars" like prizes, but marks and competition loom very large on the horizon of both child and teacher. Teachers may pretend not to take marks very seriously—"our pupils take examinations in their stride". Children may pretend to look down on the child who triumphs in exams, but really they take the competition very earnestly indeed. It is difficult to strike a happy medium between ridiculing examination marks on account of their known unreliability, and using them superstitiously as the true measure of success and failure. As a parent you will probably look regularly at your child's homework and its marks. You will certainly see his termly or annual report, which indicates his position in various subjects.

The intention of marks is to inform you and the child about his level of achievement and to encourage him to learn more. Nobody is much encouraged by getting very low marks, and you can help your child by trying to discover what caused a low mark and by practising ways to improve on the performance. You may help him to discover how to improve it for himself if you ask him to explain the teacher's comments, and if he does not understand them, he can be prodded into asking at school. Even a child who has succeeded may be unaware of the nature of his success: was he just neat, or original, or hard-working, or imaginative, or all of these things, or what? Although, in an ideal world, teachers would find time to go through every piece of work with each child, in practice they cannot often do this, and parents can help by interest and discussion, at least until the stage when the child knows as much or more than the parents do.

Most children find some difficulty as they progress from twelve to fourteen, because teachers from whom they used to receive top marks tend to mark more strictly as the children mature, and the highest grade goes down from ninety or a hundred per cent to seventy. This puzzles child as well as parent. Is it an improvement to go from a score of eighty per cent at twelve to one of sixty per cent at fourteen?[1] Neither you nor the child can tell from the mark itself. If you glance also at the position it may give some extra guidance, but it is hard to be sure. Again, this is another area where, if you are in doubt, it is as well to talk with the teacher.

The parent's function here would seem to be twofold. First, to supplement the school's efforts by showing interest in the child's work and performance. Second, to stimulate the child to do as well as he can without overburdening him with too heavy a weight of competition. Unless he is totally without ambition, he is bound to have to deal with the stress of competing—with other children as well as with himself and his past performance. To win is just as stressful as to lose, for he cannot do better next time.

The child who cannot talk about his learning difficulties, or who is simply chided for them, is unlikely to meet the challenge of learning readily, or to gain increasing confidence in the handling of his knowledge and skills which ensure self-respect and competence. By the age of fourteen a child may have some idea of the sort of career he has in view, and this can be a help in underlining some of the skills and achievements that are needed to enter that career. If these skills and achievements are realistically possible for the child, the parent and teacher may use them towards a creative end.

Note

1. Fashions in grading fluctuate, and teachers generally also try to be specific in their comments, but the principle remains that the child's assessment of their academic status is liable to go through a period of insecurity.

CHAPTER THREE

School, home, and work

T welve years of age may be early days to begin thinking about the kind of work that could best suit your child when he leaves school, but it is not too early to consider how, in due course, he can be guided towards making a realistic decision for himself. [Nowadays more and more children stay on at school beyond the statutory leaving age, and such children may well] have an advantage in stability and maturity when they do leave which outweighs the temporary gains of earlier salaried employment.[1] However, the decision to stay on at school is in many ways similar to that made when the child decides to leave school: it is a committal to a new way of life that will affect his whole future.

The preparation for this critical decision about work and further education cannot easily be postponed until the age of fifteen, for by this time the whole issue will be highly charged with emotion. The child will feel a desire to become independent—a wage-earner— but at the same time he will fear being plunged into the indifferent competitive adult world for which his achievements do not yet fit him. In the tension of these conflicting urges and feeling an inner need not only to be free but to repay his parents for the long years of childhood dependence, he may take any job that is offered, or that fits into a fantasy picture of work carried over from earlier childhood: the secretary marries the boss, the garage mechanic wins the Grand Prix.

At twelve years the child will not be in a position to know what he wants to become when he leaves school. Indeed, in an age like the present, when it is likely to be more important to be adaptable and flexible than to be fixed in one trade or skill, it would be unwise and undesirable if the specific decision were made so early. Nevertheless, it is important for us to talk with him about the world of work from time to time and to listen to his ideas and aspirations when he expresses them—as he surely will. It is this listening, much more than any direct advice we can give at this stage, which is important in helping the child to feel his way.

His ideas will often be unrealistic, even silly. It is the parents' job to provide him with information when he asks for it, but not to pass judgement upon his explorations for a role in life. He will do that himself when he is ready, for it is a matter of maturation as well as of knowledge. Most of us can remember how, after protesting that we were determined to become a fireman or a ballet dancer, these particular careers suddenly dropped out of our ambitions—we did not want to any more, or we knew we could not. An ambition that is wrong for us will drop out if it is not artificially sustained by rebellion against parental pressure or ridicule

It will happen sometimes that a child is absolutely certain at an early age what he wants to be. Special interests, talents, and the acceptance of family traditions have decided for him. Such instances are, however, the exception rather than the rule. When pressed for an answer a fourteen-year-old will usually provide one, even though it makes nonsense. For example, one boy of this age was asked what he planned to do when he left school. "Dunno", he said, and carried on with his carpentry. "Try and think, Robert", insisted the teacher. So he stopped working and after a few moments came up with the response that he would like to be a butcher. The teacher asked what made him choose that. "Well," he said, "I've always been fond of animals."

Most children simply do not know enough yet to decide. They do not know about jobs—what are the real salaries, prospects, long-term satisfactions, or social conditions. A boy talking of being a merchant seaman may not have thought how this would fit in with family and home life. Children do not know about themselves, their real abilities, their emotional satisfactions, their fears, and their ways of fitting in with other people. A girl wishing to be a nurse may not anticipate the stresses of caring for chronically ill people, or for ungrateful patients, or of having to submit to strict authority, or of bearing the responsibility for sudden and vital decisions. And finally, they do not know about the aptitudes and intellectual qualifications required for many jobs, so that in consequence, they sometimes have unrealistically high aspirations and sometimes unnecessarily low ones.

Adults, also limited as they often are to knowledge of their own field of work, cannot always provide the most up-to-date information about other people's work, and, as parents, we may have an erroneous idea of our children's powers. It is important, therefore, for parents to go and talk with teachers about both these matters. Schools will usually have a careers teacher who will offer information, and usually also have a teacher who knows the quality of the child's work and application. Armed with this information, the parents can hope to give active advice and encouragement that is at the same time founded on reality. The timing is important, for the child does not want to feel pushed out into the world, or to be held back. He has to feel our interest in his plans, but not to be burdened with our anxiety. It is a useful guide towards knowing that he is nearly ready to make a sound decision when, in the judgement of his parents and his teachers, the proposals he is making tally with what we know of his capacity and his achievement. At the earlier part of the twelve to fourteen period he is only gradually beginning to get a better idea of the sort of person he really is, and it will take him some time to feel his way imaginatively towards the kind of work he will finally be able to do. That will mean accepting and coming to terms with his limitations (parents have to do this too), but sometimes he will find in himself unsuspected powers of perseverance that will enable him to struggle towards something that he has a great urge to accomplish, and that he knows he has a say in choosing.

A child will often take an older brother or sister, a friend, or a relative, as a model for ideas about a career. It is always a great help if father and mother enjoy the work they do, no matter what it is, even if it is not the kind of work that he feels he would like to do himself. The parents' enjoyment can come from the actual work itself, or (in more repetitive jobs) it may be more in the comradeship and feeling of belonging to the firm.[2]

Parents and family have far more effect on children than do schools. If they are at variance with one another it is hard on the child. If they are together, they can do much to provide those opportunities for practice and real decision-making that will facilitate the child's eventual decision based on a self-knowledge and knowledge about his career. Children arrive at this decision later than we may expect, but in these indirect ways they are preparing for it earlier. In the preparation they are bound to make mistakes. For example, given responsibility for their own financial allowance, they may overspend, or may lie to conceal their overspending, but it is better that they do so now and learn by the experience. To always be protected against making mistakes that have real consequences is to place adulthood at risk.

Notes

1. At the time this book was written, the school-leaving age had recently been raised from fifteen to sixteen. Roland Harris (Martha Harris's husband) had been instrumental in this move.

2. Although the concept of job security within any organization has largely melted away, there are many ways of enjoying the experience of belonging to a work-group with a useful purpose, thereby satisfying the emotional as well as the financial need to work.

CHAPTER FOUR

Hobbies and interests

Play is children's work, it has been said,[1] and certainly when children are very young they concentrate intently on their play—building a sandcastle, drawing a house, being mummy and daddy or, a little later, cops and robbers. By the time they are twelve to fourteen they have less time for play, and we adults spend much of our time in driving home to them the difference we have invented between play and work. Work is virtuous, realistic, often rather unpleasant in a boring way, but serious. What's more, it is how you earn your living. Play is just a pastime—escape from reality, profitless and only to be tolerated because it gets you back to work. This distinction between work and play is one that, if he ever bothered to think about it, the young child would find incomprehensible. Like the adult who is immersed in his work, he finds the same pleasure in all experience. Admittedly, we are very guilty about our pleasures, and we have devised many types of work that seem specifically designed to ensure that no pleasure can be obtained from them, but we still acknowledge that all work and no play makes Jack a dull boy.

Necessity for play

What does a child get from play, from hobbies, games, and entertainments? He gets what he needs. Playing with a construction set or tools, with a bicycle or boat, breeding mice, catching fish, painting, taking photos, and so on satisfy an enormous range of individual needs. Some of these may be simple sensuous pleasures, like feeling the wind on your face as the bicycle rushes downhill. At the same time the bicycle may be the means of escape from tyrannous adults. It is freedom—power to decide where you are going on your own. Yet again, it is a way of belonging to a special group, all careering along together, or a way of venturing alone on distances through places like a wood at night, which might be too scaring otherwise. It is danger—but it is safety too.

Play is a way of gathering experience and of shaping powers: the power to be with others and to form social ties with them, the power to be quite alone with the nature of things—like the fisherman on the canal bank. It can satisfy deep drives, like the need to create or to cherish—as the girl making her own dress [or jewellery] or the boy with his pet rabbits,[2] or the need to destroy, but to do so safely, so that no unbearable guilt follows the impulse, as we also see in organized "war games" such as rugby or hockey.

Many forms of play—perhaps most—satisfy not one but a whole complex of needs. For example, collecting meets the urge to possess for oneself, to rival and at the same time to share an enthusiasm, or to understand something in great detail, and these more generous traits may cancel out the others. It is a way, too, of dealing with fears about one's own capacities—fears about one's courage, for example, or about being attractive. Dressing up for a party at twelve years is taken very seriously, but a rebuff met there is not the end of the world. The boy swimming a bit farther than he has ever done before can keep near the side of the pool and not lose face with himself.

Often in this age group the need to test out one's reaction to fear, to bring internal uncertainty into touch with external danger, becomes very strong, and it is hard for the parents to decide just how far to let the child go with his experiments. The boy climbing the cliff is seriously tasting a little of the flavour of death. He is no longer resting on the safety net of fantasy as a younger child might.

When he gets to the top it is as a man, and it is the sort of climb that, in one form or another, all our children have to make. We cannot hold them back for ever—we can only see that they are not driven to the attempt through any indifference on our part or in rebellion against our refusal to let them grow up.

When a very young child breaks up a toy we may get annoyed, but we usually understand that the child is saying something to us that is of furious importance and that is quite different from—let us say—the message conveyed by the breaking up that follows from curiosity and exploration of how the doll or toy is made. So we are tolerant, and help the young child by being very supportive and cuddling and talking to him. The twelve- to fourteen-year-old is still in need of this support, though it cannot easily be offered so openly. He cannot ask for it in quite such a childish fashion. Confidence in his relationships at home enables the adventurous hobbies—climbing, camping, skiing, swimming, cycling, exploring—to be undertaken without the need for rashness. It becomes a point of pride to be competent as a way of repaying trust. Important skills, as well as important personal adjustments to the inner self and to outer reality, are thus developed through play. Practical issues are the provision of genuine opportunity. The fourteen-year-old girl who wants to make real clothes for herself on a real machine with material she has chosen is practising a hobby, not a game.[3] Similarly the boy who wants to put up shelves in his room will need something better than a child's set of tools. Proper tools, though sharp, are in fact less likely to cause injury than the imitation tools, and far less likely to thwart the desire to be genuinely constructive. If the child has a pet, say a dog, it is the child's responsibility to look after it and train it. Whether he succeeds in this or falls instead into a way of pampering it one minute and ignoring it the next or neglecting it, is one index of our own success in bringing up the child. We may indeed well find that we need to rescue the dog from his forgetfulness.

Reading and television

The age of learning to read became lower and lower after the establishment of television in people's homes.[4] And there is no question that television can offer some fine and extraordinary opportunities to perceive the world beyond one's doorstep. All the same, a purely habitual, indiscriminate watching of television is a very second-hand sort of hobby, like watching football but never kicking a ball. For adults, it becomes a fantasy world to divert attention from our increasing incapacity. For children, it can be a way of escaping from acquiring the competence that accompanies real learning, a way of avoiding pain and difficulty and, in the end, even pleasure.

At school, and in most learning skills, books are a more important source of information and tool of thought than television can be. Twelve to fourteen is late to begin thinking of the quality of books in the house. Reading is a skill and a habit that needs to be picked up earlier if it is to give lasting pleasure and help, but it is worth maintaining this if it is already established, for reading is the best of all indoor hobbies. It can bring fantasy and reality closer together than anything else—it can widen experience and allow the privacy that, in the end, can exist only in the mind. Fortunately, just as many adults manage to sleep comfortably in front of the television set, so many children manage to work, read, or play while the television is on, just as they also manage to convert the sound of the radio or hi-fi to a familiar background boom that is less troublesome than silence.

The pleasures of discussion

At this age talking can become one of the greatest entertainments— gossiping about friends, family, shared activities, and finding from schoolbooks and television all sorts of new and exciting issues from the wider world to be debated.

Marion, aged nearly fourteen, arrived home from school one day quite elated. She had discovered the delights of disciplined discussion: "We had the first decent discussion in the Religious Studies lesson today—the first time everybody didn't shout everybody else down . . . the first time we all had respect for each other's opinions." Marion had always been a child with very decided wishes and views. In her last school report her class teacher commented that she showed a lively interest in all lessons and school activities, but needed to learn to listen to other people sometimes instead of being so convinced that her way of doing things was always best. Her mother recalled that when she was aged two and a half and they went shopping together, Marion would fling herself on the pavement in a frenzy and yell if she did not want to get on the bus home. The only thing to do when she had these fits of passion was to turn a deaf ear to the yells and pick her up firmly until she realized she was not going to get her point that way.

Throughout her childhood, issues would arise when Marion was determined to have her own way regardless of the convenience of anyone else in her family. She tended to ride roughshod over her older brother, who was a much milder and more retiring character than she was. Her parents learned to take a pretty firm line with her, but after the tumult and the sulks were over they would talk to her about her behaviour and often find her thoughtful and amenable to reason because, with all her greedy determination, she was also a loving child who was concerned about hurting others.

When she was thirteen her class had a new teacher for Religious Studies. The teacher was fresh from college, idealistic, and a believer in free discussion but not quite up to the skylarking potential of a class of high-spirited thirteen-year-old girls. Marion would come home and regale her older brother triumphantly with accounts of the noisy debates that took place about everything under the sun when no holds were barred and nobody listened to poor Miss P. A little later, however, a note of exasperation came into her accounts. She indicated that the fun in baiting naïve Miss P was wearing a bit thin because she really had some interesting things to say. Just when the debate became interesting, some stupid girl would break in and spoil it. That day her father asked her why, if the lesson was interesting, and some of them really liked this chance to talk about important things, they went on trying to make a fool of Miss P. Why couldn't they learn to listen to her occasionally and let each other have a turn, too?

Marion explained that even when a teacher is really nice you have to see whether she can keep order, so you try out all your tricks; but then it gets annoying if you think you might like her lessons and she cannot keep the noisy people under control. Her father asked her why, at her age, she always had to have a teacher or a parent to keep control. When did she think she and her friends might be old enough to get together to do things and decide that they would have to control themselves? If they wanted to enjoy their debates they had to try to let each other have a chance. Marion continued to argue with him that it was the teacher's job to keep order and if she could not do it then she was no good as a teacher. But she evidently pondered on this conversation and later talked with her friends about it. The first decent discussion in their Religious Studies lesson was the result.

As a rule, children of this age greatly enjoy talking, not just of their immediate concerns but of the larger world about them, about ideas, about the way people behave. Discussion is a means of getting to know this expanding world better and of feeling their way towards finding their place in it. This kind of talk—playing with ideas—is as important to them as free imaginative play is to the three- to six- or seven-year-old. Just as children playing together can only enjoy the game within a secure framework where there is agreement to give and take, so the young adolescents can enjoy the discussion only when they are prepared to give each other a turn.

In Marion's class, talking for the sake of doing the teacher down and showing how much stronger they were became a bore because they were then at odds with each other; it became a free-for-all which led nowhere. It became interesting only when the aim to triumph and disrupt was relinquished, and the play of ideas became a working towards understanding what each of them had to contribute to the topic.

Marion was, no doubt, able to contribute to this more satisfying state of affairs not only as a result of the conversation with her father but also because of the repeated experience in her childhood years of having her more bossy, violent, and greedy tendencies checked. Her father in particular, who was rather quiet and contemplative like his son, and unlike his wife—who had more in common with Marion—was often genuinely perplexed by Marion's self-willed obstinacy. He would try to puzzle out with her what might have led to some particular clash with her mother. His toleration and talking and wondering about her feelings and behaviour—which was in many ways alien to him—would increase her tolerance and lead to her identifying herself with a parent who was prepared to accept and consider foreign ideas and behaviour while not abdicating from his own standards.

Notes

1. By Melanie Klein.
2. Or the many ways teenagers have of making music, including computer-aided, immensely popular these days.
3. Even though dressmaking is less often practised since clothes became cheap, teenagers still invent their own clothing, accessories, and hairstyles, and practise similar craft or music-recording skills through which to creatively announce their identity.
4. This was a recorded statistic at the end of the 1960s. Since then, of course, educationalists have become more worried about the addictive qualities of the television and computer screens. The central distinction here is not so much whether they are indulged to excess as the *quality* of the experience—whether it is genuinely informative (or entertaining), or being used as a substitute for experience, justified on cynical grounds such as "hand and eye co-ordination".

CHAPTER FIVE

Family relationships

B eing a pioneer has its privileges as well as its hardships. If your teenager is the first in the family to reach this exciting stage, he or she needs a little recognition of his fledgling status to encourage him to feel his way towards earning a place of greater responsibility in the family group.

It can be an uncertain transition, from being one of the children to becoming one of the grown-ups—maybe at times finding your-self regarded as a deserter by younger brothers and sisters and envied for what they see, or think they see, you growing into. This envy can take various forms, but the most hurtful to the young teenager is ridicule: ridicule, for instance, of changing appearance; of efforts to smarten up and appear more attractive; of pimples and breasts and pubic hair and uncertainly pitched voices. So your first teenager has great need of matter-of-fact acceptance. He is breaking new ground for himself and for the other children, and he is likely to be shy about making mistakes and looking silly.

The ones who come after will profit a little from his pioneering, and so will often try to grow up a little faster, stay up a little later, dress a little sooner in the latest fashions, and generally benefit from their parents' experience in getting used to having a teenager in the home. On the other hand, they have never had that experience of being the first of the family, admired as well as envied for pointing the way to the others.

Sometimes the youngest may want to hold on to his childhood, the privileges of being the baby of the family, by not growing into adolescence—as, for instance, Sam (who appears later in this chapter). Sometimes the parents—usually mother, who does not want to lose her children altogether—may collude or provoke this reaction.

Rivalry goes on

The world of the twelve- to fourteen-year-old is expanding rapidly, and as he grows older the possibilities of friends and interests farther away from his family are opening up. This very likely means that he will not be shut in so much with his rivalries with brothers, sisters, and parents. He can escape more often; but rivalry does still tend to go on, though in a different guise.

The young teenage girl can often feel bitter about her somewhat older and probably slightly more self-assured sister, envying the privileges perhaps that she derives from being already at work or at college. It is in the nature of things to see the privileges—the money, the boyfriends—and not the work that goes with the new situation. In some cases, when the younger child's ambition is stimulated by the closeness of her elder sister's emancipation, you might perhaps feel that you can entrust her with grown-up privileges a little earlier than you accorded them to the older one, provided some responsibilities are attached. It is not much help to your daughter in the long run to make her a present of freedom just because she is jealous of her older sister. This freedom is gained more surely if she does something to earn it, and therefore can more truly feel that she is growing up. For instance, spending money is valued more in the end if it is designed, in part at least, to pay for some necessities like clothes, which your daughter has the chance to choose for herself. And, no doubt, you will have to grit your teeth and watch her make mistakes, but you may also find she learns to do better by herself than you did for her. She needs the latitude to make mistakes; it is best to do so where it matters less.

Take, for example, one thirteen-year-old girl who, when she was a child, had beautiful curly hair just bordering on the frizzy, much to the delight of her mother, who had straight hair but grew up in the days when curls were fashionable. Rebecca's elder sister also had fairly straight hair, which, to the younger child's chagrin, hung in a thick fashionable curtain over her eyes. The hair became a focal point for grievances and irrational accusations of her mother, who had so unfairly discriminated between her two daughters. Rebecca then began to spend her pocket money on setting-lotions, rollers, and iron grips with which she anchored the upstanding fuzz close to her head every night. Despite family discouragement and pleas for the curls, she persisted for many months, and finally managed to get her hair to hang tolerably stiff and straight (except on rainy days). It was a fair replica of her sister's hair and quite becoming too, much to everyone's surprise.

In Rebecca's case, rivalry drove her to emulate her sister's hair— to become the same or as good as her. There were other areas in which she did not feel so keenly that she just *had* to be like her sister, and where she avoided clashes by aiming for a different goal.

Brothers and sisters: can they harm each other's personality?

This is a question that many parents have asked at different times in the course of the growth of their family. In early years the arbitrating parent tends to concentrate on protecting against physical damage: the surreptitious clout or pinch that the baby or younger child receives. That kind of damage is on the whole easier to look out for and to stop than the more subtle kind of hurt to feelings. Not that brothers and sisters can grow up together, if they have any liveliness or spirit, without hurting each other's feelings many times. It is practice in experiencing and in surviving emotional upheaval within a family protected and contained by their parents' kindly attention that helps children learn to cope with the hurts and upheavals they are bound to receive in the larger world throughout life.

More lasting harm can be done when there is a constant pressure by one or more of the children to take up a particular role or to react in an expected kind of way that prevents him from developing freely. Parents may collude, or give the lead in maintaining such pressure, without being in the least aware of it. When your child comes to this early adolescent stage and begins to be more aware of hitherto unfamiliar reactions and conflicts in himself, it is wise to treat these seriously and to see that he has a chance to express them, and to consider whether maybe he is being unduly hampered by any of the other children, and if so, whether you can do anything about it.

Often, at this stage, children do tend to feel hemmed in, kept down, and prevented from growing up, by parents, of course, but also sometimes by brothers and sisters. This feeling always derives, no doubt to some extent from a sense of obstacles within themselves, from their own personality. It is easier to put these obstacles on to some source outside themselves: to pick a quarrel, to blame some other member of the family. It is easy to justify that quarrel and forget the quarrel with yourself if the blamed brother or sister—or parent for that matter—is indeed at fault: if they are, for instance, bossy or greedy or bullying.

However, it may not necessarily be the brother or sister who is overtly bossy and dominating who has the most hampering effect on the development of another. It can sometimes be more difficult for a child to free himself from a seductive influence that encourages tendencies that already exist in him against really growing up.

As an example of this, here is a short account of the interaction of three brothers. Sam, aged thirteen, was sent to talk to a child psychotherapist by his family doctor, who knew him well. He was the youngest in a family of three boys. The eldest was charming, though rather lazy; the middle boy, who was the favourite of all, was very bright, pushing and hard-working, and competent in everything that he did. Sam was a school failure: touchy, morose, and on very bad terms with the middle brother, whom he accused of always trying to make him feel small. They had to share a room, and Sam used to set up elaborate barricades so that he did not have to see George when he went to bed at night. He was on very good terms with Stuart, the eldest brother, who used to do his homework for him and mother him in all sorts of ways.

Sam saw his problem as George, who kept him feeling inferior and sapped his confidence. Stuart appeared as his good angel. There was a question in the mind of the psychiatrist who first saw the family as to whether the most practical thing might not be to try to persuade George to "lay off" Sam. George was not willing to be involved, however, and it was arranged that Sam should have regular talks with a child psychotherapist.

Gradually, in the course of these talks, a rather different picture emerged of the relationships of these three brothers, a picture that changed as Sam began to get a better grasp of his own personality. As he grew a little less afraid of his aggressive feelings and became able to experience his own competitiveness, he began to stand up to George a bit more instead of sulking and hiding in his den. There was a little more ordinary rough and tumble between them, but in a non-malicious way that resulted in their growing closer together and eventually seeming to become very good friends.

As Sam grew closer to George, however, on the basis of becoming more of a boy and sharing boyish interests, he grew more doubtful of himself in relation to Stuart. He began to realize that he used Stuart in a way that was really hindering him from growing up, and that in so doing he was responding to a need of Stuart's that made it difficult to extricate himself from a role that he no longer wanted to play. He could slip into it only too readily when things became difficult—when he wanted to slide away from trying to work and taking part in life.

He began to realize that there was a large part of him that wanted to go on existing as a sort of parasite baby that was excused all difficult things, that could just go on dreaming and being comfortable. It seemed as if this part of him fitted in very neatly with a strong drive on Stuart's part to feel that he was the provider of the family, the most admired, on whom all relied—secretly, a better and more indulgent mother than the real mother. To have a little brother who depended on him and who looked up to him supported this theory.

When Sam, in his treatment, began to struggle towards finding an identity for himself, he began to realize that the most insidious enemy to his growth was not so much discouragement in straightforward competition with his middle brother as the temptation to give up when things were difficult and to let the eldest one take care of it all for him. As he was approaching adolescence, the position of the family baby was becoming more and more hampering to him. He had not known whom to blame for his feeling of being stuck, nor how to think about it himself, without some help.

CHAPTER SIX

Discipline, encouragement, and protection

T hese things are inseparable. A child of this age still needs the help of parental discipline to guide him in disciplining himself: the discipline is valueless unless it is accompanied explicitly or implicitly by encouragement towards some more desirable way of behaving. It does involve protection from being governed by unruly disruptive parts of himself that are likely to disturb not only the group in which he lives but also his own inner harmony. Having said that these three things are or should be inseparable, let us now consider them one at a time to see how they interrelate.

What immediately springs to mind, probably, is the problem of how to get the child to obey his parents, to obey the laws of society, to keep to the boundaries of what is fair and permitted to him as his part in the family, the school, and the larger world. Around the onset of adolescence, antisocial acts come to be viewed—with reason—in a more serious light than had earlier been the case. Antisocial acts stem from unsatisfactory relationships in the home. It is fairly obvious that parents who have little sense of social responsibility, who go in for getting as much as they can for as little as possible, who behave with violence whenever they are crossed, are likely to produce delinquent or violent offspring. It is not so obvious how hard-working and apparently responsible law-abiding citizens manage to do so. It may be worthwhile to look at an example of this.

William, aged fourteen, is now on his way to an approved school after his appearance before a juvenile court. He is the elder of two brothers, in a family that is financially comfortable. His father earns a good salary and likes his job; his mother keeps a very nice home. But his parents have never been happy together since the early days of their marriage, which was made in haste because Mr T somewhat reluctantly thought it was his duty to marry the girl he had made pregnant. A couple of years after William's birth they had another baby, a little girl this time, who had Down's syndrome.

This tended to drive the parents still further apart. Mr T turned more and more to his work and male cronies and opted out of the family, although he would make an effort from time to time to take William out and do things with him. The little girl was eventually sent to a home, and Mrs T tried to fill the gap in her life by some part-time work that interested her. She was nevertheless devoted to William, waited on him hand and foot and relied on him to make up for the disappointments she had experienced in her marriage and with her second child. Mr T found William disappointing, felt he was a mother's boy and did not know how to make friends with him. He felt it was not good for the boy to be mollycoddled. Instead of being able to discuss this and to come to some agreement with his wife as to how the boy should be handled, he had spells of "trying to make a man of him", trying to toughen him up. When William could not respond to this he would become sarcastic and ignore him for a while. Mrs T would secretly make up to William with extra pocket money and special treats when his father's back was turned.

Around the age of twelve William began to get more involved with friends outside his home. One day, together with another slightly older boy, he stole a motorbike and rode some twenty miles away from his home, in such a way that they were bound to get caught. He could not say why he had done it; neither could the other boy. They were both put on probation. After about a year he broke out again and did almost exactly the same thing. He had a very severe talking-to from his father, headmaster, and the magistrate, and remained on probation. Then a year later he stole a delivery van, in company with two other boys, neither of them his former partner in crime. This time they truanted from school, stayed out all night and stole various articles from a general store. This time he was finally sent to an approved school.

The psychiatrist and educational psychologist who examined him and talked to the parents found he was polite and co-operative in the tests that he was asked to do. He tired very quickly however, and looked away when confronted with anything difficult, or when he was asked to think and explain why he had broken out in rebellion again. They found him to be rather more than average in intelligence despite his poorish school performance, and certainly capable of planning and executing a less certain-to-be detected crime, had he wished to do so.

It seemed that he had unconsciously worked it so that he was bound to get caught. He had been warned that the next time he got into trouble he would be "sent away", and it seemed that he was asking for this, and asking to be taken into the care of safer parents than his own. One could see the taking of the motorbike and of the van as an attempt to ride away from home. This would be not only his actual home and his divided and unhappy parents but also the whole unhappy experience accumulating in his own mind, which he could not think about, sort out, and make more bearable.

The fundamental unresolved disagreements between his mother and father meant that, for most of his life, he had operated under a very unstable government, with no secure framework, and an uncertain discipline. The shock of being sent away from home made the parents finally decide that they must do something about trying to come to some better understanding with each other in order to be able to help him in the future. They are taking the opportunity that was offered them of regular interviews with a case-worker with special training in working with marital difficulties, and are already finding this helpful.

The great pity is that this was not considered, maybe was not possible to arrange, much earlier, before matters reached this stage. As far as William is concerned, his future stability is likely to depend greatly on his experience in the approved school. Fortunately, it is one in which most of the staff have worked together well, supporting and learning from each other over quite a long period, and he will have the opportunity there of being contained within a consistent but kindly disciplinary framework. Moreover, he will be with teachers who are aware of the need to co-operate with the parents. They are aware that these parents are guilty and unhappy, and need to be helped if they are to realize how necessary they still are to William, and to find ways of coming together to provide a greater security for him.

Encouragement

This, as we have already suggested, is a necessary accompaniment to discipline. It is of no use forbidding and setting limits, most especially for those growing into adolescence, unless this serves some useful end. "Do this because I say so" is no longer satisfactory, if it ever was, as more than a hasty practical measure. Your young adolescent needs to know that prohibitions are dictated by some concern for his greater benefit or growth, always bearing in mind that this must also take into account the rights of others. He may not always be able to agree with you; indeed, he will disagree strongly at times. His objections or lack of response to rules and prohibitions should indeed make us, as parents, examine our own motives and reasons for imposing them. It could be that we are still treating him too much as a child, not allowing for his growing independence and capacity to take responsibility for himself; it could be that we find it a threat when our children are growing up and are no longer dependent upon us, and that we feel done out of a job as a result of this.

We need to notice just where he is in terms of developing capacities, to know what we can safely allow him to do and what we can reasonably ask of him as a contribution to looking after himself, and also to the family in general. Every step in this direction is an encouragement to that part of himself that really wants to grow up. He also needs a model before him towards which he can strive hopefully, but not uncritically. The best model is parents who have learned to get on, to love each other despite the difficulties they have run up against in their relationship with each other, and who have included their children as an essential part of that relationship.

In William's case we can see that encouragement was absent. He had parents who were running away from facing their problems, and so could not give him the security and attention he needed to encourage him to work at the business of growing up. So the onset of adolescence was too much for him, and he had to break out and run away from it all.

Protection

More will be said about this in later sections of the book. But it is worthwhile considering it here in relation to William. If his spell in an approved school is going to do him any good at all, one suspects that both school and parents will need to collaborate and try to provide a background of being held and protected against his impulses to run away from trouble. He needs to be protected from teaming up with others who are seeking a quick and supposedly easy way of earning their living through crime.

Rules, regulations, and punishment

Obviously, necessary rules and regulations change as the child becomes an adolescent. We expect him to be able to regulate himself better. So, indeed, he can for a great deal of the time, but we have to expect surprises. In many ways he may be more unreliable and disobedient than he was a year or two ago. It is part of the growing-up process to question more the things that parents and teachers expect him to do. It may also be part of growing up to defy these expectations at times, and to feel that he is being mighty clever and independent if he can gang up with others with this aim in mind and get away with it. For many youngsters this is a necessary stage before they are able to accept rules and responsibilities as being reasonable and meaningful.

It is a stage that tries us out as parents and teachers and, if we are to keep the respect of our children and pupils, we have to be prepared to look at our standards for them, and ask ourselves whether they are reasonable. When possible, talking it over with the child can help sort it out for you both, and it may enlist a more willing co-operation. It may also succeed in getting his more grown-up self on your side. As many a parent will know, however, there may be times when talking things over together just will not work, when you have to be prepared to withstand arguments about being unfair, unfeeling, and old-fashioned. Stick to your guns and hope for another occasion when you can approach things together in a more reasonable way.

It is a help to the young adolescent to have some of his battles in the home, to try them out where they originate, and work over some of his resentments where they belong. He will appreciate it if you are also strong enough to withstand him when necessary. For many of his arguments and rebellions against his parents are really arguments against himself and, although he and you may not know it, he is often really asking for his saner and more reasonable self to be supported. He is looking to you for arguments that can be used against the voices that tempt him to despise and turn away from his parents and from consideration for others.

He will often use his parents' arguments against his friends at school, and his friends' arguments against his parents at home. Better to be able to have a dialogue of this kind, heated though it may sometimes be, than to have to agree in both places just for the sake of fitting in and meeting with approval.

Not all young adolescents have to argue it out or rebel before they come to some sort of peace with the world and with themselves. But some kind of self-questioning and questioning of society is necessary if the child is to grow into an adolescent and then into an adult human being; if he is not to remain, emotionally speaking, tied to mother's apron strings. "I'm fed up with all my friends", said a thirteen-year-old. "They've got no opinions of their own. All they say is their parents' opinion, and they think their parents are God and know all about everything." "And whose opinions do you use to contradict them?" asked her father, who had a pretty fair idea from previous listening that he was often quoted as God at school (although without acknowledgement and though at home he was treated as ignorant and old-fashioned, intolerant of modern progress).

Pocket money

It is important that children in these years be given an opportunity to learn about the cost of living, food, housing, clothes, holidays, and so forth. It is helpful for them to begin to handle not just pocket money for sweets and fun, but also to manage some small allowance from which they have to save up and provide some of their own necessities, such as clothes. This will help them to know how to organize their resources when they eventually have a job and branch out on their own. Some children like to get little after-school or Saturday jobs, such as paper rounds or helping the milk-man. Schools sometimes frown on this on the grounds that it can interfere with homework—which of course it may do at times. Or it may be said that it is not good for children to have too much money; they should learn to do things as a matter of duty, be expected to pull their weight and contribute to the family without payment.

There is a great deal in this point of view, but perhaps one should examine one's own motives in the particular ways and cases in which one applies it. It is poor indeed if children grow up—and if we encourage them to grow up—so ungenerous that they begrudge expending themselves on any task not rewarded with payment. From very early days we can expect that a child should contribute something, however little, towards looking after the home and the rest of the family. School continues this process in that it requires participation in the general running of the school, of the little society in which the child is living. Such an expectation is paying respect due to him as an individual who is valued for what he is able to do at whatever particular stage of development he has reached. "To each according to his needs, from each according to his capacities."

Our tendency to feel that money is demoralizing, a temptation to greed, a sort of addiction like drugs, is one which needs examin-ing. How much are we trying to idealize our children, trying to keep them unsullied by vices that we do not like to acknowledge in ourselves? How much, at the same time, do we fear in them the same liability to be corrupted by money that we have uncomfort-able suspicions of in our own characters?

CHAPTER SEVEN

Courtesy and consideration for others

W e adults often think in terms of discourtesy and rudeness when we consider children in early adolescence.
There they are, rushing for the bus and getting on before
us; failing to offer their seat to the old lady standing up; throwing
drink-cartons on the pavement; shouting across other people's
conversation. Do they greet a visitor coming into the room, say
thank you properly when given an unwanted present by an elderly
relative, hold the door open for the person following, clear up the
mess they have made in the kitchen when helping themselves
between meals, help with the washing up before being ordered to
do so, accept with proper self-criticism dad's sarcastic comments
on their appearance or their extravagance? They do not! Quite
the contrary. It is a relief when they are off to school and their
teachers have to cope with their boisterous and self-centred
egos.

To think of them only in this fashion is, of course, to display the
same discourtesy of which we accuse them. There are some parents
who persuade themselves that "our Johnny isn't like that—it's the
crowd he mixes with that does it'—not a comment that Johnny
himself would probably welcome.

Courtesy may be thought of simply as a rather mechanical code of manners and behaviour imposed by the conventional expectations of society—a substitute for true liking, a sort of cosmetic geniality. But it can be much more than this. It can be the outward expression of an inner social grace—a true feeling of considerateness, sympathy and impulsive respect for other people. When we do see discourtesy in our child, of what sort is it? Is it thoughtlessness, with no conscious hostility in it? Is it habitual and of long standing, or is it a thing of the moment? What we do about it, and what degree of success we may have as parents may depend very much on the answers to these questions.

Adolescence, as has been said, is the second great period of extremely rapid growth in the child (the first is in the womb). He or she may be suddenly physically clumsy and will certainly be self-conscious about appearance. Doors will slam, and food will be spilt; hair will assume unnatural styles and colours; and spottiness is a terrible persecution of nature. It is only to be expected that, caught between lost childhood and unrealised adulthood, these children will react in a decidedly prickly fashion to any ironic or jibing remarks and reprimands; they feel safer with their own group, and resent our intrusion, as we perhaps resent their youth. The onus for being courteous lies also with the adults at this stage. Youth will pass, and the young will conform soon enough, adopting the deliberate disguises of adulthood.

Much childhood discourtesy is connected with the desire to be self-responsible, independent, grown-up. It emerges in the rebellion which refuses to obey just because adult authority commands. Or if it does obey, it is only under constraint and in fear of punishment—so that when the immediate constraint is removed the obedience, and with it the apparent courtesy, are thrown to the winds. The schoolboy may wear his cap [or other item of identification] when he enters the school gates—but he stuffs it in his pocket once he is round the corner.

It is therefore a step towards courtesy to explain why certain things must be done, to request rather than to order, to expect a helpful response rather than to insist only on a submissive one. Children, like adults, have an aggressive component to their nature that helps them to survive and to create; but they also want to participate in the adult world, to have their opinions considered with respect, and refuted—if at all—by reason. It is thus helpful to consider that, when children are aggressively rude and resentful, they are usually expressing a need which we have not realised or satisfied. They will usually respond seriously when they are taken seriously. When aggressive rudeness is of very long standing and has become a way of life it is like bad weather—long foretold, long lasting. If such rudeness is towards the parents it is a sign of fairly deep-rooted and unresolved hostility which cannot be corrected by simple command or punishment, but only by greater self-knowledge on the part of both parent and child. When it is towards brothers or sisters, parents can help to overcome it by considering very carefully whether they have not unwittingly favoured one child more than another in ways which they have not perceived or intended, but which the child perceives or fancies he perceives—the balance can then be discreetly corrected. The twelve-year-old is old enough to be able to talk about these things, though even better is the change in the parents' attitudes and actions which does not need to be directly expressed in words. When aggressive rudeness is shown by the child, not towards parents and intimate friends, but towards other people and especially towards people from other classes it will often represent a certain timorousness, taking refuge in clinging to the home habits and background, and adopting a sour-grapes attitude to the success which is at once envied and feared to be unattainable. This again is hard to correct, for the child naturally identifies with his parents until he has the confidence to be independent; this may be assisted gradually through good schooling and the experience of achievement, or through a lucky friendship, or when the child finally grows up and leaves home. It will certainly never come merely through punishment or rejection, and this is very trying for those of us who are in a hurry and have enough problems of our own.

A great deal of childish behaviour is conditioned by the circumstances in which we place the child, and by the teaching we have given him at home and at school. When a child has to preserve face with his gang it is hard for him to immediately obey a parental interruption. After five hours at a desk it is not surprising that the crowd running for the bus does get noisy and pushing, thoughtless or even bad-tempered. After our stressing the importance of telling the truth for many years it takes a little time for the child to get used to giving a polite "thank you" for something he does not really want at all. All around him the child sees and hears the adults doing what he is told not to do—struggling, grabbing, telling the socially appropriate lies, satisfying their own convenience rather than the values they affect to hold; and, whatever they say, he imitates them. Fortunately we sometimes do better than this, so there is some hope for courtesy, after all.

School and parents certainly try to improve manners. From the start the good junior school helps the children to help each other—putting on coats, carrying books, working together and so on. Early training by parents and teachers at an age when rebellion and the stresses of adolescence are absent can be vital in establishing the routine of courtesy for the later years, and all society relies on this. It is not difficult to set up useful habits at the right time; it is, however, difficult indeed to reverse habits once they are wrongly established. Much patience, and much self-awareness, is called for if courtesy is to become an inward growth and not an imposed and hence unreliable regulation; and the parent can help the process even at a late stage by acknowledging a courteous action when one is performed, and not merely taking it for granted. There is a sort of mirror in society, wherein "please" and "thank you" reflect "thank you" and "please". Adults know this, but children have to learn it. Therefore we must have patience.

CHAPTER EIGHT

Your young teenager and sex

Many girls begin to menstruate during these years, and some earlier. There is general gossip among them as to who has, or who has not, and, for the unitiated, "What's it really like?" As already suggested (in *Your Eleven-year-old*), it is a help if they know the basic facts about the significance of menstruation before it commences. These will not necessarily stop girls from exchanging their own fantasies and dramatized misinformation, nor, indeed, is it necessarily desirable that these exchanges should be discouraged.

Fears are usually lessened by being voiced, unless you have as a dominant person in the little group of gossips one who is too fond of stirring up the fears of the others in a cruel way. In that case the vulnerability to the horror stories is increased by ignorance; ignorance of the actual experience of menstruation, and also of real information sanctioned by mother and the grown-up world.

To continue with the story of Jenny, mentioned in the previous book: Jenny, who was younger than the others in her class, menstruated shortly before her twelfth birthday. Some six months later she was on a picnic with four of the other girls, and the conversation turned to babies, sexual intercourse, and menstruation. None

121

of the others had apparently begun to have periods and were speculating as to whether it hurt much, how much blood you lost, how many people had to lie down or take a day off school when they started. Three of the girls were whipping each other into a rather delicious state of apprehension, but a fourth was really getting quite upset. Jenny was being ignored as she was considered a little too young and sexually backward to be involved in this. Suddenly she said with throwaway satisfaction, "Well, *I* can tell you—I've had it now five or six times and none of that's true, it doesn't hurt a bit." Then followed the collapse of the more "knowledgeable" gossips, after which one of them said, "And they say that you start to have it when you're beginning to be mature enough for sex, but you can see that can't be true or *she* wouldn't have started before the rest of us!"

Jenny was an example of a girl whose puberty took place relatively early and was not heralded by the more obvious signs of physical development. Her companions, at any rate, considered themselves more nubile in appearance and in interests.

Following this is an example of an older boy whose development is delayed in a more general way.

Adam, aged fourteen, is the youngest in his family. He has two elder brothers and an elder sister. He is five years younger than the brother next to him in age, and arrived rather unexpectedly at the tail-end of the family, just as his mother was thinking about going back to do some part-time work to help the family budget. He was a slightly premature baby, small, pretty and rather delicate: a poor feeder. When he was a few months old his mother had to help nurse her own mother, who had a stroke and then died before Adam was a year old. Throughout this time Adam was a quiet retiring baby, ate very little and made few demands for attention.

He continued to grow into boyhood in much the same way, a nice child who was protected and carried along by the rest of the family. He never seemed to branch out on his own, tolerated school, but sat dreaming at the back of the class. His aim, as one of his teachers said, seemed to be to get by without being noticed. He lived for the weekends, when he would join in anything the family were doing together, or sort out his collection of cards and stamps, or maybe go to a football match with his father or one of his brothers.

Now he is nearly fourteen and his parents are beginning to worry about what he is going to do with his life and how he is going to earn his living. To a great extent he has been protected from the rough and tumble of life. He has retreated from the knowledge that he has learned so little by not involving himself in competition with others and by burying himself in the shelter of a home that made very few demands on him. In this last year or so he has been showing few signs of the strivings, self-questionings, and awakenings that herald puberty.

It is a development that takes place at a very different time for different boys and girls, as I have already mentioned. The spurt of growth that ushers in this stage usually comes later in boys than girls. One would expect Adam, who has been cautious and rather slow in growing right from the beginning, to take his time in approaching adolescence. But it is realistic and sensible for his parents to get rather worried about his future now, as long as they do not become so overwhelmed with worry and self-reproach for not being alive to the problem sooner that they try to force him to work and to stand on his own two feet in a way that will terrify him, make him feel quite hopeless, and cause him to shut himself away more securely from the outside world.

He has a family who care for him, protect him, but who have finally woken up to the fact that he cannot be the baby of the house for ever, but should in the normal course of events reach fulfilment through a family of his own. How can they help to prepare him for this?

It would be a good idea for them to talk this over with someone of expert and more general knowledge in the development of children and adolescents, who can help them to use their own unparalleled and particular acquaintance with him over his childhood years to review and come to some plan of procedure—with a therapist possibly, or a teacher at his school if there is one specially concerned with general development and careers guidance. Talking about the problem to a sympathetic professional person with a wider experience is likely to help the parents in their own thinking, and will enable them to decide whether it is practicable for Adam to help himself by this kind of approach.

They may be unlucky and not have the chance of consulting a helpful professional. It will, in any case, give them a better idea of how best to help Adam if they talk it over themselves and perhaps also enlist the attention of the older children, who are often near enough to the younger child to be able to understand his feelings from the inside. Talking about it together can help the family as a whole to have a more complete view of Adam and of how each one of them has been thinking and behaving towards him. A fresh look at their relationships might give them ideas on how to encourage him towards striking out a little on his own.

It does seem, for instance, that in his first year the general family sadness, especially that of his mother, was likely to confirm him in his rather hesitant lukewarm approach to living and self-assertion. This hesitancy and shyness seemed, in turn, to evoke from the older ones an especially careful invalid treatment. It may be that his mother, feeling guilty about her preoccupation with mourning her own mother, and also her initial reluctance to have the baby at all, tried to over-compensate for her earlier lack of welcome and of involvement by being too careful, too fearful of asking him to do enough for himself. As he was the last baby, there was never any competition for the role of the frail and helpless one. A pattern like this can persist overlong if it fits the needs of both parties.

Adam's slow, finicky feeding—he continues to be a poor eater, even now at the age of fourteen—whatever the initial physical causes, would indicate a choosy, uncertain attitude to life. Feeding is one of the earliest ways of absorbing our surroundings, of taking in life; and feeding difficulties are often linked with psychological difficulties in taking in emotional experiences of which we are afraid.

Children can be afraid of their anger, of their greedy desires. They can be too afraid to know that they have such desires, if they do not acquire the confidence to express them in a situation where the desires can be tolerated and controlled.

Adolescents' theories about sex

Knowledge of the facts about sex helps to counteract some of the wilder beliefs about sexual intercourse as a very frightening and damaging affair. It will not dispel them altogether, for they play some part in the development of every boy and girl. They re-emerge in every young adolescent to complicate his relationships with those of his own and of the opposite sex, and to complicate his attitude to his parents.

We can help him as parents if we have sorted out our own feelings about sexual relationships sufficiently to let us put ourselves in his place, to feel for him imaginatively and remember ourselves at his age. If we can do this we are less likely to act with prudishness and alarm when we see signs of his curiosity coming out in furtive smutty ways—indeed he is less likely to be so furtive and guilty about it.

His fantasies and feelings about sexual relations at this time are very much coloured by a revival of fantasies about the way he *wanted* them to be at times between his parents when he was an infant, and sensed and was envious of the private emotional and sexual tie between his parents. This secret relationship between his parents was for him, in the depths of his infant mind, one of idyllic mutual pleasure and gratification. But it was also one of cruelty and terror, in as much as it was coloured by his attributing to the parents all his own violence aroused by being excluded. His understanding was further distorted by his own spoiling wishes, which enabled him to disparage the parental relationship so that he should not suffer too greatly from not sharing it.

So, in adolescence, when heightened sexual sensation revives these buried infantile emotions and fantasies, he feels a little nearer to the wonderful all-satisfying "in-love" sensual experience, desired in infancy, but also to the strange cruel frightening one created then by his envious wishes.

The central sexual fear of the boy is one of being shut up inside some bad place, unable to escape, of losing his penis there, of losing his mind. For the girls it is a fear of being invaded by something terrifying, sometimes fantasized as a wild beast that tortures, robs, and deprives her of the ability to have babies. But as girls often fantasize themselves to be boys, and boys have a feminine side, they have both classes of fears.

These fears are, for the greater part, quite unconscious. Girls and boys look for a realization of them in pornographic literature, in horror films, in stories made up and passed around by others of their own age who are more disturbed and vocal about their fears. They are expressed in the graffiti in public lavatories. For the most part, the expression of these realizations of disturbed unconscious fantasies and impulses probably does little harm. It can, in fact, be helpful, in that boys and girls gain relief from overwhelming feelings of guilt and shame through realizing that others feel the same way.

The telling of these stories, or seeing them expressed in films and literature, is helpful only when they can be recognized as stories and not taken for truth. Thus, harm can be done when maybe one more than usually anxious and sadistic adolescent sets out to terrify others, to rid himself of his own fears by evoking them in some more vulnerable and gullible companion.

Here is an example of a story that was passed around a group of young adolescents. It was started by one of the older boys, one who was physically precocious, poor at work, but a great teaser of the girls. The story was about one of the girl prefects who was away from school for some weeks—in fact after having her appendix removed. The boy began the rumour that she had been having sexual intercourse with one of the young games teachers, whose penis was so big that it stuck inside her. He said they had to get a doctor to cut it out, and now she was in hospital and no one knew whether she would recover. A number of boys and girls in the school half believed this—in the way they would have taken a horror story, even though they were partly sceptical. The story would probably not have come to light but for one of the girls. She was very upset, cried, and told her older sister, who had just left the school. The sister had been on good terms with most of the teachers and, after consulting with her parents, went to see the head-teacher, who then dealt with the situation rather wisely by discussing it with the small group she thought was mainly involved in spreading it. Such a discussion is not an easy thing to manage, because it requires that the teacher, or the parent, as the case might be, should have worked through his own feelings of shame and guilt and embarrassment about his own immature and distorted sexual fantasies. Treating an episode like this in a more dramatic way, with blame and with veiled allusions to the wickedness or dirtiness of those concerned in spreading the story, would merely have added to the wickedness or dirtiness, would have added to the guilt surrounding sexual matters, and driven those affected to even more furtive ways of satisfying themselves.

Masturbation

This is an age when budding adolescents of both sexes tend to be plagued with secret guilt about the recurrent urge to masturbate, to play with their own sexual organs and get pleasure from fondling parts of their own body. The guilt is not just about the actual physical manipulation, but about the daydreams and the more unconscious fantasies that accompany the bodily sensations.

The young adolescent's physical development, in the normal course of events, is also a sexual one, and he has to deal with the messages that he is receiving from his body by feeling, discharging, weaving them into stories. These sensations revive the buried sexual excitements of early childhood: the fantasies he weaves are repetitions of those born in an earlier stage of development, with all the misconceptions which that entailed. These are added to and modified, but never entirely done away with in the light of later experience.

It is useless if you worry about this or get angry with your young adolescent if you suspect that he is masturbating too much. You cannot stop him by prohibition. If you try too hard you are probably still caught up in the echoes of your own past, but remaining, adolescent fears. The child who goes on masturbating and dreaming about sex is likely to be one who has the greatest difficulty in really getting to know and to like others of the opposite sex. Masturbating or dreaming about sex just to get satisfaction for oneself becomes fundamentally modified only when the adolescent gets to know and care for someone as a person in their own right.

The ancient bogey tale that too much masturbation leads to madness is, of course, nonsense; yet it has a basic element of truth. It can be part of a self-exciting circularity that substitutes daydreams for reality. Too much dreaming can cut us off from reality and ourselves. The cure is to try to get better contact and orientation with people.

Sex in books, films, and television programmes

It is a little difficult, as a parent, to lay down the law about whether certain books and films should be forbidden to children of this age, or even a little older. The film certificates seem to take care of this as far as the cinema is concerned, but even there you get those children who take pride in looking older than they are and in seeing the forbidden, sometimes to enjoy and sometimes just to boast. Moreover, one does not necessarily agree with the censor in his judgement about what is likely to be harmful in the case of one's own particular child.

In a way, we as parents—if we use our imagination and are in touch with our children as they develop into adolescence—have a better chance than other adults of gauging what is likely to be a "bad" influence upon our own children. On the other hand, we can sometimes be the very last people to know it, when the reliving of our own unresolved pubertal guilts gets in the way of our being able to appreciate how our children are dealing with them.

At this stage, lack of interest in books and films with sex interest is more worrying than its presence; but its presence may not always be noticeable. Young adolescents tend to feel guilty about it, or sometimes just private. They may not want their preoccupations to be obvious, especially to parents and maybe even other members of the family. But they do want to look and learn how people set about love-making, need to think about it and rehearse it in their own minds long before they get to the point of trying it out.

On the other hand, there are circumstances in which young boys and girls can become too involved in fantasies about sex. Some types of literature or films and pornographic pictures can have an inflammatory, inciting or guilt-making effect, especially when sexual relations are depicted with violence or a degrading element.

These perverse fantasies exist in every adolescent and in all of us, and sometimes it can be a relief as well as a shock to see them expressed, to see them in the light of day, as it were. But there is a difference between seeing them expressed, especially if it is within the framework of something that attempts to be a true work of art, and really wallowing in them in a manner that takes you right away from a world of caring, tender relationships.

What to do about it is another matter. As often, simple prohibition probably will not work. It may simply lead the child to be more secretive, unless you can talk to him and get him to talk to you, to see that you are not against sex in every form, and that you do not

regard him as incomprehensible and beyond the pale of your tolerance. Schools can [and these days generally do] provide realistic
and informative talks and films about sex education. Maybe, with
a little help, your young adolescent can begin to see that there are
more and less lovely or demeaning ways of expressing it. If your
relationship is such that you cannot talk to him—and it is not so
easy to talk to children of this age on this topic—it is perhaps better
to leave it alone and do what you can to encourage him in friendships with reasonable boys and girls of his own age and to
appreciate less sordid and inflaming expressions of his interests.

Protection against sex crimes and sexual promiscuity

Long before your children are this age you, and the school, will
have cautioned them against going with strangers, in particular to
look out for themselves in solitary places or when approached by
people in cars. The dangers of seduction—particularly for girls—
are no less at this stage than they were earlier. But the part that the
young adolescent plays in sexual relations with an older person—
and legally, sexual intercourse with a child under sixteen is a
crime—is likely to be a more active one. It can, therefore, be more
difficult to protect a young girl who is beginning to mature sexually, and to become attractive to older boys and men of an
unscrupulous kind, from allowing herself to be exploited sexually
if she does have inclinations that way.

   She needs protection, and is almost certainly aware of it,
however much she may protest. She needs to know that her parents
take an active interest in the kinds of boys that she goes out with.
A group of girls just in their teens were overheard talking with a
mixture of envy, disapproval, and pity about another girl in their
class who was allowed to go around with her elder brothers and
their girlfriends and come in at all hours of the night. They envied
the "experience" she was getting and which she was imparting to
favoured friends. They envied, too, the notoriety and self-impor-
tance this gave her, and were annoyed that she managed to get
away with it. But they did genuinely pity her for having parents
who just did not seem to care enough to make it their business to
know what was happening to her.

The young girl at risk in this way is not helped by her own combination of sexual impulses and a more than usually strong—if largely unconscious—rivalry and envy of her parents' sexual relationship. It is unconscious in so far as it is a reawakening of her early unresolved childhood conflicts about the parents together. She may not now feel consciously that there is anything at all to be jealous of in the parents' relationship; she may indeed feel that she herself has life before her and is going to have a much better time.

This makes it all the more likely that parental restrictions are likely to be felt as interference—keeping her down, not wanting her to grow up. So it is a pity to strengthen that conviction by simply forbidding. It is obviously better, if she wants boyfriends at this age, to invite them to the house, not just to assess and criticize, but to take an interest if you can. A relationship that is set in an ordinary and open social framework is easier to manage and to discuss. Our young teenagers are likely to feel much safer when they are away from us if they feel we are taking an interest and want them to enjoy themselves, but are there to save them from their inexperience and impulsive unreasoning actions.

CHAPTER NINE

Friends

F riendships at this age are often intense, often stormy, and sometimes very short-lived. The best friend of today can be the worst enemy of tomorrow. It may even be that last week's friendship is re-established as though the quarrel had never been. The intensity of emotional involvement is, on the whole, a more obvious characteristic of friendship between girls than between boys, who perhaps tend to go on a little longer finding companionship in sharing activities than from the need to really get to know and become involved with one another. On the whole, society expects boys to be a little shyer of expressing tender feelings. But differences in expression of feeling between the two sexes may be more to do with differences in the way that they are *expected* to behave than in inborn differences. The differences in the way that girls and boys are expected to behave are very rapidly being blurred these days in many ways, as are their interests, clothing, and activities.

However, in the years of early adolescence boys and girls, though interested in each other and troubled by unfamiliar sexual urges, are not, on the whole, really interested in making love themselves. Unless overstimulated by competitiveness and group pressures, they tend to prefer to be lookers-on, watching films, reading pornographic literature, having daydreams, and so on, but they are afraid of coming too close to another of the opposite sex. It is fashionable, of course, in many circles to have a boyfriend or a girlfriend at this age; but this tends to be a matter of prestige, of aping your elders, a quick way of seeming to be grown up.

None the less, this is a time when it is both fruitful and necessary to get to know others of your own age and of the opposite sex. To do so in a group is both a protection and an enrichment. Early teenage parties and youth club activities, for instance, are experiences to be talked over with your particular friends after the event. You compare notes about your conversations, encounters, and feelings to discover how your judgements of new acquaintances differ from those of your best friends and to learn from experience how well founded or not they have been. Gossip can be not only entertaining but also informative about the actions and relationships of others.

Ups and downs in friendship

"What *is* of any importance to you at the moment?" asked the exasperated mother of a thirteen-year-old girl, after a fruitless attempt to talk her out of a bored and gloomy mood that was enveloping the whole family like a black cloud. "My friends!" was the immediate, snappy answer—the first definite response to the many attempts to find out what was the matter and to cheer her up. "But you're always quarrelling with your friends and saying they're awful! Do you really mean they matter more to you than your family?" asked her mother in hurt bewilderment. "You just don't understand do you?" was the reply; "We *like* to quarrel—it gives us something to be miserable *about.*"

Not an unusual dialogue between a mother and her young teenager. When she thought about it afterwards this mother did begin to understand a little better. Friends are useful to pick a quarrel with when you are in a black mood; you do not know why, and you do not know who to blame. If your parents are kind and helpful you can feel too much of a pig for snapping at them and upsetting their feelings—that is, if you have kindly, well-meaning parents. At this age, when feelings can swing very rapidly from elation to boredom and misery, from confident expectation to persecution and withdrawal, it can be safer to enact them with others of your own kind, going through the same perplexities as yourself. So the young girl who tells her mother than her friends are the most important thing in her life is also conveying that her own state of mind, her perplexing and contradictory inner life, is the most important thing to her at the moment. She can only come to life at the time if she can live it out and fight it out with her friends. Friends are valuable at this stage not just to talk and do things with, but also to fight with.

It is easier to combat in one of your friends something that you can't stand in yourself. It is easier to do this than to be aware of it in yourself and to struggle with it there. The important thing about fighting an unpleasant trait in a friend, rather than in an enemy whom you keep at a distance and refuse to acknowledge as being in any way like yourself, is that if your friendship is based on some real respect and liking, there is chance you will come together again and find that you have faults and unpleasant qualities in common, as well as pleasanter things. In this way the young adolescent gets a feeling of his own qualities and learns that they are to be found in his friends and in himself.

Not that we should dismiss too lightly the degree to which quarrels and broken friendships make young sons and daughters suffer at this stage if they are capable of enthusiasm and love. Some of the suffering will indeed stem from wounded vanity and self-regard, as well as from jealousy, but it is through experiencing these feelings that one learns how to live with them without being too devastated by them.

Some young people are so exclusive and ask so much of their friends that they cannot forgive a wound, and a friendship once broken seems broken for ever. These sudden and final ruptures are much more likely to be due to wounded vanity than to real differences of opinion: to an inability to allow the friend to put something or somebody as more important than themselves for the time being. These young adolescents were the young children who never really came to terms with sharing their parents' love with the other children; who never became reconciled in their hearts to allowing their parents to enjoy time and interests together away from the children.

They may have become young adolescents, in fact, without ever first managing to enjoy being a child among children. They remain secretly very uncertain somewhere, unless constantly reassured that they are first in somebody's affection. They tend to look for friends, now and later, who will reassure and admire and protect them. The need for the friends' love tends to cloud perception and appreciation of his real qualities.

We all seek reassurance to some extent, of course, throughout our lives. No one is so secure that he has no need to be liked. There is no one whose judgement is not at times liable to be clouded by this. In this, as in other things, our children watch us and take us for models without realizing that they are doing so. They watch how we behave with our friends when they are there, and when we talk about them in their absence. They tend to do as we do, not as we teach, even though they may come to criticize our actions.

So, if we want to help them find their way towards lasting friendships it is not, on the whole, helpful to take sides in their quarrels. If they do confide in us we must beware, however, of treating the matter too lightly, even if it seems trivial. If we can accept quarrels and differences of opinion as necessary and painful accompaniments of even close friendships we can act as a sort of listening post where they can hear themselves speak and maybe come to evaluate the truthfulness of what they are saying. It is only after they are confident that we have been interested in their particular trouble that they are likely to listen to any advice from us, or any judgement based on our own experience, when perhaps they can be comforted a little by being told that broken friendships are not necessarily the end of the world.

CHAPTER TEN

Bad companions

As parents we all no doubt have a tendency, when our child is getting into trouble, to want to pin the blame on so-and-so's badly brought up offspring. Some of us may even have paid a visit to our innocent's school to explain with indignation how unjustified they have been in finding fault with Tommy, who was led astray by bad companions.

Now it may be that Tommy is being led astray by others: to steal, to bully, to commit acts of hooliganism, for instance. We then have to ask ourselves why, if he has been brought up to think that these things are wrong, he lets himself be led into doing them? What kind of satisfaction is he getting from behaving in this way? Is it, for instance, that he would really like to bully his little brother or sister and has never dared bring these desires into the open? Has he been prevented by authority from expressing them, but lain in wait for a chance to indulge them somewhere else, given the backing and collusion of another or of a group?

Not, of course, that one would suggest he should have been given the opportunity to indulge these impulses on his little brother earlier on. Nor, for that matter (if he had been allowed to do so), would he have "got them out of his system". The bully tends to become confirmed in his bullying if he gets away with it (as we can see from the various tyrannical and oppressive regimes that exist, and have existed, throughout the world). But if there is a part of the child that is violent and is directed against the weak, it is important that this should be known, not hidden. It can be known only if it is expressed in some way, and it is likely to be expressed in an undisciplined action before it can be contained and modified in work.

This early adolescent stage, as we have already said, is one during which emotional upheaval disturbs the status quo and stirs up rebellion in young people against authority that they may have accepted until then. It leads them to act at times in ways that can surprise them and surprise their parents. And if these are antisocial acts they have to be taken seriously as expressions of anger, of destructiveness against authority, against parents, maybe against a child's better self. "Taken seriously" means thought about, talked about, understood, not ostracized and driven underground again. They may be driven underground, for instance, if the child is made to feel too guilty about his misdeeds, and this may lead to a still greater conscious or unconscious grudge against authority that will find an outlet in some indirect way.

Need for protection from bad companions: the pull to be like the rest

These young people, just like ourselves, are made up of many parts, and pulled in different directions by different affinities. They do not yet belong to the world of grown-ups or even to the truly adolescent world, but they are looking to these worlds for models of the life that they would like to lead and the comforts they would like to have.

If they have failed in childhood to become reconciled to being children, to accept with a good grace some necessary dependence on parents and parent-substitutes—teachers, for instance—then in early adolescence they begin to see the chance to get their own back for what they experienced as the humiliating dependence of childhood. This is rather a strong statement about a state of mind that probably exists fleetingly in all adolescents, to some degree, among other mixed attitudes to the grown-up world. In some adolescents however, though they be quite unaware of it, it is so powerful that it leads them to team up with and often to idealize others who are anti-authority in a variety of ways: who think it clever to cheat, to steal, to take drugs, or to bully—to do what, in fact, they have been prevented from doing before, which includes most especially sexual promiscuity.

The need to be one of a group, to lose their uncertain identity among others of the same kind, is for many at this stage quite overwhelming. Feeling at odds with your parents is only too likely to increase dependence on a group. You can feel justified, do not need to feel guilty, if all your friends have the same trouble with parents. We do need to protect our children from dependence on undesirable companions, from feeling that their best friends are those who are clever enough to get away with defying all the outworn rules. It is probably no use, however, to forbid certain friends just like that. This is likely to cause resentful defiance in a young adolescent of spirit. Or another who is too afraid to defy you may very likely feel more scared of rejection himself because he has chosen this particular friend to express antisocial tendencies that he himself has harboured secretly. If you cannot tolerate the friend, he feels that— did you but know—you would not tolerate him either. This fear drives him further away from you.

Before setting out to try to put a stop to some friendship that you feel is damaging your child, it is as well first of all to try to get to know as much about it as you can. If you encourage your youngster to bring his friend home you have the opportunity to look and see for yourself. It may be that the friend's parents are also uneasy, and that you could find mutual support in talking the matter over. It is, in any case, advisable to talk to your own child about what is worrying you, and maybe to lay more stress on the dangers of the effect they have on each other, rather than to treat it as a case of a silly victim led astray by a thoroughly bad lot, which is demeaning to your own child and—he may feel—quite unfair to the other. He is then all the more likely to feel that he has to defy you to protect his friends.

The bad influence

And what of the situation when it is your child who seems to be the one who leads the others astray? If he is the gang-leader in delinquency it is no use—no help to him—to blink at the fact. It is much better at this stage to think hard, and then, if necessary, to try to get help by discussing matters with his teacher and maybe other experts—social or child psychiatric workers or probation officers, for instance—to consider what might be done to turn his energies into other channels before matters go too far.

Certainly one is not suggesting that every young person who is the leader or instigator of antisocial acts such as stealing, vandalism, etc., is likely to grow up to be a criminal. Many who go through such a stage now and in later adolescent years live to become pillars of society, and castigate their own children for acts that they do not care to remember having committed themselves. So, when we get heated about our own young reprobate, it is as well to cast our minds back a little and to think how we might best have been handled by our own parents at this age. It is also as well to think a little about our own present conduct, and to consider those actions and attitudes which—even if within the law—might give a sharp-eyed young adolescent sanction; for instance, to feel that it is clever to get away with paying for less than we owe, or to get our revenge for real or fancied humiliation.

Unless our child feels that we are, on the whole, sincere in keeping within the law, or in our consideration for others, we do not give him much incentive to follow us. If he knows that we sometimes have a struggle in doing so, at times not even realizing that we are failing, but that we still find it worthwhile to go on trying, he may feel more encouraged to try himself. One can also point out to him that the child who leads others in delinquency also probably has the power to lead them in more constructive ways if he wishes to do so.

When a child steals

Lying, stealing, cheating, and similar delinquencies are not isolated deeds, but actions done by children (or adults) in particular situations and for particular purposes of which the actors may often be unaware. We are not always surprised at these actions, nor do we always condemn them; a very young child often steals or "takes things", and he as often lies or "tells stories", and we count it "naughty" but not really "bad". Similarly, folk-characters and real-life characters of the Robin Hood type can seem so normal, so much just projections of our everyday habits and wishes, that even though the law may be furious with them, we may sympathize with or even idolize them, especially if they steal from non-people (such as large impersonal or government organizations) and preferably without violence. Such characters do not seem dangerous to us, any more than the rage of the infant is dangerous; in fact they may be clever, brave, ingenious and, within their own circle, even loyal and sociable. And we do not have to envy them, for they will probably get caught.

But, very naturally, this is not how the parent normally looks on the stealing of a child or twelve to fourteen, especially when that child is his own. And it is, in truth, not a light-hearted matter. We would expect a child to have worked through the tendency to steal—which often occurs at some time with very young children—by the time he is twelve or more. We are frightened for ourselves—for the good name of the family—and even more for the child, for society cannot ignore the type of theft that the young delinquent is now capable of, and in which he will, if unchecked, become habitually more capable and hurtful as he grows older. "What on earth did you do it for?" exclaims the injured parent. And the child answers, "I dunno," or, if pressed for an answer, he will lie.

A parent can do harm in this situation if he is over-controlled and fails to admit his concern. Total calmness may seem to be indifference or an icy rejection. In a curious way the child may not want to be "understood"; he may wish to be blamed, and so get rid of some of the feeling of guilt. Even more harmful and bewildering to the child (unless delinquency is his normal family environment, in which case, of course, it will not seem delinquency to him) is the action of the parent who colludes with the child—who lets him keep the tennis racket he has "found", the calculator or mobile phone he has taken, or who does not trouble to ask where some new property has come from. In fact, a child's sense of justice seems usually more primitively Mosaic than any adult's, and he expects the retribution of an eye for an eye. The colluding parent may be accepted and exploited in further delinquencies, but will not be trusted. Since the child cannot tolerate this situation, he will either have to reject the parent or to collude in turn in a self-perpetuating delinquent pattern of behaviour.

What, then, can be done when the stealing is more than a simple once-only matter for which an equally simple reparation can be made? There is no easy answer. The punishment or "good talking to" may ease the parent's or headteacher's feelings, but it is more likely to make the child a more adept liar and a lonelier thief than it is to cure him. When a child steals at this age he is telling us something, possibly too private to talk about in any other way; that is why he cannot answer the straightforward question "Why ever did you do it?" It is something lost in the past and re-emerging in the present as a powerful anxiety that can be quietened only by stealing, as an itch is temporarily soothed by scratching. But then it starts up again, more raw than before. The stealing does not effect a cure. What has been lost can be established only in the personal history of the particular family and its relationships: some sort of trust, perhaps, in the security of his position in his mother's affections? To find it again requires a good deal of self-searching in parents and child, and a searching without recrimination in an effort to try to reshape the past in a more trustful present. Only the family itself is likely to have the concern and the patience to bring this about, and, indeed, only the people intimately involved *can* do it, even if professional help is available. It is not realistic to expect society to participate in this reshaping except in a quite external way, and so the whole process will be more stressful now than it might have been when the child was younger; now there will be more social distrust to overcome and more restrictions to tolerate. The parents have to trust the child's feelings; school or other people will not, at least for a testing while, trust his actions; and this fact has to be borne. The child struggling with his tendency to steal does not want to be spied on, especially as the fact that he *is* struggling shows that he carries his own "policeman" about with him; but it would be irresponsible and no help to him to place him in positions where stealing is easy. He may, for example, have to be separated from his mates with whom he may have found, or bought, a sort of popularity by being the daring one: stealing not for the things stolen, but for the status acquired as one of the gang. But it is no good blaming his friends for his actions.

Stealing to buy friendship and popularity—sweets from the self-service store, subsequently shared out round the class—is commoner in children younger than the twelve-to-fourteen age group. In older children stealing tends to be to buy status. The thief has money to contribute to the group's activities, a bike [or skateboard] or other game to lend. Some ways of trying to solve these problems suggest themselves—letting the child have friends home; letting him have a reasonable amount of pocket money, or take a small job to save enough to spend on something he really wants. These may help, provided the stealing does not go too deep; and parents must be prepared to allow for waste and mistakes. The child given his own post office account to use as he pleases cannot be relied on to treat it like a responsible adult, but may have to go through the process of "stealing from himself", as it were. That is, at any rate, a lesson, and if he proves capable of learning from it, things will probably be all right.

"Straightforward" stealing, motivated by simple greed, can be fairly brusquely dealt with in traditional ways, and usually vanishes quickly, unless the greed is for that earlier loss mentioned above. The parent who talks with his child about things in general, who listens seriously to the child's opinions and offers a serious reply, will usually know better than any teacher or policeman whether the stealing is "straightforward" or not. It is often where there is no communication between parents and children that the secret modes of stealing or lying have to be employed. The emptiness within the child caused by the gap in his relationships is filled by taking by stealth, and telling stories to himself. But as stealing always really means stealing from "mother", it increases the gap between child and parents and he then feels even more guilty and estranged. The more guilty he becomes the more he is likely to be driven to harden himself, pretend he does not care and has every right to make away with what he can get.

It seems a pity to end this little book on the theme of difficulties. These are years of excitement and promise for children who are becoming young adults. But rapid growth does tend to be accompanied by anxiety and sometimes by greater difficulty in managing the more demanding and aggressive aspects of one's own nature. So this is a time when our sons and daughters may cause us furiously to think for ourselves and about ourselves.

Sometimes we feel that we know our youngster well enough and have enough confidence in ourselves to be able to hold a watching brief when necessary, or to battle through difficulties and sort out problems and delinquencies with him when this is necessary, helping him in this way to a flourishing and manageable adolescence.

If we do find ourselves in continual trouble with our young adolescents, and unable to talk without making matters worse, then it is advisable to think of discussing things with someone else who is not so emotionally involved in the situation. As before, this may be a friend, a teacher, the family doctor, someone to whom we feel we really can talk. This may be enough to help us decide when it is necessary to try to get some more specialized professional help, or when—with a little more tolerance or firmness or a new look at the situation—we can use the unique knowledge that we possess of our young people's personalities to enable them to express themselves more fruitfully.

BOOK THREE
YOUR TEENAGER

Introduction

T his little book, the last of the series, concerns young people of fourteen, fifteen and over in their last years at school, and those proceeding to work or to further education. They are continuing that long adolescent process of emotional upheaval and reorganization which is necessary before they come to a more mature realization of their identities.

The uncertainty in these young persons about what kind of individuals they are turning out to be, and in what kind of a world they have to find their way, is often shared by parents. We have to get used to the idea of seeing the child whom we have reared becoming more of an equal and a challenge to our authority. We are driven to question the way in which we are exercising our authority and experience, and to ask how we can still protect without stifling.

How has the teenager whom we see passing from our care grown out of the child he was just yesterday? What part did we have in that growth? Do we still need the child, or is our life complete without him?

These questions are not answered here; they cannot be answered simply, or by prescriptions by some "expert". But it is possible to suggest some ways of considering these, and other, questions which our teenagers evoke in us if we are still alive and open to experience. If that is the case, and we are able to see the world anew through the eyes of the teenager while retaining our own role as parents, we do not need to get estranged from the younger generation. We can feel that we have a part in its promise, its performance, as well as its follies.

CHAPTER ONE

The teenager at school

Can parents help in the school?

The teenager is thinking of leaving school, but for the time being he is still there. In the next section we shall consider the actual period of decision—to leave or to stay; just now, we may consider the teenager in the school itself.

Parents these days take an increasing interest in the internal workings of their children's school. It is not the closed environment it was some years ago. After the statutory leaving age was raised [from fifteen to sixteen], the rule of the teacher became modified by the incursion—at first tolerated, then welcomed—of members of the community outside the school. These include workers from specialist helping agencies, such as churches, educational psychologists, youth workers, social workers; and also, increasingly, members of the local general public, such as parents with some particular skill or knowledge, who are willing to talk to the school or to certain groups within it.

Schools are often especially willing to make use of such help with the "outward-looking" curricula that they need to construct for the adolescent students in their final years at school. Such curricula may include activities in small groups outside the school, visits to places of work or of cultural interest, and so on. In direct preparation for public examinations the teacher must still be the specialist, of course—he has the knowledge of the subject, of the examination requirements, and of the techniques of teaching. Most parents cannot be of much help here; but in all that area of the curriculum that is outside the sphere of examinations there are places where the school might welcome an interest from parents.

Providing special help outside school

Some parents are frightened of school; many schools are frightened of parents. So, generally speaking, it is not within the school that you will be able to help your teenager or his group. It would clearly be a bad thing to be seen to take an exclusive interest in your own fifteen-year-old; your co-operation with the school would have to be of a general, not an individual, nature, otherwise child and teacher alike are embarrassed. So the help you can give to your child is mostly given outside school.

Arranging special tutoring in some subject with which the child is having difficulty is one form of help, though it is one to be approached with caution. For the average child, a blockage in learning at this level of adolescence is seldom a measure of the intellectual difficulty of the material. The material, after all, is tailored to the powers of the average child. You are not likely to make the best special tutor of your own child, though it is not impossible for you to act as tutor.

Usually, however, if there are emotional complications connected with the learning difficulty you may well be involved in them. Father may think himself—may even be—a clever fellow and well able to instruct his adolescent daughter in some problem of mathematics. As often as not, alas, he proves to have very limited patience, and the daughter seems particularly obtuse with him. Alternatively, being aware of this danger, he is deliberately and excessively tolerant of mistakes, gentle in tone, concerned, and careful not to be a bully in his clear and simple instructions, as they seem to him—yet still the teenager does not learn. He begins to believe that, after all, she *is* stupid. She begins to believe it too; and begins to be very angry. So things go from muddled to incomprehensible. "I hate maths!" This need not happen, but is a sequence to watch out for if you do decide to play tutor to your own teenager.

Preparing the ground by being a learner too

It is sometimes possible to prepare the ground for direct help of this sort by showing a willingness to learn yourself. Done artificially, "once-off", as it were, such a procedure is unlikely to be effective. Boy or girl will see the hook under such a sudden and uncharacteristic interest in a point of learning. But if you have shown all along a general interest in your child's learning, you may be able to capitalize on this when some temporary learning crisis occurs. The perfunctory "What have you been doing in school today?" followed by immediate re-immersion in the evening paper or the television is not, to the child, evidence of a general interest. Nor is a dutiful cross-examination that will be felt as a chore on the parent's part and as a persecution on the child's. After all, not all subjects are interesting all of the time.

But in the relatively adult studies of the pupil in adolescence and late adolescence there are bound to occur themes of general concern—from current affairs, maybe, or scientific discovery, or technological processes—about which you could learn from your child with interest. If he finds you glad to listen it will help when he may need to listen to your guidance. Or, if you do not know enough to act as a direct guide and instructor, he will be able to learn with you as you work through some chapter in the textbook together.

It is an enlivening experience for parents to find that their minds can still tick over. To have given up learning—as so many of us adults have—is not an inspiring example to the young learner; and to have so much knowledge that we never use except to pass it on to our children is equally dispiriting. These are extremes to be avoided if we are to hope at any time to give some special help to our youngster.

Learning with friends

If you cannot help with school work there is usually a school-friend with whom your child can co-operate. This is to be encouraged, and these days in school it generally is—the old idea that working together is somehow "cheating" (though it can be that) has largely died out. Many learning procedures—for example, projects, or the new overlapping subject areas—require co-operative working. Young people often choose friends with similar interests, and minds are sharpened by contact with each other. Two people find it easier to confess to a difficulty than does the isolated student, and so are easier to help. Tests and examinations are not the only means of identifying the pupil who is simply copying his friend's work; and, in any case, a natural proper pride more often than not turns the passenger into a partner. So, by co-operation or by accepting help from an older brother or sister, the teenager makes failure less likely and success more frequent. Nobody learns so well as the pupil who is experiencing success.

Making use of the teacher

There is always the further possibility of helping your teenager by an approach to the school itself through the headteacher. It is rare for the class teacher, subject teacher, or member of staff acting as school counsellor not to be glad to discuss things with you. Clearly this is a matter for discretion. A pupil sometimes fails to "hit if off" with a particular teacher, and the failure, whatever its cause, rubs off on the subject taught and the work suffers. A simple grumble at the teacher, or outright blame for a child's failure which has complex origins, is unlikely to improve matters for either teacher or child.

Irene and the art teacher

Here is an example of a child helped through this sort of parent–teacher discussion.

Irene was a fifteen-year-old, an only child who, according to her parents, had never given them a moment's anxiety. She had always had friends, "nice boys and girls like herself". At school she had always been among the best in most subjects, but showed especial gifts for art and would probably go on to make a career for herself in this field. During the past year she had had a new young art teacher at school who evoked great enthusiasm for his subject. Irene, one of his favourite pupils, had in particular put in a great deal of extra work after school and during breaks, making great progress in her art. Suddenly, however, her work became very careless. She spoiled some of the materials by leaving them lying around carelessly, failed to turn up for work she had arranged to do, and was silently defiant when reproached about this.

Her art teacher approached Irene's house-mistress about this in some puzzlement, wondering whether there had been a general falling-off in her work. Bewildered and hurt at the change in Irene's attitude to him, he asked whether she might be taking out on him some grievance that originated elsewhere. He felt that her attitude was affecting the rest of the class. Irene's house-mistress consulted her parents to see if they could furnish any clue, as Irene herself, when questioned about her changed attitude to the art teacher, could not say much, looked sulky and upset, then finally burst into tears. Her parents could not offer any explanation. They had noticed she seemed more moody than usual during and since the school holidays. She would shut herself up in her room for longer periods than usual and had less interest in the painting that formerly occupied so much of her time.

In discussing things with Irene's other teachers her house-mistress heard that her work in other subjects had not deteriorated noticeably. However, one of the younger teachers immediately hit upon a likely explanation for her behaviour. She said that the art teacher had got married during the previous holidays. Only one or two of his friends among the staff knew of this, but almost certainly the news would have percolated to Irene and her friends.

This immediately made sense. It was likely that the marriage could well be hurtful to the dreams of a favourite adolescent pupil, and maybe was also resented by some of the other girls in the class. Perhaps the art teacher had intended to keep it a secret in order to avoid this possibility. Of course, whether he wanted to announce his marriage or not was his affair, but an inkling of the effect it could be having on Irene could, once recognized, help him to tolerate a little better—without feeling too wounded in a personal way—a period of resentment and defiant behaviour on her part. Friendly, matter-of-fact discipline on the teacher's part is much more likely to help a young girl live through this kind of hurt than is a pained and non-comprehending response.

Sharing knowledge

Apart from personal matters such as those concerning Irene and her art teacher, schools do differ enormously in their facilities, their programmes, and in the qualities of their staff—this is a national problem. In practice, each parent has to work with the school the child has [unless they resort to changing schools], and each child does the same, accepting the rough with the smooth in a realistic way that is not entirely passive. Working together, parent and school, is best done by assuming initially that the teacher is an honest and concerned professional, anxious to help your child— and this, fortunately, is nearly always the case.

So, a teenager having learning difficulties may be helped if you explore the likely causes with the teacher—not dictate them to him. There is sure to be something he knows about Tom that you as a parent do not know, and vice versa. Teenagers can be secretive because they have an extreme, snail-like sensitivity. A boy, for example, may seem lazy to his teacher; his homework is never finished, or is untidy. Teachers are human too—the teacher may have responded (although inadvertently) to the boy's "don't care" attitude by not caring himself to devote special attention to helping him. You may know as a parent that the boy in question really spends ages over his homework, but cannot do it. The "don't care" attitude he shows to teachers masks his self-despair at not manag- ing. Major changes of attitude may result from this little discovery, and the teacher may be able to rescue the boy from his impasse. Alternatively, the teacher may have a more objective and valid understanding of a pupil's intellectual capacity than you have as ambitious—perhaps over-ambitious—parents. He can then help the parents to adjust their expectations to their child's real potential in that particular school situation, and so modify the pressure that may be causing failure even where the child could succeed.

How much your teenager should know of your discussions with his teacher admits of no easy answer. One thing is certain—your visit should not be used as a threat. No normal child *wants* to fail.

The teenager, confined in his own habits of secrecy except among his mates, may welcome with relief the knowledge that his difficulties are now in the open. He can now say, "I don't understand this", to the teacher. On the other hand, more good may be done by the teacher being able to change his approach without the stimulus of your visit being apparent. The teenager is thus allowed to retain his privacy, and will feel he has worked through (and in consequence will in fact work through) to a better relationship with the teacher. What he feels was his own achievement becomes just that.

On not seeing eye-to-eye

These reflections have so far assumed that the teenager does accept, even like, his school and its programme, and that underneath some particular learning difficulty there is a real wish to succeed. These assumptions may, unfortunately, be false for many children. There is little doubt that, in Britain at least, there is often thought to be a wide division between the objectives the school sets up and those seen as important by the pupils or even by the parents. The school, for example, may say that it ranks self-development (confidence, personality, interests, and awareness) above vocational training or academic results.[1] Leavers at the statutory school-leaving age, and their parents, seem to reverse these rankings. So, pupils do not always perceive the relevance of their studies to their lives; they feel irresponsibly detained in a dependent juvenility. They fail in their exams, lose self-respect, and compensate by losing respect for their school.

In adolescence, genuine or fantasized awareness of the difference between adulthood and childhood dependence is vividly felt. At the same time, the adolescent feels understandable panic at the imminent need to be independent and self-supporting. If there has been a failure to see eye-to-eye between the young person and his school environment and values, it is intensified at this stage. This is not the place to enter into discussion of educational objectives in detail: suffice it to say that they have at least become a subject of constant agitation and review in the profession.[2] Whatever happens, and whatever changes may be made to the school-leaving age, it is a fact that although a child's schooldays come to an end, education need not; and, happily, we find that many formerly disaffected pupils may mature rapidly and sensibly once out at work, often indeed returning to further education when they realize they want it and are not driven to it.

Objectives with which we can all agree

We can more profitably consider some generally agreed objectives to see if parents can help their teenagers at least with these. Speaking and writing well and easily, being confident and at ease, judging right and wrong, getting along with other people without sacrificing your principles—these seem to matter to everyone. How unlikely it is that we shall speak well if we rarely converse; or be at ease with different types of people if we can think only in our own limited parochial terms; or judge right and wrong if we have never seriously considered what is going on in the world; or get along with others if we remain locked up in the superiority and seclusion of our own little family circle!

It has often been said that children identify with their parents. That they do so results sometimes in the adoption of similar views, sometimes in the rejection of these views, but nearly always in the style and manner of the parental outlook. We may hold broad and generous views meanly, and stern opinions with tolerance.

The teenager enters the adult world

The teenager is not only a learner. He is a person in himself, though what that self is he may not rightly know—the teenager's search for identity is discussed in Chapter Seven.

The exciting part of the parental share in a teenager's education comes when the problems of particular school subjects are left behind. It is exciting because the teenager is so nearly adult. Indeed, older teenagers can be greater pontificators and appear older wiseacres than any adult. Despite their sanctimony, we as parents have to consider our child's views as valid expressions of opinion to be weighed in their own right against ours, when there is disagreement.

The teenager impinges on his parents' world

Bringing up a teenager thus implies being willing to review our own standards and judgements, as well as to criticize his. We can only expect to educate him by re-educating ourselves. This does not, of course, mean acquiescing in all his opinions and giving up all our own dislikes to take over his. No growth is possible that way. But reviewing opinions entails discussion. It entails agreeing—even if only agreeing to differ—after having first listened to the evidence. Confidence for the teenager, as for all of us, comes not from experience alone but from thinking about that experience; discussion is the exchange of thought. It is a common finding in schools where free discussion in small groups is encouraged that otherwise "difficult" pupils become, for the time being at least, amenable to argument and open to evidence. They may relapse immediately afterwards, but that is because the habits and defences of a lifetime are not easily altered.

Unless your teenager is very self-absorbed, he will be bound to gather his opinions from television, newspapers, books, the world about him, on a thousand topics of critical importance to the shaping of tomorrow's world. It is important to his education, to his ability to move freely in society, that he voice and test out these opinions so that they do not harden into banal clichés. We as parents can help him in this, but only, I think, if we do so for the interest's sake—the topics must matter to us too, and the education will follow automatically; for us, perhaps, as well as for our teenager.

Speaking well

People without a long formal education—that is, the majority of us parents—tend to think of "good speech" as a particular manner of enunciating our words, a special sort of accent, a polite way of saying—nothing. This, of course, is not so. We have all met the anxious person who puts on a thin gloss, like a lipstick, of refined accent in order to seem at ease in a social group when really feeling profoundly ill at ease. Good speech is not such a gloss, not such a veneer. It is the outcome of the interdependence of experience, interest and awareness, and of language and its structures and vocabulary.[3] This sort of good speech is not restricted to one particular social class [or ethnic group]. It enables us to construct new forms of experience and to mix easily with groups and classes other than our own: with, that is, the great social class of the truly educated people, the people who are still learning. It is by taking an active part in this process, in which in a sense we are all equals, that we parents can help our teenagers and keep their respect as well as respect them.

When our child does better than his parents

One further point, concerning a tension arising from another source—success. Adolescence is the time when it may emerge, as happens increasingly often in our society, that children have had more education and training than their parents. The young person may not only be an emotional critic but also a better-informed one than his parents of the way of life his parents represent. This can be painful to both sides.

A teenager from a working-class family where perhaps there may have existed a stoical or contented tolerance of a routine and repetitive but secure means of earning a living, may in one sense hunger to stay safely cocooned within his parents' social horizons. The parents may even disapprove of, or resent, the acquisition of knowledge—the ways of elaborated speech and thought that go with education in depth, the tendency to see too many sides to an argument where they see only one, the "right" one.

So the growing and learning teenager may see the homeliness that he half longs to retain taking on something of the quality of a dream, a fantasy, which he can no longer accept as his real aim in life. He may suddenly find that he has gone further and will go further than his parents can manage or even want for themselves.[4] Work, from being something to put up with for the sake of the car and the Saturday football match [or holiday abroad], might become a special form of enjoyment; and enjoyment may be something his parents feel ought to be paid for by grudged toil and discomfort. Fortunate—even if at times unhappy—are the parents with an adolescent in this state. They can help him or her best by saying,

"God speed!" and letting go. If they can manage this, their teenager will come back to them not under constraint but in his own way and with free affection.

Notes

1. In recent years, of course, this has changed in Britain with the publication of school league tables, and, if anything, the pendulum has swung in the opposite direction, though it will no doubt swing back again.
2. And these days—some would say excessively—by the government.
3. The concept of "good speech" is unfashionable at present, owing to the prevalence of political correctness (the result of fear of social upheaval) that interposes a screen of uniformity instead of genuine communication as in King Lear's "speak what we feel, not what we ought to say".
4. A problem particularly, perhaps, with immigrant families these days, even those whose credo is educational success.

CHAPTER TWO

Work and further education

Growth continues, learning continues

Fifteen. At such an age the teenager comes to a crack in the ice over which he must leap at some point if he is to go further. Much of his growth, mental and physical, is completed. The great physical spurt of early adolescence is dying away. Mentally, he will go on growing for many years to come, if he is fortunate and lively enough not to subside into a comfortable early middle age. But this growth will be at a slower rate and probably chiefly in directions that his own selective interests dictate.

Who decides?

It is a critical time for decisions, at least in our society, where administrative convenience imposes synchronization on a wide spread of personal, psychological, and social divergence. The teenager is urged forward and held back by forces inside himself, and also by social pressures and restraints. So it is no wonder he sometimes makes rather a mess of his great leap forward! Perhaps he makes the wrong decision about his future plans—decides to enter some dead-end well-paid job when he could have tried for a more testing and rewarding career. Perhaps he rashly aims much too high. Perhaps he takes part in delinquent or semi-delinquent adventures. Perhaps he just shuts his ears to all the contradictory voices calling "Do this!" "Do that!" and leaps blindly forward and away to escape. "Who are all these people who want me to be just like them?"

A decision can be modified

Fortunately, society generally is much more aware of adolescent need and conflict than it used to be; teenagers, indeed, are much more vocal in expressing themselves on this score. Being more aware, as well as being driven by its own technological and industrial requirements, society has increasingly built in to its procedures ways and means of allowing for change and development in young people. An educational decision made at fifteen—say to leave school and study no more—is not irrevocable. The boredom that comes with a mind unused can be alleviated later by various means of entry into further education—home studying, part-time, or sponsored by industry. It is not an uncommon experience to find staff at these institutions of higher education welcoming particularly the more serious motivation and maturity of outlook, the self-disciplined hard work of entrants who have had a taste of the ordinary world of work before coming to—and succeeding at—college.

Similarly, a new flexibility has entered into many trades and professions. The old concept of a particular skill to be learned and practised for a lifetime has not only lost its finality, but has been expanded by the recognition that what is also wanted is an ability to learn new skills, since the processes by which we modify and use the physical world continually change, indeed are changing at an increasing rate.[1] This is a fact that can be distressing to the middle-aged, but should also be a hopeful safety-net for the teenager whose mind is still open.

Anxieties about work

Nevertheless, the teenager's anxieties about work and educational decisions are very real. Let us consider a few of their sources.

Crises, even when long expected, always take us by surprise. Long before fifteen, I dare say, you and your child's teachers talked with him about his choice of career, or about leaving school or staying on for A-level exams. To have discussed this problem early was wise, since it may have prepared the ground for a decision when there was as yet no great involvement or emotional stress about its rightness or wrongness. The anticipated results seemed safely far off. Now, all of a sudden, they are at hand, and decisions are for real.

Sometimes it is almost as if the earlier careful introduction had never taken place, and parents who had hoped the dilemma already resolved may be irritated by the whole business being reopened. "But we discussed all that last year . . ." Endless patience and reconsideration are necessary; the only once-for-all events are birth and death.

One source of anxiety is that the ideas which it had been possible to consider fairly coolly and reasonably have now been coloured by strong feelings within the teenager himself. "It's *my* life we're talking about." He or she has to finally abandon the fantasies of easy and early success of the secretary-marries-the-boss type (the fairytale princess) or the unimaginative lad stumbles-on-a-brilliant-invention type (the frog turns into a prince). Yet your child does not seem to welcome the staid routine course that we parents may, for safety's sake, propose to him.

Furthermore, strong pressures of necessity and time impose themselves from sources outside the teenager, and are indifferent to him as a person—statutory regulations, or perhaps the need to contribute to the family income. "Playing it cool" is a technique adolescent songs and sayings often advocate, presumably because they find it hard in actuality.

Conflicting expectations

The teenager himself wants to make the decision. He wants to leave school, to earn money, to be self-responsible, to acquire adult status in all the ways that can be satisfying only when they are not granted by tolerant or reluctant parents but are there as of right—the grown-up right. If he decides to go to work he can recompense himself for the real or fancied slights that stem from the attitudes of any friends who have decided to continue their education.[2] If he decides to stay on at school he can compensate for the continued feeling of dependence and the continued stress of learning and scholastic trial by feeling that in the long run he will do better than his mates who leave. As he envies them, so they may envy him.

It is easy to see how this conflict of expectations makes any decision stressful for him. The part of him that wants to leave, to be grown-up, doubts as well as desires his ability to succeed or even to survive—a tough guy can be very tender under the skin. Someone deprived of self-respect by failure may well lapse into some form of delinquency. The teenager also wonders—for in British society, especially in the south, there is something of a stigma attached to leaving school at the earliest legal time— whether he could not have done better for himself by staying on, and this even when he has managed to convince himself that school is "a lot of crap".

The part of him that wants to stay on and take further examinations and training has equally no lack of doubts. Does he just want to stay protected, still a child at home? Is he incapable of making a final decision—has he always to put things off? Is he just letting himself be pushed around by the ambitions of his parents, or of his teachers, or by his own unwarranted vanity? Many teenagers have a poor enough opinion of themselves by the time they reach the upper levels of the secondary school—it is one of the fruits of the educational system.

Parental pressures

The desire to test and the fear of testing their own potency as adults may thus be equally strong in teenagers who have reached this time of decision, the threshold of adulthood. Sources outside themselves contribute to the conflict. Whether he leaves or stays on at school, the teenager knows he is reacting to his parents' wishes. Maybe a feeling of guilt or indebtedness at what he owes them compels him to a decision either to achieve higher education or to abandon it in favour of a quick financial return. We parents can, inadvertently or deliberately, be very skilful at levering our teenager into the slot we favour—"Of course dear, you mustn't let yourself be influenced by what your dad wants you to do . . ."

For boys, and increasingly for girls, parental pressure may result in education being presented as a course of hoops to be run through as quickly as possible, perhaps tempered by the older but equally unconstructive view of education as one of the social graces. Both girls and boys embody their parents' hopes, whether happily or with resentment: perhaps dad had wanted to be in a profession and "only managed a trade", or mum regrets having operated the cash-till at the local supermarket part-time to help out with family finances when she "might have made something of herself". Boys as well as girls feel, as they come to the time of the leap into adulthood, that—by, as it were, a second birth—they are both losing and rejecting something safe and, even if constricting, precious: their mother. This, however, is certainly an idea no self-respecting teenager would allow himself to express.

Fortunately, most youngsters who leave school to go to work are able without loss of face to stay at home and, while retaining this protection, avoid any guilty feelings by contributing part of their new wages. It is as important for the teenager as it is useful for the household purse for parents to allow and indeed to expect this contribution.

The loss of friends

The teenager wants to be grown up; he also wants to remain a child. At least as much compulsion to break away or to stay on at school comes from his friends as from his parents and teachers. Even with the "streaming" of academic groups at school he will find some of his acquaintances go one way and some another, for streamed groups are not identical in social background and ambitions.

There will be some inevitable wrenches here. It is clear that whatever protestations of eternal loyalty may be made, there is the beginning of a big drift apart when some members of a group start on further academic studies while others go out to work. It is like giving up reading comics [or watching cartoons]—at a younger age one cannot believe that this will ever happen; but it does happen, and a return is inconceivable. The lost friends or habits drift in one's memory into indifference or a safe nostalgia, and already in late adolescence we acquire that signal possession of adulthood—we have a past.

If there is a fairly equal division of numbers in a school group or a group of friends at this point, the parting of the ways after the teenager's decision is more easily accepted: friends are lost, but friends remain.[3] However, if the division is very unequal—perhaps only the one pupil stays or leaves—then the feeling of loss of comrades can be profound indeed for the single chancer. It is as little consolation to say, "You'll make plenty of new friends", as to say to the jilted fiancé that "there are plenty more fish in the sea".

Feelings exist, though unexpressed

By and large, in society we survive by hiding our feelings from each other. In this way we are less of a burden to others, and they to us. "How are you?" is not really a question we want answered! But in a close society—and the family is the closest—we cannot operate at this comfortable social distance without the family disintegrating. The tie between parents and adolescent child is such that we cannot hide our feelings, though equally we rarely verbalize them. But they emerge and are noted. When we *can* hide them it is by a sort of anaesthesia. It is prior to a breakaway, a final rejection, an acceptance of difference, even an amputation. The adolescent of fifteen, at the end of school or the prelude to a career, may find an amputation the only way to get clear if parents are too clinging; but usually he may not be so ready for the breakaway as he affects to be.

Helping towards independence

How can we help him make the transition to final independence?

Most important of all, we inherit the relationship we have built with him in the past. The feeling-relationship that emerges now without words emerged formatively in our teenager's childhood, and now it is simply expressing what was largely decided then. In the lost boyhood of Judas, Christ was betrayed—or could he have been rescued? There is little purpose in being over-dramatic about this at this stage, like somebody indulging in a death-bed repentance! Most of us as parents have neither failed abysmally nor succeeded perfectly; we all have something still growing towards a good outcome in our tie with our children.

This good outcome we can cherish in various ways. First, it seems to me, we can try to feel ourselves back into that contradiction of arrogance and abasement that the teenager experiences and presents himself as being. By our re-experience of the contradiction in our imagination we are able to adjust the tone of our unspoken feelings to a genuine sympathy that helps the young person to feel understood—not tolerated, patronized, allowed for, neither foolishly adulated nor unjustly castigated. This adjustment of tone comes from a state in which we are, not a magical formula we can employ.

This "being understood" offers to a teenager some of the same security that the younger child feels when his parents justifiably undertake the role of arbiter or restrainer. But with the teenager the relationship is more nearly equal—it is not one of judge and judged.

It is sometimes tempting to underestimate the acuteness with which the teenager experiences the contrary pulls we have discussed above. We are tempted to say, "Yes, we have been through all this too, and look—we have come through". But have we come through unscathed? Are we justly so well satisfied? What have we lost en route? We can, as parents, be sure that the teenager will perceive and chafe at our complacence, and resent it when it seems justified, as much as he may deride it when he notes its basis in a limited achievement. "The trouble with you is, you're dead!" stated one teenager flatly to his crushed, ironic elder.

The teenager's feelings are intense, the dilemma is real. If we think we know the answers pat it is likely to be because we are out of touch with the feelings. The teenager's self-pity annoys us, and the teenager's rage infuriates us because it condemns us. We forget all too readily that most pity is self-pity ("There but for the grace of God go I . . .") and that the teenager spurns our proffered advice because he is less, not more, egocentric than we are—he cannot stand the world we have made for him as he sees it. We call him immoral ("What are young people coming to . . ."), but he is more often violently and passionately moral, or at least moralizing, and this morality is at odds with our own social structures.

Well, this may be so, or may not: it is intended here to be simply a way of suggesting that if we as parents think of rescuing our teenager from his sea of troubles we have to get wet ourselves. If there is one thing a teenager cannot stand it is not being taken seriously at his own level. This is the level of feeling.

On giving advice

There is another level at which we as parents can help. This is the level of ordinary information and guidance, a level at which advice can be offered, especially if it is requested. Generally, it is more suitably our parental function to consider advice than to give it.

It is often a useful protection for our parental role if we can seize the opportunity to work through other relationships with our teenager in a functional way—those of the teacher, the club leader, the careers advisory officer, the local employer who is a friend of the family, or the godparent, if there is one. These people, being less emotionally implicated, may often find their advice acceptable where the same advice would be suspect if offered by parents; equally, if the teenager prefers to reject it, he can do so without fear of hurting our feelings. Our function as parents is thus to take the heat off the advice—to play it cool. It is not so much to be reasonable or rational; it is to engender or discover a situation where reason can be allowed to operate. The teenager is not merely a mass of conflicting and intense feelings, after all. He is also a developing rational being, given at times to exaggeration, to self-deprecation and to self-aggrandisement—but withal no fool in his self-assessment and insight: likely, indeed, to be less blind in this than we are about him.

Thus, given the real chance to know what opportunities are open, not only in general but with particular reference to him and his abilities, he is as likely as anyone to weigh up sensibly what he might best do. We can help him by getting him the appropriate guidance from people who have the requisite knowledge to sort out the real options, and who are not emotionally involved with us. Then the teenager can choose his own ambitions, and not merely shoulder ours. It is our task to nurture ambition, and to discourage folly: to expect realistic self-understanding, but to protect against unnecessary and crippling pessimism.

Time for thought

Finally, there is one special way in which we can ease the pressure for our teenager. This is by giving time, without putting a price tag of guilt on it. Fifteen is a critical age in our social system, but it is not *that* critical. We have often spoken of the enormous range in the speed and maturity of different children's development. Some children genuinely take longer than others to find themselves, to find an identity they really want to live up to. Some deceive themselves and are for ever putting things off. But parents are the only people who can or will afford the opportunity to experiment in this. To allow delayed choice without letting this dwindle to spineless vacillation calls for some nice judgement—a useful guide is the quality and strenuousness of the teenager's work and thinking at the time. Giving time may be a gamble, but it can be a wise one. There is, indeed, no risk at all if the decision is based on a real awareness of adolescent feelings, and on a respect for one's child as a person in his own right—a respect which is normally returned.

There is then no need for gratitude to fester into guilt, or for our pleasure as parents to be soured by the suspicion that we are simply projecting our own thwarted wishes on to our child's adulthood. This is adequately expressed, I think, in the folk joke in which proud momma speaks to her inadequate son: "You can be whatever you like, sonny, as long as it's a doctor or a lawyer."

Notes

1. Here, also, the pendulum has swung since the technological revolution and the "global economy", the loss of expectations of job security, etc.
2. These days a much higher proportion of young people go on to some sort of further/higher education and this has brought its own set of problems; e.g., qualifications that appear to have become less meaningful . . .
3. In many parts of Britain there is a parting of the ways even among those staying to do their A-levels or NVQs; children may change schools at this point, or go to different sixth-form colleges from their secondary-school friends.

Leisure interests and activities

After the party

Parties, picnics, holidays, expeditions, dates—all these social events that bring together boys and girls are eagerly anticipated and prepared for in adolescence. The preparation, the looking forward, can interfere grievously with work and humdrum ordinary activities in the days between; and the days afterwards can be frittered away in despondency, mourning for moments of enjoyment just past, the anticipation of a phone call to follow these up, or simply a flat feeling of disappointment at expectations that went largely unrealized.

A sixteen-year-old girl, talking of her reactions at leaving a party after she had been enjoying herself very much, said that she suddenly found herself so depressed that she had an irresistible urge to pick a quarrel with her parents or her younger brother the moment she got up next morning. She realized it was totally irrational, and that the feeling was a familiar one from long ago. She then remembered how, when she was quite a small child being brought home from a party or from some family outing where she had enjoyed herself, she would throw a tantrum, kick, and scream. She could not bear the good time not to go on for ever.

The teenager has something of the small child's intolerance of frustration. Whatever he wants, he wants now, and wants it always. This applies to many things—to the whole field of sexuality, for instance. The small child who has not managed to come to terms with his desire for instant gratification, or who has not been given parental help and firmness towards accepting some limit to his demands, has more difficulty in struggling with the problem in adolescence. Sometimes he is not really prepared to try to struggle with it at all, but prefers to devote his energies to finding instant and easy solutions. Most teenagers probably do both to varying degrees.

"Will you come and join the dance?"

To boys, who are seldom as confident of themselves or as socially mature as girls, the dance, the disco, the social gathering are not always totally enjoyable. Witness many a school dance, with the boys cowering in glum silence or glum male conversation round the edge of the floor, unable to pluck up the courage to dance, while the girls are left to dance together. For the adolescent youth able to exercise the social graces easily there may be a mixture of envy and professed contempt from other boys, especially the younger adolescents, who still feel gawky and maladroit. It is probably wise not to insist too earnestly that your teenager should partake zestfully in all these social occasions—he may be frightened off altogether, or at least for longer than is necessary.

The adolescent boy finds it hard to be conspicuously separated out from his self-consciously "masculine" mates, especially if he has been confined to a single-sex school, or if it is common in the social life of his parents and their circle for them to assume male superiority. Equally, however, parents may wish to take opportunities when these present themselves to really encourage adolescent participation, and even a simple practical step such as suggesting dance lessons can relieve a great deal of the anxiety for him (many types of dancing are now taught outside, and occasionally inside, school). He is sure to regret his social gaucherie if it is allowed to persist too long.

It is only too easy to laugh at the shy boy, even when as parents we half-realize that he may feel our friendly mockery more intensely than we would wish. It is difficult for all teenagers, but possibly especially so for boys, to develop that subtle and rather heady mixture of social flirtation and sexual seriousness that dancing affords. This was possibly why the set formalities of the dance floor were in previous generations so insisted upon: they offered an introduction and at the same time protection against emotional involvement. Something equivalent to this may be seen in the modern habits of what seem to be far more emotional and unrestrained dance steps, yet in which the "partners"—when there are partners—dance apart and without contact. So, gradually, and with some reasonable chance of success if parents do not impatiently insist, the ease of social mixing and the serious importance of the search for a lifelong partner emerge from awkward adolescence.

As the young person grows in adolescence the social gatherings become a means of meeting someone special, a boy- or girl-friend to fill the need that is increasingly felt for a close relationship with one of the opposite sex. Some go to the club or disco largely in order to be a social success—to collect scalps, to find evidence of their own desirability, of being more popular than their friends or enemies. But these motives exist alongside the need for a close companion who will understand without needing to be told, who will be both loving and lovable, desired and desirable, and a protection from loneliness. The search for this ideal companion is discussed a little more in Chapter Six.

It is all the simpler, of course, to help this happy development if boys and girls have had throughout childhood natural opportunities of mixing socially—at home in a group of acquaintances, friends, brothers and sisters; at a co-educational school or at least in a school where boys and girls from neighbouring schools meet frequently for plays, music, debates, and in formal and informal societies. Such a natural and frequent interchange helps to do away with the anxious pressure of sexual isolation with its aggressive, belittling failures of relationships.

Recreations and their meanings

The teenager's recreations have an important personal significance.

The bicycle, the motorbike, or the racing canoe are not merely technical objects to the lad who polishes, cleans, tunes, and exults in them: they are not even simply objects to express a masculine boast of power. They are just as importantly love-objects, towards which the youth has what is for all psychological purposes an erotic affinity. "She's a beauty", he will say of his boat or his bike, stroking its gleaming paint and chrome. Such a machine has the same animate significance that a horse has for the horse-mad boy or girl. The teenage boy dreams of and recalls his achievements on it, "doing the ton" or striving against the current, achieving moments when he was, as it were, one with it and it responded to his every desire. So he can show off in public, and impress his enemies and his cronies; and in private he can enjoy an idealizing relationship that does not have the dangers of the mocking, assessing, and demanding glances of a real girl.

This period and type of recreation has its very real physical dangers, which are part of the attraction—the young man proves to himself that he is not a coward. Since we do not have initiation ceremonies to bring the young into adulthood by some trial of courage or endurance, the young contrive them for themselves.

Adolescent driving and road safety

In view of the increasing threat to life and limb on the roads, it is probably worth having a moment's thought about the teenager and the family car, or whatever vehicle he aspires to drive as soon as he is eligible for a licence. It is not accident that insurance rates are higher for those under twenty-one; and we know that the motorbikes beloved of so many young men are more lethal to them than any other vehicle.

For so many boys a fast vehicle driven furiously becomes a symbol of potency, and is so regarded by their girl-friends. The more skilfully it is driven, of course, the less dangerous this particular expression of potency becomes. It is what motivates the love of speed that may cause the danger: it may, for example, be motivated by aggressive competition with neighbours on the road, or with some unseen internalized picture of a father who must be outstripped and outshone. Girls also have this sense of rivalry, but it is usually expressed in different ways.

It is a worrying thought, however, that at a time when a young boy or girl most wants to learn to drive, and has the necessary keenness of eye and quickness of response, inner uncertainty makes them at this very time particularly susceptible to dangerous aberrations. So what does one do about it? We can hardly make them wait until an age of staidness. We can only see that they are properly instructed and hope that whatever other teaching they have had about courtesy and consideration for others, and whatever opportunity they have had to identify with us as parents concerned for their life as for that of others, will carry over and become part of their driving performance.

In some things parents have, if necessary, to make firm decisions. For example, adolescents are much given to feelings of omnipotence (as is the adolescent still evident in some adults). The accident cannot happen to *them*. If, despite that, it does happen, then the other driver was to blame. So they will sometimes think it is a joke or a dare (even while denying any risk) to drive without a licence or insurance. This, of course, is not only illegal but in our crowded society is immoral too, for an accident may well affect the innocent bystander.

Recreation as an escape

The teenager's attitude to his motorbike often lasts at least to middle age, and we find the same adolescent self-assertion and anger then, but rendered if anything still more dangerous because of weakened physical judgement. But then there is also a quieter component in our recreations and pursuits.

In part, this feeling for his bike arises from the use the teenager makes of a hobby as a way of escape from areas in which he feels thwarted, threatened, unsuccessful. Chess-playing is an example. Chess is a game full of violence and aggression: what is more, this mental violence is sustained often over hours of play. Yet it is a safe violence. No harm is done except to some opponent's pride or one's own; and pride, we know, can seldom be killed. Furthermore, chess offers a pattern for all idealized loves. Its laws have no exceptions, its obedience is perfect, it is entirely controllable and reliable. Symbolically, it is black and white, good and evil, with no ambiguous half-shades. And so it satisfies a sort of fairytale instinct in us.

Most games offer similar satisfactions, as do the various types of collecting—anything that satisfies obsessional rules for the perfect matching and completion of sets.[1] Football is a "perfect" battle, like jousting in days gone by, spoilt only by human lapses into petulance and anger which create real bruises but are still very strictly controlled. Most parents feel, and wisely, more worried if their teenagers can find no such outlets than if they occasionally devote too much time and energy to them.

This too, however, needs to be watched; and a little discreet pressure applied (a reminder of urgent work to be done, for example) if it becomes clear that the hobby is commandeering all serious purpose and so defeating its real value as a safety-valve for dangerous, hidden pressures.

Recreation as re-creation

Recreation is not all escape. It is much more important as a means whereby the teenager can re-create a part of his life. This begins to occur when, as an addition to other life-work instead of as an escape from it or from failure, the teenager uses his recreation in a more creative way.

This may emerge obviously in the arts—in painting and drama, in writing, in scientific invention and experiment, in the crafts of woodworking and dressmaking, and so on. It is also present in those "escape" recreations discussed above, when the game of chess or of football is achieved at a level at which standards of performance are realized, or appreciated, or striven for, which reveal an excellence in itself, the excellence of a creative act. The boy fishing has forgotten the world not simply because he is escaping from it, not because he is living out a petty derivative of an earlier hunting existence, but because he is concentrating on a self-justifying standard and excellence of sensitive technique—in this case, a feeling for some aspect of the natural world and man's relationship to it. The feeling doubtless has its dark side. Through it he expresses savagery and love of plunder, and he will no doubt boast of the size of a fish he catches—this is his public face showing the expected reactions. But privately he may notice the leaf falling into the water, or the shadow in the rock pool, and these recollections may refresh him for all his life, though he does not speak of them.

By these elements in our pursuits we are refreshed. We are not tired and irritable as people tend to be when they have merely run away from a greater difficulty. Recreation becomes re-creation.

Parents who watch their teenager's hobbies and passions may often notice when this truer satisfaction is being obtained. It will usually be accompanied by a happiness that does not need to reject other responsibilities, and by satisfaction and success in other spheres. Thus, adolescent recreations are in themselves usually neither good nor bad. They act to the discerning parent as a useful barometer showing when all is clear, or when the weather is too oppressive for the teenager to venture out into the "real" world without some sympathetic help; or when real storms are brewing.

Note

1. Including computer-games these days, which do themselves often come in sets and series.

CHAPTER FOUR

Family relationships

On being parents of teenagers

How does it feel to be the parents of teenagers? Teenage sons and daughters can make us as parents feel middle-aged or even old. It can hurt if we have not been sufficiently aware of the value of time to note the passing of the years and the way we have been spending them. A teenager makes us aware of our own buried adolescence—and how else should we be able to be in touch with him, to feel how he feels? He puts pressure on us then to contrast our adolescent dreams of possibilities in life and in love with our present state.

This pressure to do some stocktaking can be painful if we have been avoiding it. For mothers who have given up work to bring up their families, or who may have married so soon that they have never had any experience worth mentioning of working outside the home, the teenager who is becoming independent can bring the warning of redundancy. This may come with the first child who reaches that stage, or it may be put off till the last one gets there. In some fairly large families, when the last child becomes adolescent and is on the verge of leaving home, some of the elder children may already be married with children of their own, and the mother may continue her mothering function as a grandmother, and so manage to put off the day of questioning.

This is how an intelligent but depressed woman of barely forty talked of her situation when her second and last child was about to leave home:

I married at nineteen and had my first child before I was twenty. We had very little money, and the first years we were so busy with the babies, trying to make ends meet and to put by a little to get somewhere decent to live. As the children grew older I used to wonder with a chill what I would do when they were grown-up. I was never one for gossiping a great deal with the neighbours, but when the children were around there was plenty to do: cooking, and mending, and entertaining their friends. My husband and I get along all right, but somehow it doesn't seem enough to do just looking after him now. I hardly had time to do much before I was married—just a little office work, that anyway didn't interest me greatly. Somehow it was just a means then of filling in time until I did get married.

I did have spells of feeling a bit low and wondering what I was doing with my life, even in the busy years when there were a lot of children about the house, but I would say to myself then, "You're a mother, you've got children to look after, what more do you want?" and then I'd work myself out of the blues. I didn't want my son or daughter to feel held back in any way by me, I didn't want them to feel they had to stay at home or near home to keep me company, and I think I've succeeded in that.

I remember how panicky I was in my teens in case I never got away to be married. I was the youngest in a large family, and my parents were much older when I was growing up than I was when my children were. The way I was brought up it was taken for granted that the youngest girl would probably stay at home with her parents until she married, and some girls, of course, never did marry. So I think that I probably got married in haste to get away and have a home of my own.

I don't regret it, but here I am with my husband, who has his job and his friends, and I don't think we really know how to talk to each other. The children are the great thing we've had in common all these years—the children and their friends. They were my job:

my husband still has his job, but has always assumed it was too technical to interest me greatly. Anyway, I do want a job and an interest of my own, but I don't know how to set about it.

This mother probably speaks for many, some of whom may be much less aware than she is of the burden that it can be to teenagers to feel that their parents, and especially their mother, have come to depend upon them for a reason for existence. This is a burden that the teenager himself is only too prone to feel for reasons of his own, which we shall consider a little later, but which becomes doubly heavy if in fact he is being asked either explicitly or implicitly to carry the responsibility for fulfilling unrealized ambitions, unfulfilled possibilities of happiness for his parents.

To wish to live on through one's own children, and maybe to see them accomplish more than we have managed, that is surely one of the legitimate pleasures and desires of parents, but a desire that, if too tenaciously held, can be sapping to the vitality both of our children and of ourselves. Indeed, they cannot do for us what we have not managed to do, and if we are going to be truly able to appreciate their success and allow them to have it without appropriating it for ourselves or feeling unduly envious of them we have to come to terms with our own failures or disappointments first. For most of us have these.

Disappointment with one's children

Among the disappointments, not the least is that we may be forced to recognize in our children traits that we really dislike and disapprove of. We are bound to ask ourselves how much we are to blame for these, and we may indeed recognize our own hand in bringing them out in our children's character. We may feel also that there are unpleasant qualities in a particular child that are peculiar to himself, and so have to struggle to be able to contain our dislike of these while trying to accept and appreciate as best we can his total personality.

For much of the suppressed dislike that some parents and children entertain for each other from adolescence onwards springs not only from a recognition of unpalatable qualities in each other but also from the bitterness evoked by unfulfilled expectations, a kind of disappointed love: "To think that a child of mine could turn out to be like this . . .", etc.

A few words will be said presently about the teenager's disillusionment with his parents.

Parents can help each other to adjust to their family's growing-up

The quality of our marriage in middle-age is not only viewed critically but tested by our adolescent children. They consider whether ours is the kind of marital relationship that they could conceivably wish to develop in later years, and their critical appraisal, whether overt or implicit, stimulates us to have a look at ourselves if we can bear to do so.

As marriage becomes a nearer possibility for them and they talk about it to their friends, they look more closely at the marriages of their friends' parents as well as of their own. When their assessment is made, they tend to become much more preoccupied with their own dreams of marriage, and of how their parents will seem to the boy- or girl-friends whom they bring home.

As parents, we can find it wounding when we have to take second place when children to whom we have been very close become adults. Father is traditionally jealous of the young men whom his adolescent daughter favours, and thinks none of them is good enough for her. Then there is mother, who clings to her son and warns him of the guileful scheming girls who are out to catch him.

These stereotypes may make us stir uneasily. If we do not recognize them we may be too near to them to do so, and in that case our own marriage is in a sad state. For teenagers threaten to bring more strongly into focus the dissatisfactions of the marriage that has been child-centred to the exclusion of a living and mutually rewarding relationship between husband and wife—a marriage where each has been using the children to obtain satisfactions that should more properly come from the bond between each other. If there is health in the marriage, however, the growing up of the children gives parents an impetus and an opportunity to turn to each other and to develop other interests.

A teenage girl's view of her parents' marriage

Virginia, the younger of two sisters, is chatting to her mother during one of her periodic bursts of confidence. She is comparing her views with those of a close friend of the same age who belongs to a French provincial family:

> Christine and I had an argument about how you should bring up your children. She said that falling in love is one thing, but when you are married and have children they are the really serious thing, and you work and make sacrifices to educate them and bring them up as well as you can. She said that she knows the children are much more important to her father than her mother is, and that her mother is quite agreeable that this should be so. Her father is strict with them all. They expect it, and don't bear him a grudge when he comes down all heavy-handed if they have been misbehaving themselves. They can usually rely on their mother to soften him up a little . . .

> I shouldn't mind him being *strict* really if he were my father. I think you need that sometimes, even at my age, if you aren't going to be absolutely useless in any civilised society. Some of my friends make me feel quite ashamed sometimes, the way they carry on at school and about their parents. I don't think it's right that children should be more important to their parents than the parents are to each other. I realize that now that I'm beginning to think of when I shall get married myself.

> I know my future husband is going to be much more important to me than you or daddy—it's bound to be so—not just because we'll be in love and all that, but he'll be the same generation. That means sharing experiences in a way you can never do with your parents, finding things out together without feeling that one of you has the advantage of knowing better through having lived a lot longer.

> I do think you and daddy are more important to each other even than we children are to you. I used to think about that when I was younger and feel sulky about it, sensing that you talked about things that I couldn't share. I didn't ever really feel you didn't love me or take a lot of trouble to make me happy. But I was jealous: you know I used to say that I was born jealous!

> But now I'm glad that I *had* something to be jealous about. I don't quite know yet the sort of person I shall want to marry, but I do know

the kind of relationship I shall want to have with him, and I think
that I'll feel quite free to set about looking for it in my own way.

How attitudes to parents change

To quote Mark Twain, "When I was fourteen my father was so
stupid I could hardly stand to have him around. At twenty-one I
was astonished at how much he had learned in the past seven
years!" This expresses very nicely the change that many teenagers
undergo in their attitudes to their parents, when they feel sure
enough of themselves and their own grown-upness, and of their
capacity to use their own intelligence, to give their parents their
due. When we feel that we have something to give, that we are
capable of some achievement, we can afford to be more generous
and to see in others the virtues that they have.

So, if our teenagers are going through an estranged over-critical
phase and we feel we cannot do much about it, that our well-meaning overtures are met with scowls and sighs of exasperation, it may
be worth while saying to ourselves that this can be a passing phase,
and perhaps like Mark Twain they may suddenly discover that we
have been developing! . . . if, indeed, we have been. For it is not
quite so easy to slide from being the parent of a child to having to
recognize in him a teenager who is rapidly becoming an adult. One
does not manage this without a great deal of thought on a number
of occasions.

Recovery from disillusionment

The young teenager can go through a stage of disillusionment and
exasperation with parents discovered to be far from infallible, and
who may be less important in the world than he, in his childhood
idealization and ignorance, had supposed them to be. Parents may,
indeed, have invited by implicit encouragement his initial over-
estimation. On the other hand, children like to feel that their parents
are important, not only because they *are* important and necessary
for their nurture, but also to increase their sense of status with their
companions. So, when they find the feet of clay and realize that as

young people they are going to have to work to earn their own status and their living, they can swing to the other extreme in their disappointment. Then they invest parents not only with the short-comings that we as human beings surely do possess, but tend to project into them the failures of understanding and limitations by which they are themselves assailed. When father is stupid his son feels superior by comparison. There may come a time when a better grip and organization of the son's capacities allows him to look at his own stupidities and to be less alienated from the father whom he has made his scapegoat and driven into the wilderness.

From parental discipline to self-discipline

At eighteen the adolescent comes of age legally and is an adult who can be held responsible for his own actions.[1] But even before this it can be very difficult to discipline and control an unwilling adolescent who, in extreme situations, can simply clear out of the house and fend for himself.

In practice, the clash of opposing wills and values between parents and teenagers is usually very much a logical development of their early childhood relationships. Adolescence tests the parents' flexibility and sensitivity to the changing needs of each young person, and their capacity to perceive and adapt to growth. In earlier adolescence there is often a paramount need for fairly firm control and some parental supervision over late hours, parties, and so on. But to be accepted without continuing resentment, this supervision has to come from parents who have managed to spin over the years a strong thread of basic trust that will withstand the adolescent strains.

How firm should one be—how firm can one be? The degree varies with each young person and at every stage and age.

Here is an example of undesirable friendships that illustrates the difficulty of this question.

Rosalind: undesirable friendships

Rosalind was fifteen and a half years old, the youngest of four children in a professional family where the three older children had completed very successful careers at school. She was an after-thought, born five years after the previous child. During her first year of life her mother was in hospital for two or three brief spells, for a condition suspected to be serious, but which cleared up eventually.

Rosalind was a delicate, pretty baby, tenderly cared for and spoiled by all the rest of the family including her mother, who was anxious lest her little daughter should grow up insecure as a result of these early separations. She grew up as the family mascot, included in everything, allowed to stay up at night to join in the parties of the older children and was much more in the company of grown-ups and of older children than of her contemporaries. Although she grew out of her delicacy in babyhood, she continued to make the most of any little illness, and was prone to take to her bed when work at school was difficult. Although quite a bright girl, she never did well at school and appeared to have decided that her brothers and sisters were the clever ones of the family. She was content to admire them and to participate vicariously in their success without apparently wishing to compete or emulate.

Just before Rosalind's fifteenth birthday her sister Phyllis passed her university entrance exam and at the same time became involved for the first time with a steady boyfriend. Rosalind reacted to this with a series of minor ailments and unaccountable bursts of tears. She became moody and secretive, and shut herself in her room for long spells.

She then began to be intimate for the first time with a couple of girls in her form who were contemptuous of school and of adults in general, just waiting for the day when they could leave to live a gay untrammelled life. Through them she met and began to mix with a group of slightly older boys who had all left school, but who were neither in nor showing any signs of moving towards steady jobs or a responsible style of life. She and her friends became especially entangled with three boys of eighteen, one of them a runaway from his grammar school and with a background much like their own. The other two were poorly educated, rather dirty, but very superior young men, contemptuous of all who take a humdrum job or who try to get on in life. It was not clear how these three did manage to survive—there were suspicions that one of them at least was a drug pusher.

Rosalind gave up any pretence of working for the public GCSE[2] exams that she should have been taking in a year's time. She became estranged from all the members of her family, especially from the sister in whom she used to confide. Her parents were extremely perplexed about how to handle the situation and how to get close to her. They allowed the little group of boys and girls to meet at their house and tried not to seem disapproving. They approached the parents of the other girls to try to work out some concerted action. One of these other couples had apparently taken a strict prohibitive line with their particular daughter, only to find that she was deceiving them and meeting the boys behind their backs. The other couple showed very little concern and took the line that you cannot stop this kind of thing and that the girls would grow out of it eventually.

In fact, they took much longer to grow out of it than was anticipated. Rosalind's parents tried to reason with her, to point out that she was ruining her chances by neglecting her work for friendships that could not lead anywhere. When remonstrated with, she became tearful and prickly, and accused her parents of not allowing her to grow up, of being middle-class and contemptuous of people who were less well off than themselves. Her parents were hurt by this change in attitude towards them. They had never been accustomed to having to exert any firm discipline with her or with any of their other children, but began to feel that she did need some firm direction to save her from herself at this point, as they realized that she was extremely unhappy.

One could look at Rosalind's involvement with this doubtful little group of boys and girls as a desperate attempt to break away from too great a dependence upon her family, in order to find a way of life and friends of her own. This is what she maintained she was doing; she felt outraged at their criticisms of her friends. It would seem that her sister's academic success and serious romantic relationship triggered off in her the panic that teenagers so readily feel about being left behind in the race and about being able to have a life of their own.

This panic was likely to have been increased in her by the fact that she had continued to trade upon her position as the youngest and much protected baby of the family, to let herself be carried by the indulgence and affection of the others, to avoid facing her own limitations. Frustration, jealousy, and envy are always inevitable to some extent when you are trying to do something yourself and comparing yourself with others. Having lived so much through her sister, she had managed to avoid any close acquaintance with these emotions. The sister's impending departure and total absorption in the boyfriend must then have been a considerable shock to her.

The need and the attempt to find a group of one's own friends, both boys and girls, with whom to argue and to exchange ideas and to identify is, of course, a normal part of adolescence. When the teenager is on basically good terms with her parents, when she respects and values their way of life, she is likely to find for herself a role and social circle that, however it may appear to differ from that of her family, is unlikely to be totally alien to their values. In choosing such an antipathetic circle of friends, Rosalind expressed her resentment and repudiation of her family.

This may be a kind of revenge for her parasitic dependence upon them throughout her childhood. She managed to bring about in her association with the semi-vagrant boys a situation where *she*—despite her voiced contempt for the parents' middle-class values—was in the superior social and monetary position, where she was the giver. Thus, she may have been trying to compensate for the hurt vanity she felt when comparing her achievements with those of her sister, a sister whom she could no longer consider to be her own special property. Also, by idealizing the special quality of these boys who had no thought for the morrow and who were kept by society, she made an alliance to justify her own lazy parasitic way of living off her charm.

This situation is one in which for Rosalind's protection her parents need to exert some firmness in at least restricting and limiting her contacts not only with the boys concerned but also with her two girlfriends. They have to be prepared for rows and resentment, but if they can tolerate the expression of these without feeling too hurt and reproachful it could be of some help to Rosalind to have her quarrels and her fight with them out in the open, to realize that it is possible for her to be nasty, to be disapproved of, but yet accepted in spite of that. If they can listen to her complaints, however unfair they seem to be, they may recognize that at times she will be trying to convince herself, as well as them, that she is being ill-treated in order to avoid feeling badly about herself.

For her own self-respect she needs to be helped towards some course of study that will lead to earning her own living. Many boys and girls of her age, and later still, have little idea of what they want to do with their lives. They require both encouragement and toleration while they make up and change their minds, their training courses, or their jobs. It is particularly important that Rosalind should be given some hope that she will eventually be able to manage something worthwhile on her own—in time and with effort. Should none of the members of her family succeed in gaining her confidence sufficiently, it would be worth considering whether she might speak more freely to any of the family friends who are less intimately involved in her conflicts. As has been suggested in Chapter One, there may be a teacher with whom she could talk more easily about the work situation and who might be able to suggest special coaching. In the town in which Rosalind lives there is no possibility of obtaining psychotherapeutic treatment or consultations for teenagers—even if she were willing to consider undertaking this.

One has to consider, of course, that it may not be possible to help Rosalind to see herself and her friends in a different light, to bring her back to the fold in spirit as it were. In a year or two's time she could leave home and earn her own living and choose her own friends. Pressure that parents can bring to bear becomes less effective the older the teenager becomes. In such a case we may have to endure the pain of seeing our young son or daughter making some grievous mistakes, and rely on the hope that they do carry within them some basic values and good experience from their years of family life that may eventually enable them to learn from their mistakes. The very last thing we should do, if we can avoid it, is to cut them off in disgrace, thereby making it impossible for them to move closer to us at a later time when they might be more ready to do so.

Changing relationships between brothers and sisters

Patterns of interaction between brothers and sisters can alter greatly as they near adolescence. The difference between the first adolescent in the family and those who are still children may for a time seem to be much greater. Then, as the others also enter this stage, if rivalries are not intensified, or differences and dislikes sharpened, a kind of camaraderie sometimes develops between adolescent brothers and sisters that helps them in stormy passages with parents.

This happened in the following instance.

Joanne and Lisa—teenage sisters

Joanne, aged fifteen, had recently grown much closer to her eighteen-year-old sister Lisa. For years she had been struggling valiantly to emulate and surpass her, not usually with a great deal of success because of the three years' difference between them, and because Joanne had in the past always tried to outdo Lisa at her own game. Then over a period of six months or so, she seemed at last to begin to feel that she had her own talents and interests. She started to develop an identity and style of her own. She had always been an impulsive, greedy, self-willed child, frequently in trouble, but quick to repent, and full of promises of reform. In adolescence she showed the same traits, but became more conscious of them and troubled by her conscience for longer periods at a time.

She often went to her elder sister's room for late-night chats before going to bed. One night when she and her father were on easy confidential terms, he commented on the recent friendship between the sisters, and asked what they found to talk about these days—was it mainly boyfriends? "Sometimes," said Joanne, "but much more than that. When I've been up to something I know you wouldn't like, and I feel bad about it, I don't dare tell you, but I go and tell Lisa." "Oh," said her father, "and what does Lisa say to you?" "Well," said Joanne, "you'd never guess—she looks as if butter wouldn't melt in her mouth, and she never gets into trouble, but she's got a mind or her own and she thinks for herself. Just like Satan she is! She says, 'Don't mind about what mummy and daddy will think—you want to ask yourself what *you* think, and do what *you* think is the right thing for you.' She doesn't know how wobbly my mind can go, and how it changes when I get with different people. But all the same I feel better when I talk to her—she's got some sensible opinions, and she lets me know them without making me feel guilty like you and mummy do. You can't help lecturing me when I've done something silly—at least, I always feel you're going to—it comes to the same thing . . . I mean you can't really help it—you're my mother and father and she's my contemporary."

Just as the parents—contemporaries and partners—through talking together can remember, compare, and contrast their own adolescence, and so discover the similarities and the differences they find they have in common with their children's generation, so can the adolescent children find comfort through exchanging views about their parents. Thus, they may find some common ground for understanding as well as, perhaps, for disagreement.

Note

1. When this book was first written the age was twenty-one, though it was pointed out that "the date for this may be advanced by three years in the near future".
2. O-levels when the book was written (changed throughout).

CHAPTER FIVE

The teenager and society

Teenage rebellion

For many teenagers the upsurge of life and the changes that they feel within themselves are too exciting and explosive to be contained within themselves or to be worked out in the immediate circle of family and friends. They need the wider field of society to express themselves, and they try to bring about changes there. Rebellion against authority at home is taken, for example, into the field of political activity. Of course, there are those who come down so hard on any tendency within themselves to rebel, or who may be so afraid of doing without the protection of authority, that they ally themselves strongly with the reactionary and over-conservative. The process of working through to some real appreciation of what is worthwhile conserving from the past, from the parents' world, and deciding what should be rejected and what is within the realm of possible modification, takes a while—indeed the rest of one's life if one goes on living mentally.

It is difficult for parents, and for the older generation in general, to take adolescent portentousness and arrogance about social ills quite seriously. It may remind us of our own adolescent aspirations,

and of our failure to realize them, if we have simply abandoned them rather than modified them in the light of increasing
experience.

Politics in the world

Margaret, aged sixteen and a half, the eldest child in her family,
flounced upstairs to her bedroom after yet another row with her
father. It started as usual with an argument about politics, and
became increasingly acrimonious, with Margaret accusing her
father of being out of touch with the modern world, and her father
countering by telling her "not to teach her grandmother to suck
eggs"-he had been through all these enthusiasms when he was her
age, but he had learned a little more about the world since then and
had a better idea of what was possible.

Later in the evening he excused himself somewhat shame-
facedly to his wife, but said he could not stand his eldest daughter's know-all airs and sanctimony. The storm over, he tried to
broach the subject with Margaret and asked why they could never
have rational discussions.

"You never take me seriously, you can't get used to the idea that
I'm not a child like the others any more. My teachers listen to me at
school. I'm supposed to be one of the best debaters in the class, my
friends respect me, but either you think that I'm rather quaint, or
when I show you I do mean what I say, you think I'm just being
rude . . . you don't seem to understand that we really think about
these things, and care about them. We may be wrong, but you don't
seem to think of the possibility that we might just be right. Living
longer needn't mean that you get any wiser. Anyway, even if you
are wiser, if you are right you ought to know that you can't force
me to think the same as you do, that I need time to learn to think
for myself and try out my ideas."

This is the kind of clash that often arises between parents and
young people who feel sore that they are treated with less respect
at home than they are in the outside world. They can feel despair-
ing of ever becoming grown-up individuals at home, of shaking off
their childish past. So they become over-emphatic in their effort to
assert themselves.

And, of course, there is often a great deal of truth in their complaints. It is not always so easy for parents to adapt to the stage which the teenager has reached, especially as for a while it tends to be a pretty erratic one: the responsible thoughtful young adult of one day can suddenly be the heedless infant of the next. Until he comes downstairs in the morning sometimes you have no idea from which side of the bed he has crawled out!

Just when we are getting used to the idea of being able to regard our teenager more as an equal than as a child, he may behave in such an irresponsible way that we feel let down, exasperated, and all the more so for knowing that he "could do better". It is maybe worth considering that sometimes he may feel let down by himself, and if so, it is not necessary to rub salt into the wound.

When he harbours suspicions that he is unreliable or at times pretentious, he can be very touchy at being treated lightly. Just because he feels passionately about tolerance, justice, freedom, loving his neighbour, and so on, he hates to be reminded that these are virtues that so often elude him in practice in his own closer relationships.

Society and the internal wars

Teenage students traditionally tend to be world reformers: acutely aware of the corruption and greed in governments, their ruthlessness for power, and lack of concern for the underprivileged. For the would-be reformers it is not always so easy to see among the established elders those who are also aware of these things, or easy to be charitable about the imperfections and the inherent difficulties in mankind that make it such an uphill job to struggle against them. Until we feel more at home with our own inconsistencies, it may be easier to find an enemy in the outside world to express the contradictions of our own nature and to argue against them there.

"I always seem to be in opposition", said one sixteen-year-old boy rather ruefully. "At school I'm standing up for my parents and some of the teachers and their views, and at home I'm always arguing for my own generation."

A clear-cut division between the rights and wrongs in the causes one supports and in those one fights against is a way of gaining some relief from those differences within oneself. The cause that is most vehemently attacked is often one which threatens to remind us of those areas within the self which are most difficult to accept. There is no war more bitter than a civil war, because the enemy is so close and carries so many reminders of one's own nature.

Idealization of other societies

In an attempt to get relief from the contradictions within the self it is sometimes not enough for the teenager to fight them out in the context of his own home and the society in which he has grown up. The need to "get away from it all", to "drop out of the rat race", can lead to a longing for far-away places, and for remote ways of solving one's personal and social problems by adopting, though still a stranger, the modes of other societies. In attempting this we may forget or ignore that we take ourselves and our problems with us. The story of Julia affords an illustration of this.

Julia: flight to another country

Julia's parents were in relatively easy circumstances, and in late adolescence she was getting on with her studies at college, though not finding these any too simple. She was aware of her parents' monetary help, but none the less felt it also rather irksome, and had decided to seek out some sort of paid employment during the first long vacation so that she could live off her own resources in digs. Her parents did not disapprove of this, and indeed rather welcomed this initiative on her part.

Predictably, perhaps, the one excursion into independence led to another, and Julia before long was living with a fellow student, a man of about thirty-five who, as it happened, though studying one of the "hard" sciences, had developed a strong interest in mystical forms of religion, especially those with an oriental flavour. He decided he would spend his long vacation travelling along the fairly well-worn path to a centre of meditation in Asia; and Julia, who according to her parents had never previously expressed any interest in such meditation, decided or was persuaded to go with him.

The parents' reactions were, perhaps understandably, panic-stricken. They saw their daughter (and we are not here discussing the truth or otherwise of their perceptions) not only "living in sin"—this they had come to accept—but living in poverty and even in danger, in a far country with no job arranged, studying or pretending to study some incomprehensible creed, and probably indulging in all sorts of self-induced or drug-induced hypnosis in the name of transcendental experience.

They acted, as it seemed to them, in a generous and reasonable way. They invited the young man to come to discuss the plan with them, and asked Julia to arrange a meeting. They even offered that, if properly in the picture, they would consider giving some financial help to the venture. But the young man refused to meet them; when the father called at the digs he denied (through the door, but without a meeting) that Julia was in the house at all. And Julia seems to have colluded with him in this rejection of all overtures.

And there, for the moment, the situation remains. Should the father do as he now threatens, and make his daughter a ward of court, thus invoking the law to impose a solution on the problem? If he does this it is not likely to be effective, since although Julia is technically just young enough to come within the purview of the law, she would not be so for long. Her father's "protection" would be seen as tyranny, there would not be time for the scar to heal, her young man's probable description of parental attitudes would seem justified, and an early and final break almost guaranteed. Should the parents simply acquiesce in the ill-organized adventure? A passive acceptance of what they evidently feel to be a rash and wrong step is hardly likely to seem right to them—and may in fact cause the daughter herself to feel rejected as not worth caring about. "You made your own bed—now you must lie in it" is only likely (however indignant they may feel) to ratify the break they, in loving responsibility, want to avoid.

The roots of the whole problem almost certainly go far back in this family's history: perhaps Julia was too protected, too little in contact with boys of her own age to be able to judge whether or not her young man is a phoney, pretending to be adolescent when nearly middle-aged. Perhaps she never did quite work through her relationship to her own parents, and still resents their unity: still needs to be the centre of attraction for a man old enough to be her father. Perhaps she has been urged to undertake a course of study that is, in fact, too difficult for her or not sufficiently in line with her interests. Perhaps she never has experienced as she grew up the stimulus of serious and active conversation about such important matters as a philosophy of life and of religion, so that coming across someone really or apparently interested in these things for the first time, she was soon swept off her feet.

No doubt there are faults on both sides for a break of this nature to take place. On the parents' side there is not much that they can do in practice to prevent the event and at the same time to keep the relationship they desire. They have made their anxieties felt, only to find them seen as irrational; they cannot appeal to any concern for their feelings as parents, partly because this appeal to a sort of pity would be repulsive, partly because the daughter wants in some way to wound. If there were some other friend of the family whom the daughter trusted and could use as a confidant—someone such as a loved and respected aunt, let us say—some easing of the situation might be contrived; but there is no one. There are usually sparse counselling services in universities nowadays, but in general neither students nor university staff today are prepared to accept seriously that a tutor is in any way *in loco parentis*. It seems as if the parents are going to have to face the severe test of seeing their daughter take a step that could be irrational and stupid, and still to retain in the long term their cherishing love for her if things go wildly wrong.

What, however, of the teenager's own attitude here? Much the best way of dealing with crises is, of course, to prevent their happening; but this depends on a long-term exchange of views and confidences, and on training in responsibility over a long period. In Julia's case this has not happened or has not succeeded. Her parents cannot talk to the man involved, since he will not meet them. They can presumably still talk to their daughter, however, and ask her to consider her own motivation, just as they are considering their own frankly with her. It happens to be a fact in the case that Julia is herself showing evident signs of great unhappiness in the whole business, as well as of sulky defiance. One might suspect that she would inwardly welcome, if not total and open disapproval, at least the chance to reconsider her own position and so save face by changing her plans of her own volition. Some hurtful things may need to be said on both sides, but if they are said out of concern rather than out of spite, they may possibly be heard in the right spirit.

The main things she might be asked to consider are, one supposes, the sincerity of her own motives for going on the trip. How much is it a real enquiry into meaning and truth? If not much, why is it necessary to give it this cloak? What is so much feared that the young man cannot observe the ordinary courtesies and meet Julia's parents? What is the justification for the furtive and secret element of denial in their relationship? What personal difficulties, anxieties about her own capacity as a woman or as a scholar, are causing her to nurse the illusion that by running far away the corruptions of our society and her own internal dissatisfactions can be remedied or even avoided? These questions, attempted honestly (and most teenagers pride themselves on their frankness and honesty) and put with consideration and not condemnation, may at least help explain, if not justify, subsequent actions. Many of the questions are to be answered by the parents, however, as well as by the girl. The rage of the teenager is often matched only by the complacence of the adult.

Julia's case, and the problem of the drop-out in general, is terribly difficult ground. There is no instant answer to its problems—any more than there are instant solutions to our social malaise or to our search for personal truth. Yet such ready solutions are proposed by the drop-outs themselves; and they are also often proposed by those who stay "in", whether comfortably or uncomfortably.

"Know thyself" is an old and a difficult injunction to obey. It is, nevertheless, an important one to repeat in our age, which, perhaps more than most, is much given, in adolescence or in adulthood, to the paranoid habit of finding faults in everybody but ourselves, and in refusing to face up to the depressive anxiety we may feel when—possibly too late—we do at least consider what we are and the world we are within ourselves.

Searching for a cause

The attempt to get right away from one's home and also from one's society, as Julia intended, in order to find the answer to one's problems, is one of the many ways in which the young person can run away from discovering himself and his identity. Another is the search for a cause to idealize, in which to immerse oneself totally, or a leader whom one can follow wholeheartedly, and who evokes no doubts. Or the "leader" may be the idea of total freedom and equality, which obliterates responsibility and envy. We find mixed motives behind many forms of idealism.

Peace movements or student demonstrations are examples.[1] In these, some teenagers are motivated by genuinely constructive courage and some are there for "kicks", or to satisfy their destructive impulses against authority under an apparently gallant banner. Many, no doubt, have mixed motives, even when the cause is a good one.

This applies to all "causes", even when they do not manifest this battle against authority. The aims of the charitable agencies for relief of the aged, incapacitated, weak, or underprivileged are entirely exemplary and offer an excellent channel for many teenagers still at school to do something constructive about social ills, and to know that they are of some use in the world. One must not underestimate the genuine altruism and generosity contained in the devotion of so many teenagers to causes and people. They are the expression of a need to love and to devote one's life to something greater than oneself—to do away with personal ambition in the attempt to make a better world. To do this with others of one's own generation is a heady attraction.

There is the temptation to write off the older generation, the parents—the mistakes of their world provide ample justification. But blaming our elders can be used to justify the flight from struggling with problems of knowing oneself, and of coming to terms with one's relationship with one's own parents, not only as they are now but as they were experienced and internalized in childhood days. Thus, although the teenager's concern for the underprivileged can be a genuine and generous one, it may also contain a very strong element of unresolved grievances of long ago, still active and unmodified: the grievances of the child who resented being kept down and felt hard done by. In doing his social work he is also redressing the injustice he feels he suffered in his more helpless days. That's fine—we would not know what it is to feel helpless and unhappy unless we had felt that way ourselves. But unless the well-doing is accompanied by some degree of continuing self-questioning and introspection, which leads to acquaintance with our own ingratitude, greed, envy, and so on, we are not likely to develop an approach to these social problems that is informed with humility and humanity. Without these we do not really learn from experience to aim for what is possible, rather than only for the unattainable ideal. Thus, when embittered or discouraged by failure and the ingratitude of his protégés, the teenager is only too likely to settle for the middle-aged cynicism and apathy that will agitate another generation of teenagers in their turn.

Richard: flight to apathy and daydreams

Richard is an example of a teenager proclaiming a concern for the world's ills, but unable to grapple with his own. Aged sixteen, he is the only child of very elderly parents who married and had a child late in life. One might, indeed, say that he has been virtually brought up by grandparents, but ones who were more than usually out of touch with the needs first of a small child and then of a young person. His school career has been uneventful, for he has been intelligent enough for his own needs to get in with a group of boys and girls whom the teachers have generally recognized as being below him in real ability.

He is a rather passive, friendly, well-spoken boy, who has up until now fitted in with the school framework and has never been a nuisance. He has often been kept at home, or has kept himself at home, for nebulous little ailments, but has always had plausible excuses, corroborated by his parents. His teachers were hopeful that, as he neared the time for leaving school, he would get more of a grip upon himself and see the urgency of preparing himself to earn his living.

Quite the contrary, however. During the past year he has become increasingly erratic about the time he turns up at school, about his attendance, his homework, and about taking any active responsibility for doing anything at all. When at school he is perfectly charming and co-operative, takes a very intelligent verbal part in lessons when occasion demands this, but will only spasmodically produce any written work that has to be done on his own. His parents are leading such a valetudinarian life, so withdrawn from contemporary society, that attempts by Richard's headmaster to get them to take a realistic interest in his future are in vain.

Most of the other children of his age in the little town where he lives have some kind of holiday or weekend job, to earn them pocket money but also to prepare them for leaving school to earn their own living. Richard has no such job, either regular or occasional, and has no interest in acquiring one, not because he has much pocket money or because his parents are well off, but because, as he explains, his needs are few. He seems to have no practical personal interest in his future, but is well read in revolutionary political thinking and proposes to devote his life to the causes of revolutionary social change, though without any clear idea of how he is going to set about it.

His headmaster's problem is to decide whether to keep Richard on at school any longer. He likes school and would be quite willing to stay on for another year or so, but without studying for any particular exam, and without any prospect of fitting in better within the framework of his school.[2] The headmaster has to cope with some of the members of his staff who are overworked already and who see a boy such as Richard as subverting the system without deriving any benefit from it. Their view is that he should be asked to leave shortly, as he is pursuing no legitimate course of study. They feel that keeping him on any longer merely panders to his assumption that he can be a parasite upon society while devoting his intelligence to studying the means of overthrowing it. The headmaster has very little hope that if Richard leaves now he will settle down in any job to earn his living, and is certain that he will sponge amiably on his parents as long as they are alive. He has discussed this with Richard, who agrees that this is probably going to be the case. This is clearly no matter of concern to Richard, who quite realizes that the headmaster might not wish to keep him on at school any longer, but bears him no grudge for it.

There is no possibility of obtaining psychotherapy for Richard. It is in any case very doubtful whether this would be of any use, as his is not an instance of a teenager sufficiently in conflict with himself and dissatisfied with his lot to want to work at trying to change it. He would first of all have to be put in touch with some unhappiness or pain within himself to have some incentive for altering himself and his way of behaving. Pain he avoids by opting out of formal responsibility and self-knowledge. He can hide his ambition and destructiveness, and this allows him to be personally amiable and liked, both by his peers and by his schoolteachers. For he has no personal quarrel with them, only with society at large.

Other teenagers not unlike him in revolutionary enthusiasm would be only too anxious to clear out of school and get away from home at the first opportunity. That could, in some, be a sign of greater health, of some ability to stand on their own feet. Richard's willingness to stay at home and at school for longer may simply be a sign of apathy, but on the other hand, there is just a chance that this experience may stand him in good stead later on if there does develop in him more of a drive to make some kind of life for himself.

With such a child one would not be too hopeful of his future development—many a teenager who refuses to try to take any personal responsibility for his life, and who has nourished himself on daydreams of a more cosmic grandeur, ends up spending periods in a psychiatric hospital, which seldom guarantees a cure, though it may sometimes be a refuge from society. Whether we can reduce their number by making it possible for them to be given more and better-informed educational facilities remains to be seen. In Richard's case it is fairly clear that the school has tried to provide something of the support and guidance that his elderly parents do not seem to have been able to give him.

The antisocial teenager

Delinquency and violence practised in isolation, or more often in groups, are the antisocial activities that the socially-minded teenager so often attacks with a vehemence matching that of his enemies. It is a common observation that young people will commit acts in a group that they would never dream of doing by themselves—when the responsibility cannot be so easily shared and thus avoided.

There was a recent television play about a gang of hoodlums [young thugs] who bashed up a man who subsequently became paralysed. The youth who had been mainly responsible for the attack went to see the victim afterwards, came to know him, and was horrified to witness the creeping deterioration that his unthinking blows had produced. He ended up in an agony of repentance, living with and taking care of the paralysed man.

A great deal of adolescent antisocial activity of this kind takes place through failure to imagine the effect it has on other human beings. In any gang there is probably a minority who commit crimes because of an active grudge against the victim, getting sadistic pleasure in hurting and exploiting. But that minority can seduce and make fellow criminals of others who are not cognizant of such impulses within themselves.[3] Perhaps some of these become shocked at what they do and extricate themselves, like the young man in the television play, but, unfortunately, this is by no means always so. Getting away with criminal acts can produce increasing cynicism, which may cover a load of guilt that is too heavy to be acknowledged. So it is important at an early stage to try to protect our teenagers from bad company if we can. In the previous book, some possible ways of doing this were suggested.

Sudden unpremeditated acts of crime—kleptomania, violence, sexual crime—may occur to the astonishment and subsequent distress of the offender himself.[4] These, of course, are not confined to teenagers alone, but continue to occur among those in whom the state of mental disorganization and the pressure of conflicting instinctual impulses—which is common during adolescence—are accentuated and perpetuated. These sudden or compulsive criminal acts come from an antisocial destructive part of the personality, which is not contained and understood, and is not therefore being modified by other reasonable social aspects of the teenager's character. They may occur in young people who are otherwise obsessively and rigidly moral.

The teenagers who are distressed (hidden though the signs of this may be) and in conflict about their antisocial tendencies are the ones who are amenable to psychotherapy and who are in need of it. Their chance of being helped by a good psychotherapist depends largely on the degree of co-operation that can be obtained with the saner and more social part of their personality. With this co-operation, they can be helped towards self-discipline and responsibility.

Note

1. Modern examples might also include animal rights or eco-movements in their extreme forms.
2. It is dubious whether a child would be allowed to remain at an ordinary school these days without being registered for a particular course, although, of course, in practice it is easy enough to formally register and just pretend to study, so it comes to the same thing.
3. These considerations appear relevant to the modern disease of youthful terrorism, and suggest the importance of thinking and understanding not in a "soft" way but from a stance of social responsibility for the failings of our own young people.
4. Take for example the recent example (2005) of the young mother left paralysed by a knife attack, whose attacker subsequently committed suicide on realizing that he must have been the one responsible.

CHAPTER SIX

Sex and love

The basis of sex enjoyment

We have made the point in various ways in many of the earlier books in this series that a child's current relationships and his physical and emotional growth continue to be affected, if not determined, by his earlier experiences. This is especially true of the sexual development of the teenager, of his feelings about himself and his body, of his capacity to anticipate and finally enjoy sexual experience reciprocally with the partner of his choice.

His capacity to enjoy his body and to be able finally to integrate sexual feelings with tenderness is rooted in the early physical and emotional relationship he had as a baby with his mother. This goes for the girl, of course, as well as for the boy. Her very first physical closeness is also with her mother, in whose arms she first begins to feel some fleeting physical identity and sense of what belongs to her body and what it looks like.

As we have already mentioned, a number of things can interfere with the mother's capacity to accept the baby in a physical and emotional way, and there are differing factors in each baby that may inhibit its capacity to utilize and to respond to what he is offered. These half-formulated secret shames about being unattractive, unlovable, and lacking in love weigh very heavily on the teenager. Sometimes they lead him to rush prematurely into sexual experience and promiscuity; sometime they inhibit him from seeking it at all.

Identification with the parents' marriage

The capacity to wait until he is really ready, and the capacity to enjoy sexual experience attended with love, depend very much on the kind of picture the teenager has internalized over the years of his parents' relationship, and on the nature of his identification with them. This will not correspond entirely with the real nature of his parents, although this, of course, must have played an important part in determining his views of them and of their marriage.

As he has grown older he will, as a rule, have come to take consciously a more objective view of his parents. He will want to repudiate or to identify with certain qualities of their characters, and this more conscious process is intensified in adolescence. The healthier his relationship with his parents, the more he will be able to question it, and to question them and their relationship in order to form his own opinions.

But the teenager is not entirely a reasonable being. If he is really having an adolescent experience that includes revival of the past as well as hope for the future, he finds that he has complicated and far from dispassionate feelings that both distort and enrich his relationships. These derive from infantile unresolved jealousies and idealizations about his parents and their relationship. From the qualities of the idealized parents comes the dream of the perfect partner. From the envy and jealousy come fears of hostile parents, the archaic nebulous forces that lurk in the phobias and night terror of the small child.

These are often left behind in the course of getting more experience of managing the external world. They are, as it were, forgotten in the middle years of childhood, which are so concerned with acquiring skills and facts to manage oneself and one's environment. They are revived in the upheaval and yet potentially integrating experience of adolescence. The only way whereby such fear can be modified, rather than avoided, is by a confrontation with, and a greater acceptance of, the terrors and guilts perpetuated by the destructiveness in one's own nature. Some teenagers do struggle to face this, though they will also project it into the larger scene of social violence and destruction, and into their more personal social circle of parents and authority figures.

Some of the young child's most violently destructive feelings are evoked by feeling excluded and frustrated at not sharing in some treat that he feels is going on. He believes that something is being enjoyed that is denied to him. The parental relationship in its very nature has elements that exclude him. If he has an appropriate close and happy relationship with each of his parents, and is included by them both in a framework that is within his compass, he is not so likely to go on bearing a grudge about the experiences from which he has been excluded.

But some children—probably most children to a certain extent—put aside the grudge rather than relinquish it, and wait until they are adolescent to get even as soon as possible. An over-authoritarian upbringing can lead them to nurse and to justify this grudge. A too-permissive upbringing gives them no help in recognizing the priorities and the need to make choices: it fails to teach them that you can spoil some things if you try to grab them too much too quickly.

The child needs not only parents who give, who gratify needs and accept with love, but who can say "stop", and *help* him to stop going on to spoil things for himself. If we have been able to say no firmly enough at the right time to our children, perhaps we will not have to say it so often to them in their adolescence, when it is not so easy to enforce prohibitions.

Premature sexual experience and promiscuity among teenagers is probably, in most cases, motivated much more strongly by unresolved childish greeds and unconscious competition with the parents of childhood than by love or even irresistible sexuality. The promiscuity obviously implies inability to be satisfied and to develop one adequate relationship.

The boy's sexuality

The boy's diffuse sexual feelings of early childhood become increasingly focused in adolescence upon the penis. At puberty sexual feelings can be experienced as a violent and exciting possession by urges outside conscious control, and the penis can be felt to be the instrument of their discharge. The urge to masturbate can sometimes become compulsive, and attended by fantasies exciting at the time but producing flatness and depression afterwards, with fear of damaging oneself, one's penis, and one's mind. Hence, so many "old wives' tales" about blindness and madness have taken strong hold and are still heard today.

In later adolescence sexual relationships with a girl or girls are sought sometimes as a defence against this kind of self-defeating masturbatory experience, and sometimes the girl is just "too easy" sexually, despised as a victim conspiring with an aspect of the boy's sexuality that gets the better of him, as it were. Such a sexuality has no tenderness or appreciation of the object towards which it is directed.

A relationship that is sought mainly in order to discharge sexual frustration is little more than the enactment of masturbation fantasies with another person, and will result in as little real satisfaction. It may be a temporary reassurance, or a triumph, another scalp to add to the collection. If it is seen as a triumph, then the teenager is surely not only competing with and triumphing over his peers, but is acting out deep-seated childish rivalries and sexual grudges against his parents. And this goes for the girl as well as for the boy.

The sexual development of the girl

Like the adolescent boy, the girl is preoccupied with anxieties about her sexual capacities. The boy's anxiety about his potency is paralleled by her fear of being frigid. These matters are so much more openly discussed these days when youth and sexuality are equated, idealized, and flaunted. The fears of frigidity and impotence express and conceal a more deep-seated anxiety about not being fully alive, of being uncreative, of having death within. This derives from a sense of undeveloped, disregarded aspects of the self, and also from the accumulation of relationships with parents who were internalized in anger and in hatred.

The adolescent girl is most conscious of the resentment and struggle against her mother. Sometimes she may still feel the rivalry

as a current and conscious continuation of ancient childish grievances. More often, perhaps, as she grows up, she is aware that it is
"her turn". "Oh mummy," sighed a young girl in exasperation as
her mother lamented the discovery of a grey hair, "I don't see what
you're grumbling about. I mean to say, you've had a jolly good
innings." She was clearly feeling that her mother's intimation of
ageing was an accusation against herself.

This is quite unreasonable, as any rational teenager would readily agree, judging by standards of external reality. But it is understandable if one recognizes that in each teenage girl there is a little
girl who at last sees herself within reach of realizing her childish
dream of marrying—not maybe her actual father any more—but
that Prince Charming whom daddy appeared to be in her eyes long
ago. Thus, she displaces her mother and occupies the enviable
central position that her mother used to have.

Her touchiness and guilty feelings about this are in proportion
to the strength of her continuing unconscious wish to triumph, on
the strength of the unworked-through infantile grudges. She can
quite easily bring to mind a shadowy picture of a displaced mother,
who emerges as a mean and grudging person, but at whose
expense she has profited. Remember that the wicked fairy, who was
at first left out of the invitations to the christening of the Sleeping
Beauty and who then appeared late, predicted that she would be
killed by pricking herself with a bodkin when she was sixteen years
old. This is a mythical expression of the fate that many a young girl
unconsciously fears will snatch away from her the promise of fulfilment just within her grasp in adolescence.

The danger from outside, from fate or ill luck, has to be avoided
and guarded against. But it is sometimes easier to bear than the
depression about damage within.

Worries about appearance

The preoccupation with appearance, the worries about spots and
acne and periods, and any real or fancied disfigurements, seem
natural enough in a young girl who wants to attract a boyfriend, to
be admired and loved, to be sexually attractive. But the worries can
be disproportionate to the blemish. Relatively slight imperfections

can be magnified in the eyes of young girls and boys and taken unconsciously as evidence of something wrong within. As they grow further on in adolescence and gain a little more confidence in themselves, their bodies, and their heightened emotions, these worries tend to be less acute. You learn to live with what's wrong with you![1]

Attitude to babies

For most girls, sex and boyfriends become linked with thoughts of having babies and a home of one's own much sooner than they tend to do with boys. And yet, during recent years, many young men have been getting married at an age when they are hardly more than boys. Many have become less ashamed to take an interest in their children as babies than perhaps their fathers were. Their long hair, gayer clothing, and slogans about "making love, not war" suggest that some of the more traditionally feminine values and apparel are not necessarily felt to cast a slur on their manliness.[2]

But the longing for a home of her own and babies probably plays a much greater part in the psychology of the adolescent girl than in that of the boy. This is at the root of a great many theoretically unplanned and unwanted pregnancies, and can defeat the best attempts at instruction in methods of birth control. It is a longing that can be sharpened by the unconscious rivalry and envy of mother still present in the little girl who is now adolescent. The pregnancy of sisters and friends, for instance—a new envy situation—may also reactivate that first unresolved one. Mingled with this can be the genuine wish to have and to love a baby for its own sake, and upon this rests the successful outcome of an initially unwanted pregnancy.

Abortion

To have an abortion or not is a serious decision for an adolescent girl to take or to be helped to take. She may have become pregnant by some casual affair, or maybe by some boy who she then realizes does not want to marry or live with her, or whom she does not want to live with after all. A baby without a father is a double responsibility, and it may well happen to someone who might in any case be hardly fit even to take a shared responsibility with a partner.

It is then hard for her, but harder for the baby. On the other hand, some girls are capable of gaining maturity by having this responsibility thrust upon them. They are so live to the fact of the baby as a potential human life from the very start that they feel the idea of abortion to be a terrible violation of themselves and of that life. To escape from the guilt and depression following on such an abortion, they may harden their hearts and become more brittle, callous characters.

Whatever the decision in the case of a young girl who has an unplanned pregnancy—whether she chooses to have an abortion, to keep the baby, or to have the baby adopted, she does need support, not condemnation, from her family. She will certainly feel guilty and frightened and ashamed, and will need help to look at the situation in a practical way.

It may be that her relationship with her parents is basically so strained that the best help they can give her is to refrain from trying to discuss too much with her directly. They should then try to put her in touch with some more professional help—the family doctor, a social worker, or someone trained in psychotherapeutic skills. In different areas different services are available, but the most important thing is to choose a professional who has some experience with teenage girls and who will really be able to understand her feelings.

Sometimes it may be that the best person to talk to her initially is her former headmistress, or a teacher who has a counselling role. But that depends entirely on the girl's feelings about it and your knowledge about the teacher. There are those from whom the teenager would need to be protected. This becomes an additional complication if the pregnancy occurs while she is still at school. Nevertheless, school and college authorities do, on the whole, take a much more enlightened and helpful attitude to such matters these days than they did in the past.

The permissive society

While penning this last section we can hear many a dissentient voice protesting that schools and college authorities ought *not* to be so lenient, that society is altogether too permissive about sexual morality—witness the alarming increase in sexually transmitted diseases among adolescents as a result of promiscuity, and the increase in illegitimate or unwanted pregnancies.[3]

But it is no good locking the stable door when the horse has already bolted. If either of these misfortunes has occurred, the first thing is to consider what is the best remedy. In the case of sexual diseases the course is simple: consult a doctor or the appropriate clinic and have it treated promptly. As already suggested, the solution is, however, not so simple when it is not a disease that is contracted but another life that is created.

Society has indeed a great deal to answer for in the shameless exploitation of teenagers for commercial ends: the seductive advertising, sexual titillation on screen and in print. But the danger to the teenager is probably not so much even from undue inflammation of his sexual desires as from the continually implied or stated propaganda that unless he is sexually "with it" he is not really alive—that he is left out, left behind in the race to grab something out of life. To have a boyfriend or girlfriend, and a bank balance—those are the two keys to life!

As parents and educators we, too, are part of that society, and therefore cannot dissociate ourselves entirely from responsibility for what is happening to our teenagers, or from what they are doing Yet it may be equally untrue to assume that we are entirely responsible for their predicaments, any more than we are for their achievements.

Preparation for sex and parenthood

We do owe it to our teenagers to see that they are properly informed on all the factual aspects of sex, pregnancy, birth, and contraception, and about the possible effects and dangers of promiscuity. They need to know our views on these subjects; but as they grow older it will be up to them to decide what line they are going to take—that is, if they are going to grow through adolescence into maturity and not remain (emotionally) retarded children who still cling to accepted but unexamined parental attitudes.

A relationship between parents founded on love and respect for each other is the best model we can offer to our teenage children; it provides a setting in which children can grow and be appreciated, but does not depend on them for its vitality. If we have achieved that, then we can but hope that they will be able to make use of this model as a basis from which to develop their own.

And information about babies and their needs? This may be one aspect of an education that now often includes other aspects of domestic and social science that could receive more attention in the later days at school.[4] In large families the teenagers learn about young children through watching their mothers or looking after their own younger brothers or sisters. The youngest children in the family, in their turn, sometimes learn through dealings with little nieces and nephews. But in these days of generally smaller families, and when families also move around much more, this way of learning can by no means be relied upon.

Matthew: teenage infatuation

Matthew is a boy of nearly eighteen now who is just about to leave school to take up work in his father's business, to their mutual satisfaction. But he had a very stormy period some twelve months ago when he and his father clashed badly and he almost ran away from home.

This clash was an unexpected development, as Matthew, the middle child and eldest boy in a family of five, had always been the good child of the family, diligent and hardworking, although not brilliant. At home he was very attached to his mother, and appeared to be like her in nature as well as in appearance. When he was a little boy he tended to cling to her and to be upset whenever she was away from home. He was rather afraid of his father, who had a more spontaneous relationship with his younger brothers. At school he had uniformly satisfactory reports, although the comment "could take more initiative" appeared more than once.

The only thing that seemed rather out of character in his otherwise rather staid and dutiful performance and demeanour at school was his speed and excellence at all forms of sport and a positively tigerish style of attack on the football field.

Until he was nearly sixteen he held rather aloof from girls and did not seem to know how to talk to them, although, as he was a nice-looking and well-grown boy, some of his sisters' friends showed interest in him from time to time. Then, at a party, he met Jennifer, tall and fair like him in appearance and also like his mother. They fell for each other immediately, and from then on were practically inseparable for the next few months, spending every weekend and every evening together, to the exclusion of any homework or out-of-school activities that did not include the other. His father described him as "tackling this girl with the same ferocity that he went for the ball on the games field".

Matthew's infatuation was at first a family joke, but he became so furious with his parents and brothers and sisters for making fun of him that they desisted. His parents began to get very concerned about the whole affair, especially as he was due to sit his public examinations in a few months' time, and upon the results of those depended his chance of a place in the firm where his father worked.

Neither his mother nor his favourite elder sister had his confidence any longer. His mother became worried that he and his girlfriend were having sexual intercourse, and tried to broach the subject with him without success. His father then decided to take things in hand, give him a lecture about what the consequences would be if he were to get the girl pregnant, underlining the fact that he would not be able to support her and neither would he have his parents' support. Matthew flew into an unwontedly violent temper and stayed out of the house for the night, which terrified both his parents, as it was intended to do.

They got in touch with the girl's parents to try to talk over the matter together. They found that the other parents were much less concerned than they were, apparently took a much more lax and permissive line with their daughter, assuming that she was well able to look after herself. They did agree it might be wise to encourage the two young people to do a little work occasionally and to limit the frequency and length of their periods together.

Matthew's father decided to make a positive effort to see more of his son and to try to interest him in some aspects of what he had planned would be his future work. They had a month or two of very uneasy relations, periods of friendliness punctuated by recriminations, sulks, and explosiveness. There was enough goodwill on both sides, however, to tide them over. Matthew came to realize that they were not trying to part him from his girlfriend, just trying to see that he would finally manage to get himself into a position in which he could take some responsibility for their future relationship.

As time went by, however, their infatuation died a mutual death, leaving not even friendship—as a result not of quarrels, but of gradual disillusionment. The chief outcome seemed to be that Matthew got on close terms with his father and became more articulate and surer of himself with girls.

Without detailed knowledge of the innermost thoughts and motives—not always by any means entirely available even to the parties concerned—it is difficult to be other than tentative in formulating the genesis and nature of such teenage infatuations. They can be very tricky indeed for parents to deal with, if they are to avoid provoking permanent ruptures between themselves and their teenage son or daughter. The fact that the parent may sometimes see correctly that the infatuation is pathological or unsuitable does not make things any easier.

That Matthew's affair died away so completely suggests that it was not founded on any real appreciation of Jennifer as a person. That she bore a marked resemblance to both him and his mother would suggest that this was a narcissistic falling-in-love with an image of his mother that was mingled with some idealized image of himself. Very often the teenager's falling in love is initially of this nature. If there is also some appreciation of the object of that feeling as a real person, then there is also the possibility that it will develop into love and respect or a friendship that has a better foundation in reality. Sometimes, of course, this more mature relationship does not develop, but the attachment remains. Many marriages have been made on this more immature ephemeral basis.

It is a very tricky business for a parent to interfere with such attachments, though easier possibly when the teenager is still at school and not really able in fact to be independent without a great deal of defiance. Even then an arbitrary and heavy hand can produce a grievance that is not easily forgotten, and the teenager can end up none the wiser for the experience. Firmness at this stage is likely to be effective only if the teenager has had an experience over the years of parents who are genuinely doing their best to understand him and promote his growth. And firmness without sympathy is just hurtful. These affairs may seem to us from our later experience just "calf love", and may be tiresome or rather amusing, but to the teenager they are terribly serious, and the process of growing out of them is a painful one that adults may help but cannot force.

Elizabeth: disappointment in love

Elizabeth is the only child of rather careful, anxious parents who have always fussed about her welfare and wanted her to do well in school. She had always managed to satisfy their ambitions and her own until the year after her O-level [GCSE] examinations. She became very panicky just before these, needed a great deal of extra help, then managed to pass reasonably well, but not as well as she had hoped.

Her teachers thought she would have little chance of getting to university,[5] but her parents were keen that she should go on to try. So she continued to study for university entrance with some others in her class. Six months before her examinations, during the Christmas holiday when she was seventeen and a half years old, she met a boy at a dance and spent most of the rest of that holiday going around with him—sometimes just the two of them together, sometimes with other friends.

Elizabeth fell head over heels in love with him, and for a while managed to persuade herself that he felt the same way about her. When the new term came and they both returned to school, he became immersed in his work and school activities, and dropped Elizabeth completely.

She became increasingly hypochondriacal and morose, complained of pains, and often refused to get up in the morning. Her parents were distressed, but her family doctor said there was nothing the matter with her, and tried unsuccessfully to jolly her out of her apathetic state. She was sleepless at night, and anxious during the day, until finally she lived on sleeping pills for the night and sedatives for the day. Then she left school and took a routine job that demanded very little of her.

Although her parents' over-fussing had contributed to her anxieties, and had in many ways been most unhelpful, they were responsible for finally encouraging her to go to a clinic where she was accepted for psychotherapy and where she showed a fairly settled resolution to try to work to understand her breakdown. Her progress in her therapy so far suggests that she will sooner or later be able to resume studying and will eventually train for work more in keeping with her potential.

It seems that she was aware of an increasing anxiety from about the age of fifteen, when she was studying for her O-level [GCSE] exams. The examination looming ahead was felt to be a very critical kind of conscience that was going to look into her and discover the poor quality of her work, her life, and all the time she had wasted. She was, indeed, experiencing in a more acute form the kind of examination anxiety that many teenagers suffer from to some degree.

With a little help she managed to get by, but continued to feel very inadequate and doubtful about her capacities. The falling in love with the boy she met in the holidays was very clearly an escape from depression and feelings of unworthiness to a dream of being loved and valued, a reconstitution of the infantile dream in which she—as a doted-on only child—had been living until adolescent questioning had deflated it.

This dream was shattered again when the boyfriend cooled off so quickly. That was too much for her to bear, and confirmed her inner feeling of being unlovable. The hostility she felt at being rejected permeated the world so completely that she had to take to her bed.

Her response, when she finally met someone who understood something of her feelings of guilt, who could look at them and help her to sort them out without blaming her, suggests that she has a real hunger to understand herself and to work towards living on a more honest basis. The outcome of Elizabeth's breakdown promises well.

Notes

1. There are also the problems of anorexia and eating disorders and of overweight young people, which at present are more acute and more widespread than at the time this book was written.
2. Although the fashions and slogans have changed, the general principle of merging traditional male and female roles and appearance continues.

3. As mentioned in a note to the previous book, although these books were written before the AIDS problem, the principle of increase in sexually transmitted diseases continues the same, indicating that the problem of genuine education (not just thrusting of "facts") has still not successfully been addressed.

4. Generally it is available, but only to the small number who choose to learn about it.

5. At that time a much smaller percentage of students went on to higher education than today.

CHAPTER SEVEN

Towards finding an identity and living creatively

Creativity

Puberty, which stimulates the wish and provides the capacity for physical procreation, is accompanied in the teenager by the desire to create in other ways. Together with this desire and the hope of realizing it, he also experiences self-criticism, doubt, and despair about his achievements.

Here is a passage from an essay by Diana, an intelligent sixth-form girl, on "Changing attitudes in the last two years at school".

Changing attitudes

Work becomes a central aspect of life and more communal. But this makes it more vulnerable, as in earlier days any anti-work statements were boasts or envy and rarely had any communal effect on the class. Those who wanted to work to get good marks did it anyway, and the others often did it secretly too.

In the sixth form though, you cannot work productively on your own—you have to discuss. Therefore anti-learning movements are more serious and result in stagnation for months. People get extremely sensitive about their intellectual ability, and so if anyone chokes the class with a sort of pseudo-intellectual enthusiasm, others just retire for fear of losing their popularity, if they can neither agree with the current enthusiasm nor convince the others of its phoniness. Then you can feel very lonely unless you are fortified by discussion outside the school.

The pseudo-intellectual activity she was referring to was almost certainly a fever of spiritualistic enthusiasm for table-tapping and for communicating with the dead, which swept through most of the upper school one Christmas term. In this essay she is making a point that is valid for the teenager if he is maturing well and creatively: that the competitive element does not disappear. It remains active in all of us to some extent throughout our lives, and shows in many ways, from the collecting of marks to the collecting of material possessions or status symbols that set us a little above our neighbours. But, as we mature, work tends to become valued for the sake of the subject and the material involved, and as something that can be added to and illuminated by sharing with others in common endeavour.

Introspection and relating to others

The ability to share creatively, however, depends upon some individual work and introspection, and also upon the examination of one's own values and the questioning of one's honesty. Here is another quotation from the same essay:

> People become more private. You begin to consciously work out your position in the world and your relationships with people. There is a sort of conflict between easing the strain in yourself, which results in acting and trying to be like someone else, and struggling to discover yourself and behave as an individual. This is particularly so in situations where you feel yourself inexperienced and distrust your own capabilities or your own attractions.

> This play-acting is often weakness rather than an attempt to deceive, but it hurts people. Sometimes they feel that they have been deliberately led on, their expectations aroused, and that they have been slapped in the face, e.g. over some talent or code of

morals or conduct you have displayed and then ignored. This can have a more bewildering effect than deliberate off-handed spitefulness or rudeness.

This attempt to be honest—to be "me"—results often in pursuits or interests embraced enthusiastically for a time and then dropped. If such unstable enthusiasm about work or friends is excessive, it may mean that the teenager is constantly approaching life with over-idealized expectations that are foredoomed to disappointment. However, some variability of interests and of companions is probably for most a necessary stage in finding themselves, testing their beliefs, and establishing the core of their identity.

The struggle to find an identity

This is the central task of adolescence. It is a long and slow process during which are laid the final foundations for the personality of the future adult. These foundations, of course, were first begun long ago in the relationship between the baby and its mother and then in that of the infant to both its parents. They have been further developed by later interactions throughout childhood with parents, with brothers and sisters, with friends, school teachers, and other important adults. They are affected at every stage not only by the nature of the new acquaintances but also by the child's approach to these and from the expectations arising from the results of his first encounters with the world. These are then transferred to subsequent relationships.

First identifications

The very first step in knowing people is to be able to identify with them, to feel your way into their minds, into their personalities, to sense their physical reactions and to learn in these ways what it feels like to be them. Little children do this quite literally when they step into Mummy's shoes and shuffle round the house pretending they *are* Mummy. The very first way of learning about yourself is also to project yourself, your unknown, unnamed needs and distresses, into your mother and (later) your father. From their greater experience of life and of themselves, and according to their openness to that experience, they may be able to respond to that need, to give you a name for it, a better acquaintance with it, and therefore a better grasp of some aspect of yourself.

This learning of new things about yourself from the way that people see you and feel you to be can take place throughout your life. People may not always reflect a correct image of you. But they may reflect accurately some unpalatable aspect of yourself that is too painful to credit. You may play-act, project a false image wittingly or unwittingly, and so receive back a false picture of yourself. This is what Diana, the sixth-former mentioned earlier in this chapter, was talking about.

Trying to be sincere

The process of finding an identity is, for the teenager, for the most part one of trial and error. He tries out many ways of behaving, looks critically on past modes of being and of thinking before he grows into some changed mode of being that he feels *is* himself. Some teenagers suffer agonies of doubt about their sincerity and find their spontaneity grievously inhibited as a result of this—an example may be found in the account of Jane later in this chapter.

This quest for sincerity and for uniqueness, for an identity that is one's own and no-one else's, leads the teenager to try to struggle free from identifications that he has made earlier in childhood in order to escape his own littleness and inadequacy. The earlier identifications may have been with older brothers and sisters, against whom, in consequence, rebellion may later be sharpest. They are the people he would have most wanted to be, and whose power he would most have wished to possess.

The more completely he has relied on living through his parents, through brothers and sisters and through authority figures in his childhood, the more difficult it is for him to extricate himself from their identities to find a style of his own. Some teenagers, of course, do not try. They remain conformist, old, as it were, before their time.

Others break out in a very explosive way, emphasizing new conformities of dress and hair that demonstrate to themselves and us the fact that they are, after all, different. This "explosive" reaction was seen in the case of Matthew, who from a predominantly "good" kind of identification with his mother in childhood switched over to being quite possessed by a possessive greedy sexuality that took both him and his family unawares. "Many teenagers", said one of them, "become pregnant to punish their parents."

The teenagers who are able to keep their heads and—despite the turmoil—to really enjoy the unparalleled promise that their sexual and emotional flowering offers them, are likely to be those who have identified in childhood with parents whom they have experienced as essentially loving and understanding, whom they have carried within them throughout the years as a protection and a stimulus to learn and develop.

Identity realized in work and marriage

The search for an identity is intimately bound up with the desire to be able to love and to work in one's own way. The teenager seeks to know and to choose the work that he wishes to do and that best expresses his talents, and the partner with whom he can best develop these—the person he finally wants to live with. This means making choices, making a commitment. If you are you, you cannot be anyone else—you are responsible for what you do. Without commitment, only a split and divided life and love is practicable— a double and cross-eyed identity.

It is anxiety about the failure to find commitment that may cause a career to be precipitately embraced, or a "falling in love" that is really a fleeing from uncertainty before true certainty has been earned. The teenager closes off other possibilities and experiences and takes refuge in what seems a planned certainty. This may, indeed, curtail the adolescent period, but at the expense of settling down prematurely into an apparent maturity. It is known, for example, that the chances of divorce increase with the decrease in the age of marriage.

Later on, maybe not until middle age, there may be depression or resentment about opportunities missed, talents not developed, relationships never explored. Then maybe the fear of being left out, left behind, of being inadequate, which was avoided in adolescence by an over-hasty flight to safety, can no longer be kept at bay.

Fleeing from oneself

Thus, for some young people, the uncertainties of adolescence, with its emotional work and self-questioning, provoke an intolerable anxiety. They go, in consequence, to extremes to avoid the struggle. They make premature choices, and so fail to pass through a fully worked-out phase to maturity.

What happens to them?

Some carry on in the same old tramlines, perhaps narrowly wedded to an ambition mapped out for them since childhood. They may become the kind of bookish, uncreative student who ages without ever really having been young, without experiencing the delights, the uncertainties, and the follies of youth. Such a person has not been able to afford the luxury of doubt. Among them is the little girl who realizes her childhood dream by becoming a little-girl bride and mother, without ever maturing to be a woman.

Others seem to find it difficult to get beyond the early adolescent stage of taking refuge in some group of peers: groups of boys go about together meeting groups of girls. As they grow a little older, individuals tend to separate out, to pair with some particular person, and more intimate personal relationships develop. Then the teenagers who are not developing, or who are developing more slowly, can feel a little lost and lonely, for they are not learning how to be more independent.

Panic may drive them to take refuge in a boyfriend or a girlfriend, and maybe eventually to marry so as to conform and be like the others, but without relish for the relationship itself. Young people like this take on the colour of the people with whom they consort. Sometimes they remain amenable to firmness, to being guided in the direction of social usefulness, but almost as easily, it would seem, they can be led astray towards delinquency, idleness, or antisocial behaviour.

Jeremy

Take the story of Jeremy, for example.

He is a boy of seventeen and a half who has not been doing a regular job for the past six months. He had an undistinguished but adequate school record, doing no more than he needed to get along with the rest of his class; then he left for a job with a firm which was arranged for him by the Youth Employment Officer. He was doing quite well there, then he suddenly left before his first year was up, telling his parents he was going into the second-hand furniture business with another two youths he had met at work.

They had convinced him there was more money to be made in this for less effort. His parents were uneasy, but were persuaded, and then paid little more attention until the police called one night to ask them questions about Jeremy's movements. It turned out that he was suspected of abetting his friends in receiving and selling stolen goods. The two friends were sentenced to a term of imprisonment, but he was put on probation. He was unusually open and guileless with his probation officer, with whom he had a number of lengthy talks. The probation officer formed the impression that Jeremy was not so much immoral or delinquent as amoral, and might just as easily have led a legally blameless life as a life of crime, depending on the company he kept.

Jeremy was quite frank that he thought he could go straight only if he was with mates who were straight: he just would not think of stealing. It was never something he had deliberately set out to do. When he had met his two accomplices he had been caught up with the idea of picking up money more easily by collecting scrap and odd bits of furniture and so on—he had not known there was going to be anything dishonest about it. When he found out that there was, he had not worried much, as they seemed to be getting away with it. But he would not go stealing or trying anything of that sort on his own. He would just as soon earn his money honestly; but he was not one to kill himself with work and struggle to improve himself—he "didn't mind a fair amount of work, but he wanted to enjoy himself".

His idea of enjoying himself seemed to consist of going about with his mates and a group of girls—"It's a way of passing the time." Some time, he supposed, he would find a partner and settle down, but he was not in too much of a hurry, wanted to "enjoy himself" first. But this trouble with the police had given him a bit of a shock, and he would like a bit of help to see that he was kept on the rails in future.

The probation officer felt that Jeremy's assessment of the situation was fairly accurate. Although Jeremy had the appearance of a teenager, there was no corresponding reality under the appearance, but rather an undeveloped child growing physically and waiting to find some appropriate slot into which he could fit himself and spend his life with as little trouble to himself as possible. The probation officer's own duty was to do what he could to ensure that the slot would not be an antisocial one.

It would not, of course, be entirely accidental that Jeremy went along with is little gang of receivers, even though he *saw* it as accidental. He was not aware of having made a conscious choice. His friends obviously spoke—as he himself stated—to that potentially delinquent part of himself that wanted to pick up things easily without having to work for them. It seemed as though there was virtually no conflict about the enterprise, that there was no sufficiently developed central core to his personality, self-respecting and respecting the rights of others, to resist the greedy, easy way of existing when this was put in his path.

Flight to drugs

This needs a brief mention here, but it is a subject too wide and controversial to do more than touch on.

Drug addiction is another kind of flight, an increasingly common and dangerous one, from self-discovery and self-responsibility.

We all use some form of drug to sweeten reality and to avoid pain. Forms range from smoking and alcohol to daydreams, flattery, and reassurance. The harmfulness of the "drug" depends on the degree to which we rely on it, and on how much it is used as a substitute for self-awareness.

The additional danger with actual chemical drugs is their habit-forming nature—the organic effects that add a bodily craving to the mental craving. It is the social seduction of the drug that usually provides the initial attraction; it speaks to that part of the teenager that is hostile to the parents and to the older generation. One young student said, "I can think of several of my friends who took pot for the first time and then could hardly wait to get home to tell their parents." The object, she implied, was to flaunt independence and to worry them.

An essential feature in the seductiveness of the drug is the conventional assumption among teenagers that it leads to a fuller living, a heightened consciousness—and if you have not experienced that, then you are simply not with it. This is one way whereby teenagers can establish their own particular in-group, where the parents in their turn become the unknowing, helpless infants outside it all.

The position with regard to treatment for drug addition is altering rapidly. It may be worth mentioning here a society formed by parents who are worried by drug addition as a problem with their teenagers.[1]

Jane—changing and resolving identifications

This is a brief account of an adolescent girl finding her femininity.

Jane is now seventeen years old, and is due to take her A-level exams in six months' time. She has always done well at school, and her teachers have little doubt that she should get good grades and be offered a place at the university of her choice. She has confounded them and her parents, however, by panicking suddenly, wanting to leave school and to get a job looking after children. She has, in fact, applied to an agency and has been offered just such a post, as mother's help to four children in the family of a diplomat who is going abroad. She seems determined to follow this whim, as both her parents and her teachers see it to be.

She is the eldest of a family of four, two boys and two girls, and until she was nearly fifteen years of age she was very much the tomboy of the family—bossy, active at organizing the other children, and very good at games. She was included in most of the school's games teams at a much earlier age than most other children. Neither her brothers nor her sister showed anything like the same drive or ability, and were at a less academic school, to the disappointment of their father, who is successful, ambitious, and highly intelligent.

At about the age of fifteen Jane's character seemed to alter. She became more thoughtful, less certain of herself, and made secret little attempts to improve her appearance, although she was extremely touchy if anyone in the family appeared to notice and comment on this. She became shyer with boys, but interested in them in a different way—no longer competing and boastful, but less sure of how she should behave, more aware of the effect she was having on them, and anxious to be pleasant. Her prowess on the game field declined, to her distress, and she found it hard to explain to the games teacher that missed goals and inaccurate shots were not due to lack of practice and attention but to a loss of her general sureness of touch. Indeed, she could not explain it to herself. She began to envy her younger sister's gentler feminine ways and greater social poise.

Her mother had been in delicate health and rather hypochondriacal throughout Jane's life. The younger sister had always figured as the girl in the family, and as her mother's help Jane was classed with the boys, but from early on was marked as a forward child and one who was going to be the academic success of the family. It seemed that when she was well on into adolescence this role of the successful tomboy began to constrict her, and she was trying somewhat hesitantly to find an identity for herself as a girl. There she felt at a disadvantage, because her sister had always been the one who was close to her mother, while she herself had been an object of pride, but also of some perplexity and disapproval. "Jane," her mother would sigh after one of her pranks, "if you'd been a boy I could have understood you much better."

During her childhood and early adolescence she felt that the one talent and interest she had that her mother understood and wholeheartedly approved of was the capacity to empathize with and look after small children. Irresponsible and impulsive in all else, she was careful and resourceful with children, who trusted her and enjoyed her company; and this made her greatly sought after as a babysitter for some of her younger cousins and for the small children of family friends.

When she became so set on leaving school at seventeen without completing her public examinations, her form teacher and headmistress, who regarded her as one of their most promising pupils, spent some time talking to her to try to understand her reasons for leaving. They arranged for her to have interviews with a psychological consultant to enable her to explore more fully her aims and motives in making what seemed to be a hasty and ill-thought-out decision.

It seems as if this decision is an attempt on Jane's part to break away abruptly from her former tomboyish, ambitious, and competitive self, which she associates with academic success and triumphing over her mother and sister, in particular. She is feeling oppressed by the role that she accepted so readily before, both at home and at school, and feels that the best way of getting out of it is to get right away and start a new kind of life. Her liking for children and her understanding of them are genuine. They are used in a positive identification with a mother who is a sweet, warm-hearted woman; but the identification also conceals an unacknowledged, long-standing rivalry with her mother over her younger brothers and sister, which has been stirred up by puberty, the possibility of sexual fulfilment, and of giving birth to children of her own.

Getting right away from the family is also, then, an attempt to escape the revival of the childhood conflict with her mother for the husband and babies. It seems as if she had avoided this in childhood days by becoming a boy, identifying with father and turning away from feminine things. Very probably it may have been harder for her to acknowledge her rivalry with her mother more fully because of the mother's ailments. This was likely to make her feel both more guilty about her hostility and also more frightened of wanting to be feminine and a mother herself, if to be a mother meant to be ill and the object of your children's envy.

Getting a job as a nanny to look after someone else's children—interestingly enough there were four of them, the number of her mother's children—is a short cut to acquiring a family herself, an expression of typical adolescent impatience, an instant satisfaction of infantile wishes. But the fact that she is going to be the nanny and not the mother, and therefore interrupt what promised to be a successful career, would mean that she punishes herself by restricting her possibilities of a more complete fulfilment and of achieving a richer and more complex identity.

By punishing herself in this way she avoids both the guilt and the responsibility that the greater success might bring: guilt in so far as success may have an inner meaning of triumph over someone else—ultimately the parents; and responsibility in so far as (to a person who has care and feeling for other people, as Jane undoubtedly has) greater achievement means being in a position to do more for others.

The upshot of the discussion about Jane's future is that she has agreed to stay on to finish her examinations at school. She is applying to university, but with the agreement of both teachers and parents that the question is still open as to whether she decides to go there or not. She may, indeed, be one of those teenagers who need to prove themselves by holding down a job first before they feel free enough in themselves to continue with further study.[2]

Learning to be more objective

The teenager who is struggling with himself and winning through to some kind of maturity is learning to contain and to live with his inconsistencies instead of being dominated by them. His improving mental and emotional organization gives him gradually a little more tranquillity, and more impetus to appreciate the world outside. He becomes more able to see people and ideas as something in themselves, less strongly coloured by projections of his own personality. He may learn to argue less fiercely, but more rationally and dispassionately. He is better able to consider the merits of the case he is arguing when he needs to argue less against himself.

Each teenager proceeds at his own pace and begins in his own time to win more freedom from himself to be objective in his learning and in his relationships. But time to grow is very often the very thing he fears that he does not possess.

Teenage impatience and panic about wasted time

It seems paradoxical that those whom the middle-aged envy for being at the beginning of life, the golden time of youth, should so often be obsessed with the passage of time, bedevilled by the thought of death, and impatient to grasp at fulfilment lest tomorrow never come. There are a number of factors that account for and intensify this panic about wasting time.

Greater self-consciousness about the nature of his work and capacity leads the teenager to assess his achievements in a more realistic way. He has examinations to face towards the end of his years at school, which are, in many cases, going to determine what kind of work he will be able to obtain, and are seen as the verdict on what he has done throughout his school career. In addition to omnipotent daydreams and also to neurotic undervaluations of one's own powers, there is probably in most of us some unconscious awareness of our own true potential. The teenager begins to have some sense of it, and thus can often be plagued by a guilty feeling of time wasted in his schooldays when he should have been learning how to grow up.

Emotionally, he often feels the acute and vulnerable sensitivity of the small child, and is only too apt to veer from a position of poised sophistication and arrogance to that of an infant on the threshold of adult life. If he has not had a solid enough experience of working at acquiring skills in his middle-school years, he feels he has little to fall back upon, and is all the more vulnerable and panicky about being unable to grow up in time.

As *all* his emotions tend to be more accessible and acutely felt, he is also more aware of his destructive ones. He recognizes, moreover, that he can actually do more damage than he was able to do as an infant, however strongly he felt then. The young child is very largely his parents' responsibility, but the teenager becomes more and more his own; and this, although desired, can be a heavy burden.

Fear of the envy of parents and of the grown-up world

This fear can, of course, have foundations in reality. It is worth taking a longer look, however, at some of the factors that make some teenagers particularly sensitive to envy, and, indeed, make them anticipate it. They are always ready to feel that they are being grudged their place in the sun, even when they have little real reason to complain of their treatment.

These grudging teenagers tend to be the ones who in childhood did not manage to face up to and to live with their envy of their parents' greater power and possessions, of their sexual and grown-up social relationship with each other. If inwardly they have not managed to accord their parents some degree of freedom and integrity, they tend to be dogged by a grudging inward image of them, by an inner expectation of being deprived of fulfilment themselves.

Conquering fears of a malign fate

We may remember from our adolescent days some nagging super-stitious fear of an envious fate which can step in to spoil things when they are going too well—"Those whom the gods love, die young". The fact that happiness is not everlasting, that it may be interrupted by misfortune, is an observation that experience forces us to make.

The teenager's sense of the precarious nature of joy, or his feeling that there are parents and a grown-up world that want to do him down, is not, of course, necessarily based on actual experience of harm done and of restrictions imposed upon him from outside. Rather, it is often related to an apprehension of the restrictions endemic in his own nature, which he has not been able to understand and manage as part of himself. Projected outside himself into the external world, these return to plague him, either in specific people and instances or in vague apprehensions.

This fear of the imminence of danger to what he loves and values, or to what he wants to achieve, lends an urgency to "gather rosebuds while ye may", and adds to his sense of time passing rapidly. The realities of the nuclear age give a good reason in the world outside for the fear—which the teenager is already apt to have—that his personal world is liable to disintegrate.[3]

Perhaps, in a very simple and stereotyped society, the social norms and practices would be so rigid and established that the many adolescent doubts, the troubled searchings for an identity that we have been discussing, would not arise. We can, however, never return to such a society, if indeed it ever existed.[4] We can only try to help our teenagers by expecting honest self-criticism in them, by responding with honesty about ourselves, and by offering the opportunity and the stability within the home for the teenager to work safely towards real independence.

This will be based on his finding himself, not on merely rejecting the faults in our adult world; and it is encouraged by our attempting as parents to understand his search, even when that takes a form that may be hurtful to us, and to which we are tempted to respond—like teenagers—with rashness, anger, or contempt.

Notes

1. The organization referred to here no longer exists, but health and social services can make known those available in a given area. For some years after this book was written there was an attempt to provide a comprehensive drug-withdrawal service, but the situation now is more patchy, with local differences.
2. Or to take a gap year, as some students did at that time, and do increasingly these days.
3. It is hardly necessary to add, fear of the modern developments of bombings and terrorism.
4. Though, presumably, the present-day increase in ethnic rigidity is an attempt to return from the "permissive society" of the past half-century to such a never-never land.

Martha Harris's philosophy of education

Meg Harris Williams

"The end of learning is to repair the ruins of our first parents by regaining to know God aright"

(John Milton, *Of Education*, 1644)

The simple vocabulary, yet finely tuned phraseology of these "little books" (as the author refers to them) conveys their counterpoint between practical commonsense and psychological penetration. They are a vehicle for imaginatively considering the true nature of education, comprising as it does both the acquisition of skills and the development of the personality. The interaction between these constitutes the finding of "identity", which Martha Harris defines as the "central task of the adolescent" (Book Three, p. 221); on this achievement rests the well being of both individuals and of society at large. It entails a continual realistic self-appraisal—though not necessarily a conscious or verbal one—testing the boundaries of relationships and of capabilities. In its most sophisticated form it establishes reliance on internal parents and is thus a private matter (as in Milton's description of "regaining" knowledge of God); but in the child or adolescent the search for identity takes place in the context of family life and the first "little society" of school (Book Two, p. 115), under the aegis of actual parents and parental figures, who therefore have a formative ethical role.[1] The evolution of ethics takes place not in a vacuum, but in an environment of acquiring skills and learning to appreciate the requirements of others.

It is the central task of parents to facilitate this process: to some extent through practical measures (proper instruction, access to information, etc.), but above all through emotional means. Acquiring a truly parental attitude to one's child is not something automatic, but necessitates an internal reawakening and self-evaluation. For "we can only expect to educate [our teenager] by re-educating ourselves" (Book Three, p. 115). Since adolescence is "a time when our sons and daughters may cause us to think furiously for ourselves and about ourselves" (Book Two, p. 141), the whole tenor of these books consists in formulating the kind of fine distinctions that enable parents to try to distinguish between their received values (those of class or ethnic group, current fashions in child-rearing methods, and so on) and the evolution of real values that arise from "thinking about" the interaction between ourselves and the individual child.[2] Ultimately, both children and parents may take their place in "the great social class of the truly educated people, the people who are still learning" (Book Three, p. 156).

"Thinking about" our child means making qualitative distinctions at points where, in the haste and confusion of everyday existence, we are liable to see things quantitatively, assuming in a woolly way that a compromise between opposites—but not too much of either of them—is a reasonable solution to the problem. These distinctions occur in the areas of (for example) discipline and punishment; encouragement and overpraising; fairness and rigidity; firmness and authoritarianism; letting go and indifference; love and narcissism; creative and destructive types of aggression; useful and self-indulgent types of worrying; "delayed choice and spineless vacillation" (Book Three, p. 167); protecting and stifling; permissiveness and neglect; liberalism and self-idealization; manners and courtesy, etc. Thinking about such matters, when stimulated by the real experience of trying to educate our child, means becoming more questioning of our own values and assumptions, more aware of our own hidden bad feelings, and therefore in a better position to encourage thoughtfulness in the child who is in the process of becoming adult. Realism consists in "learning from experience to aim for what is possible rather than only for the unattainable ideal" (Book Three, p. 199), and this is equally true for parents and children, and entails a certain self-knowledge of the "ingratitude, greed, and envy" that can cloud our judgement.

The examples given of actual children are not presented as necessarily typical. They are not there to be generalized from, as one might expect if these were simply handbooks listing the features of adolescent mentality. Rather, they are intended to "illustrate the way one would set about trying to get a picture of [an individual child's] situation and of their development" (Book One, p. 3). A more abstract purpose underlies their portrayal of the pitfalls and assumptions that we are likely to make if we come to automatic conclusions without self-scrutiny. The purpose is to spotlight the nature of developmental thinking. Reading the books carefully can help us, as parents, to identify our own adult and creative aspects by means of noticing the feelings aroused in us by our adolescent children. Such turbulent and contradictory feelings mirror the state of the adolescent himself, who is assailed by a renewal of heightened infantile emotionality, yet who may be one day a responsible adult. Through an increase in self-awareness, parents can help their child to engage that part of himself (for it is only ever a part) that desires to grow and develop. "By keeping ourselves alive as parents we help also to keep our children's interests growing" (Book Two, p. 88).

Martha Harris's philosophy of education was formalized in psychoanalytical terms in the tract written in collaboration with Donald Meltzer a few years after writing these books, *A Model of the Child-in-the-Family-in-the-Community*.[3] At about the same time she wrote her description of "The Tavistock training and philosophy", which is likewise, on one level, a vehicle for her personal views on education and how to facilitate it within a particular group, or group-within-a-group. For there are, in her view, many parallels between learning to be a parent and learning to be psychotherapist or analyst—especially in terms of the mental qualities to be cultivated. In each case, "it is not enough to love one's own children"; a particular type of generosity needs to be opened up which goes beyond possessive love.[4] Parenthood, like psychoanalysis, is to be understood as an "art-science" (Harris & Bick, 1987, p. 277). The central quality that needs to be developed is the ability to focus on the task in hand—to observe the minute realities of the child's situation, to relinquish judgement and ambition and instead to "acquire a capacity to delay, or rather to refrain from asking for, immediate satisfaction from the patient [or child] himself" (*ibid.*, p. 276). This is Keatsian "negative capability", or, in Harris's terms, "living in the question" (*ibid.*, p. 267).

In the Model, the family is described as an "educational institution" (Meltzer & Harris, 1994, p. 453; below, p. 265); it is the place where intimate learning-from-experience can meet up with acquiring social skills and quantifiable knowledge "about" the world. A psychoanalytical model of mental development envisages the personality as a complex field of possible states of mind, ranging between the mind-stretching orientation of "learning from experience" and the more superficial or imitative modes of acquiring knowledge (projective, adhesive, scavenging), with tyrannical and gang-like attitudes operating at the destructive extreme. All these various personality structures, and their equivalent family structures, can be found somewhere in these books—either referred to or described through examples. These mental states are the context in which learning difficulties occur, or are overcome. Since everybody—of whatever age—has both adult and infantile aspects to their character, and will at times oscillate between them, it is necessary for purposes of self-scrutiny to have an overall view of the possibilities. This is the "epistemological dilemma of the individual" as described in the Model: the two opposing value-systems of "understanding the world" (the adult attitude) and of "controlling the world" (the infantile attitude) (Meltzer & Harris, 1994, p. 411; below, p. 255). Here, however, I will focus on the "adult" aspect and on the principle of how to nurture it in one's child.

As stated in the Model the "adult part" of the personality begins to form early in childhood, indeed infancy (Meltzer & Harris, 1994, pp. 436–438); it is not a question of chronological age but of mental orientation. Indeed, the progressive part of a child may cause "dislocation" in a family bonded together rigidly through behavioural patterns (projective identification) as tends to happen in strict ethnic, class-bound, or ideological communities.[5] But it is "those who have failed in childhood to become reconciled to being children" (Book

Two, p. 136) who are most liable to sink into the antithesis of adulthood (gang mentality), owing to having no means of self-awareness, no internal objects securely established.[6] The concept of "work" has been lost, a concept that, like "thinking", depends on transference to internal objects. For the adult state of mind "has a sense of purpose and regards every activity as a form of work, in relation to transference figures (teachers, parents) or to those depending on it" (Meltzer & Harris, 1994, p. 437). How can this be encouraged to predominate over infantile states so that the individual's education may progress?

As Martha Harris points out (citing Melanie Klein), "play is a child's work" (Book Two, p. 95); the distinction between work and play is a false one and would be incomprehensible to the young child, who has not yet lost touch with the joyous aegis that Wordsworth called "the master-light of all our seeing". Work–play is an absorbing activity that engages the developing mind–body and draws it onwards (e-duc-ates). It contrasts with the "shades of the prison-house"—the conformity of feeling like a drudge, a cog in the machine, "overworked"—in short, the claustrum of basic-assumption values.[7] It is to alleviate the pressures of the claustrum that we all seek some form of

> drug to sweeten reality . . . Forms range from smoking and alcohol to daydreams, flattery, and reassurance. The harmfulness of the "drug" depends on the degree to which we rely on it, and on how much it is used as a substitute for self-awareness. [Book Three, p. 226]

Thus, it is motivation, rather than quantity, that clarifies the nature of a drug.[8] Adults, Harris writes, may tend to be "guilty about their pleasures" (Book Three, p. 95); and this is associated with more infantile states of mind. But the adult state of mind is in itself pleasurable and playful and requires no drugs. Ultimately self-fulfilment is the same thing as service to the world, and, as Blake was always saying, its energies and potentialities are "infinite", not subject to excess or rationing. You can have too much of a drug, but you cannot have too much of a good thing—at least, not in spiritual terms.

So these books encourage parents to seek for enjoyment in the work–play of bringing up their child. The period of adolescence, from the first stirrings of puberty onwards, is a time not only of stress but also of opportunity for children and parents to grow together. On the verge of their teenager's "leap into adulthood", the parent may be tempted to lapse into feelings of obsolescence and redundancy (Book Three, p. 163); but the author repeatedly suggests that if we can learn to make certain "realistic" distinctions, this reciprocal turbulence in ourselves can be channelled towards the rejuvenation of our own life and relationships. Then, most importantly, these may in turn reflect back on to the teenager, for the evidence of our continuing emotional growth is critical to the teenager's own quest for identity. The most valuable gift we can offer is to model the process that Yeats described as "remaking oneself". Only if the parental model does not "depend on the children for its vitality" can the children "use it as a basis from which to develop their own" (Book Three, p. 213). This means the model provided in psychological reality by the parental figures—not just their creed. For "To have given up learning—as so many of us adults have—is not an inspiring example to the young learner; and to have so much knowledge that we never use except to pass it on to our children is equally dispiriting" (Book Three, p. 149).[9] And, the author reminds us, the teenager *will know* the facts of our feeling: "the tie between parents and adolescent child is such that we cannot hide our feelings, though equally we rarely verbalize them. But they emerge and are noted" (Book Three, p. 164).

It follows that it is no use if our interest is not genuine—interest in our work, in the world around us, above all in the child—because the adolescent, like Hamlet, knows the difference between "is and seems", and his adult part wants to know what will "denote him truly" in the context of all this.[10] Genuine interest is not proprietorial but is a type of wonderment at the astonishing fact of nature that is the adolescent mind. Interest acknowledges the existence of our unpleasant feelings of irritation, anger, guilt, and can tolerate rather than immediately expel them. As explained in the Model, interest is of powerful therapeutic value;[11] as exemplified in the case of Edward, with his prison-dream (Book One, p. 8), or of Steve and the headteacher (Book One, p. 38), it is capable of penetrating the sense of self-imprisonment and drawing the prisoner out into the world of reality. Hence, the need to continually monitor and discuss the "indicators of physical, social, intellectual and emotional development" of the various family members (Meltzer & Harris, 1994, p. 427; below p. 257). Through our interest we can teach by example how to scrutinize scientifically the evidence for our opinions, and demonstrate the possibility of changing one's mind on the basis of new evidence. "The topics must matter to us too, and the education will follow automatically" (Book Three, p. 155). Interest enables us to hold approval and disapproval in abeyance while we consider more closely. We may, for example, disapprove of too much television (or computer games), apparent rudeness or uncivilized behaviour, or, indeed, of competitiveness or sports-obsession, depending on the social group to which we consider we belong. If we withhold judgement but continue to observe closely, we may discover, for example, that the significance of the television for a particular child at a particular time is to provide a cocoon "less troublesome than silence" to protect his privacy (Book Two, p. 98); or that undesirable material in his reading or entertainment may have likewise no penetrating power.[12]

For in the intimate area of emotional growth, learning takes place "through identification" ("with parents, friends, and teachers", Book One, p. 13), not through precept, reward, or punishment.[13] Once the concept of identification is established, it becomes clear why "do as I say, not as I do" does not work. Teenagers will be affected by what we mean, rather than what we say; and "We may hold broad and generous views meanly, and stern opinions with tolerance" (Book Three, p. 154). As with the question of hypocrisy vs sincerity in religious matters, it is not our social carapace but our real intentions and behaviour that count. Reliance on a veneer of respectability is merely the other side of delinquency, as in the reformed adults who become "pillars of society, and castigate their own children for acts that they do not care to remember having committed themselves" (Book Two, p. 138).[14] Antisocial behaviour derives from hidden or secret delinquency in the parental attitude, and is associated with tendency to blame others (Book One, p. 34; Book Two, p. 109). By contrast, "real courtesy takes into account the needs and potentialities of the child" so will be imbibed (eventually) by a species of reflection of our actual values, not just of our self-image.[15] "Much patience, and much self-awareness, is called for if courtesy is to become an inward growth and not an imposed and hence unreliable regulation" (Book Two, pp. 117–120).

In the same way, the child will perceive intuitively any attempt we make to deceive him about his real capacities; and our own motivational confusion will create a disabling confusion in his mind.[16] When are we really treating the child as an attribute of ourselves, "to do us credit in the eyes of others" (Book One, p. 44)? When, believing we are protecting or encouraging him, are we really protecting ourselves from our own fears of failure, or sexual furtiveness?[17] "The child does not wish to be caught in a commercial transaction in which if he delivers the goods (success) he will be loved, but if he does not deliver, he will be despised"; though this is to be distinguished from glossing over failure, which is equally unhelpful (Book Two, pp. 85–86). This failure in our own self-knowledge derives from a quantitative definition of "success".[18] Several examples are given of parents coming to terms with "disappointment in their own unrealized ambitions", which they have attempted to live through their child, or in other ways use the child as their instrument.[19] Neither guilt nor pride is "useful", since both involve blinding oneself to the individual nature of the child, the need to respect his "spark of uniqueness that was in him from the day of his birth, and that sets him apart as a separate human being" (Book One, p. 26), as in Keats's formulation of the "spark of identity" in the "vale of Soulmaking". The key to igniting the spark is "realism"—how to encourage the child's realistic capacities—and that entails being realistic ourselves, not idealizing or dismissive or domineering. One part of the child may stimulate our "overpraising", but once this is distinguished from encouragement in our own mind, and recognized as tyrannical, it is easier to resist the child's demands for it, and to ally with the more realistic adult part of the child that wants "to be understood and to relate to the world and themselves truthfully"—to become educated (Book One, p. 38).

The main function of a parent, according to the Model, is to share and thereby to modulate the child's developmental pains:

> The essence of service is the sharing of someone else's pain with a view to lowering it within the bounds of their toleration, while going beyond this limit produces indulgence and overprotection . . . *containment* of mental pain is the central concept for examining the educational functions of the family under this model. [Meltzer & Harris, 1994, p. 411]

where "pain" is the negative-capability cloud of uncertainty, not-knowing, as in Edward's "prison of not knowing anything, . . . the terror of feeling lost at school and deprived of identity" (Book One, p. 10). The parent can usefully "take on the worrying part of the excitement" of any new challenge (such as that of starting secondary school—marking, as it does, in formal terms, the "end of childhood": Book One, p. 15), but in such a way as not to deprive the child of the "real experience" of the challenge by demeaning it. So, another of the distinctions we need to keep in view—in order to make turbulence profitable—is that between self-indulgent and "useful" or "creative" worry. Worrying usefully is a parent's "work and pleasure" (Book One, p. 3). By clarifying what is meant by "useful" worry we can learn to distinguish between persecutory anxiety and that belonging to the joys and pains of development— the vitality of living in the question (Book Two, pp. 75, 86). Similarly, our own justifiable anger and irritation becomes more containable when we realize that "the qualities that irritate us most strongly are likely to be qualities in ourselves that we do not like" (Book One, p. 26), or that "children, like adults, have an aggressive component to their nature that helps them to survive and to create" (Book Two, p. 118). This is to be distinguished from the type of aggression that is really "timorousness" and that is generally directed against those who seem different (in class, sex, or ethnic group).[20] The principle is to try to harness the child's innate vitality usefully into facing the challenge of life, rather than to deny the natural role of competitiveness and aggression (including towards ourselves), in a way that will only lead to rebellion and the ideal-ization of "freedom" or far-away places later on.[21]

Behind all the specific life-challenges of new schools, public exams, new friends, etc., lies the New Idea of adolescence itself—a catastrophic change like a "second birth" (Book Three, p. 163).[22] Puberty, with its new body, heralds the unknown idea of one's future internal shape or identity. "This change and protection against this change" is what prepossesses the adolescent mind from around age eleven onwards (Book One, p. 15). The adolescent has "too many unfamiliar stirrings of growth . . . to have his feelings taken other than deadly seriously" (Book One, p. 36). Hence, his "extreme snail-like sensitivity" (Book Three, p. 152).[23] For the tomboyish girl who senses the dawn of womanhood, "a sense of reality convinces that the best must be made of a bad job" (Book One, p. 32). We can empathize with the child's resistance to the New Idea, even "mourn" our own lost childhood again, for, according to the laws of identification, "our attitude of mind is probably more important than what we actually say" (Book One, p. 52).

Martha Harris captures the poignant precariousness of the adolescent child, "caught between lost childhood and unrealized adulthood" (Book Two, p. 118). Balanced between moving forwards and gazing nostalgically backwards, the child senses "the shadow of the future cast before" (as Shelley put it), the "undiscovered country" of his future self (as Hamlet put it).[24] So, "the responsible thoughtful young adult of one day can suddenly be the heedless infant of the next" (Book Three, p. 193). It is a testing time for the parents, since previous modes of regulation no longer work, and it becomes apparent whether or not the child has imbibed some sense of self-responsibility. We need to be in touch with their "despair" of ever growing up, of possibly feeling "let down by themselves" (Book Three, p. 193), and to "feel ourselves back into that contradiction of arrogance and abasement that the teenager experiences and presents himself as being" (Book Three, p. 165).

The books map out the various sections of a child's social life in which he can explore and get a feel for his growing identity: living out internal emotional dramas among friends, siblings, the "little society" of school, school work, and the complementary work of playing—interests, games, and hobbies. All of these are fields that offer opportunities for gauging the qualities of the developing inner self—or equally, for denying, evading, or acting out. Like the games field, they can all potentially draw forth "the loss of self-consciousness that brings success" (Book One, p. 17). The adolescent child's "play" is described as a "barometer" for watching the child's condition; to see when they need help "venturing out", or when "storms are brewing" (Book Three, p. 175). Thus, in terms of the teenage boy's sexuality, he may have an "idealizing" relationship with his bike (or, these days, very often his electric guitar) that does not have the "dangers of the mocking, assessing, and demanding glances of a real girl" (Book Three, p. 172). Emotionally, he may be pursuing a search for an "ideal partner" in this way.[25] The eleven-year-old may learn from the experience of owning a pet about responsibility towards others and about the individual life of another creature

(Coleridge's "one life"), also in preparation for intimate human relationships (Book One, p. 16). The boy watching a leaf fall as he fishes in the river may drink in semi-consciously recollections that will "refresh him for all his life" (Book Three, p. 175); the experience of feeling part of a larger world—of nature—will contribute to shaping his own identity, his sense of the bounds of his existence.

In the process of imagining-into the child's emotional state, the author's language takes on a metaphorical, even poetic, quality at times. Thus, she describes the young teenager climbing a cliff: he begins as a child, but "when he gets to the top it is as a man, and it is the sort of climb that, in one form or another, all our children have to make" (Book Two, p. 97). The climb of forward development entails "seriously tasting a little of the flavour of death", without the "safety net of fantasy" of a younger child. We cannot empathize with the struggles of development without recognizing its real dangers; growing up is a serious business. Our role as parents is to distinguish between necessary and unnecessary dangers, avoiding both the "indifference which will result in foolhardiness" and the overprotection which will result in "rebellion against our clinging refusal to let them grow up" (Book Two, p. 97). None the less, self-scrutiny is not an infallible tool, and (in the interests of realism) it is acknowledged that, just as life may hold tragic circumstances which we cannot foresee or forestall, a situation can arise where the most helpful thing a parent can do for their child is to tolerate the pain of watching them make serious mistakes—even though the easier option would be to disown or abandon them emotionally.[26] Correspondingly, there can be a situation where a child wishes for "safer parents than his own" and finds ways of engineering this (Book Two, p. 111). The cliff-climbing aspect of the child is his adult self, the escapism (drugs, opting out, etc.) his infantile self. One is driven by "competing with oneself", the other by envy of internal parents. They can both end in "death", but the motivation—the danger—and so the meaning, is different.

Again, the child exploring his own identity by playing and quarrelling with his friends "gets a feeling of his own qualities and learns that they are to be found in his friends and in himself" (Book Two, p. 133). Some relationships are exploratory; others pander to that part of the child which would prefer never to grow up. Only individual thinking will alert us to the distinction. A child may choose a particular friend "to express antisocial tendencies that he himself has harboured secretly" (Book Two, p. 137). Or, an initial diagnosis may need to be reversed on closer inspection, as in the case of Sam, where the antidevelopmental tendency lodged not in the evident sibling rivalry, but in a more hidden collusion with his eldest brother and apparent protector (Book Two, pp. 106–107). The distinction between the kind of acting-out that is an attempt to evade inner emotional conflicts and the kind of playing that expresses and so helps to resolve them, is illustrated by the example of Mark, who emerged from his prolonged infantile state by "playing out the rivalry he had with his sisters in a wider field [of sport] . . . where the same rules apply to all" (Book One, p. 18). He needed the kind of status earned in an area where all are treated equally to develop his sense of values and identity.

For the ethos of a "couple family" (states the model) requires "the growth of all members" (Meltzer & Harris, 1994, p. 427; below p. 257); where there are scapegoats there can be no sense of security, and the family slips into shades of gang mentality.[27] Martha Harris cites the old dictum of "to each according to his needs, from each according to his abilities" (Book Two, p. 115), while reminding us that "an appropriate share may not mean an exactly similar shape" (Book One, p. 27). A fair share is not something externally visible, but something that can be known only through self-scrutiny, once one is alerted to the distinction between share and shape. In the same way, it is "not generally considered clever to cheat" where the teacher is fair-minded. "If we play fair with them [children], and with other people, we strengthen that side of them which recognizes and upholds justice and fair shares for all" (Book One, p. 47). As in other matters, the child will sense what is genuinely a fair share (of attention) and this will help to establish the "couple" aegis in terms of internal parents. Because the school has a semi-parental ethos, playing for the school (as in sport or music) or simply feeling part of the school has, for the young teenager, the sense of carrying responsibility for the family name, and is a means of earning self-respect.[28]

The sports field is just one of the areas that can act as a "theatre of fantasy" (the term used in the Model) for the contradictory emotions of the adolescent, who needs "war games" to develop. In the drama of the "internal wars", parents, like other figures, are not solely, or always, themselves in the eyes of the child, but move in and out of their transference role. "We can act as a sort of listening post where they can hear themselves speak" (Book Two, p. 134): hence, the attention paid to encouraging family discussion, where different aspects of the child can voice themselves experimentally, testing the boundaries of the self and its contrary inner voices. "Playing with ideas", writes Martha Harris, is "as important to [the adolescent child] as free imaginative play is to the three- to six- or seven-year-old" (Book Two, p. 100); and parents are required to stand in for facets of the child's self:

> For many of his arguments and rebellions against his parents are really arguments against himself and, although he and you may not know it, he is often really asking for his saner and more reasonable self to be supported. He is looking to you for arguments that can be used against the voices that tempt him to despise and turn away from his parents and from consideration for others. [Book Two, p. 114]

There are many forums for playing with ideas—home, school, formal lessons, and "gossip". The parental role-playing is not merely a case of being used by the child, nor of providing technical expertise in argument that may help them to stand their ground in the world; it is an exercise in reality testing, demanding the evidence for their views. It will not be effective unless there is a genuine possibility (however small) of modifying our own opinions, thus demonstrating that we have been "stimulated to take a fresh look at our reasons" (Book One, p. 35). It is associated with the more sophisticated concept of "speaking well"—not to convince others, but to know oneself and the grounds for one's own opinions, the opposite of arrogance.[29] For the adolescent is not only a tangle of feelings, but also a "rational being", and the parental role is to provide "a space where reason can operate", founded on this theatre of fantasy (Book Three, p. 166). That space is defined by the parent–child interaction.

The vitality of the inner theatre of fantasy is essential to the process of being drawn out into the wider world, the world of work and working relationships that will put to the proof the child's "realism".[30] In the later years of school, many academic subjects can take on an emotional charge, in the same way as relationships to teachers have always done. Subjects involving time and history, for example, may trigger in a stormy way the teenager's new sense of being "part of a much larger world, a world which has a history, which is much nearer and more real to them as they become more aware of having a personal history" (Book Two, p. 83). By his later teens he will have acquired "that signal possession of adulthood— a past"; he is then liable to "blame us for the world we have made for him" (Book Three, pp. 163–165). When this is happens, the teenager will require an expansion in the capacity of his internal objects in order to contain the sense of urgency springing from the clash between idealism and reality. Reality has expectations of him, ideality does not. Hence, the "panic about wasted time" that often underlies later teenage impatience and may result in breakdown or in foolhardy actions (Book Three, p. 230).

Parents who are trying realistically to evaluate their own lives in the world can help to protect their teenager not so much in practi-cal ways (which become increasingly limited as they get older) but from the overwhelming impact of their own feelings of guilt and destructiveness. Older teenagers who sense their parents have constricted their own lives—supposedly on their behalf—may develop "a grudge towards inward parents, leading in turn to an inner expectation of being deprived of fulfilment themselves" (Book Three, p. 231).[31] The guilt requires not denial (expurgation), but modulation; however, we cannot hope to modulate their pain unless we have sufficient internal reserves to rely on to modulate our own pain and uncertainties. We have a duty to our adolescent children to enjoy the work–play of our own lives, so that they can climb the cliff of their adulthood, no longer reliant on their actual parents but following that more abstract pursuit of regaining their gods within—"the privacy that, in the end, can exist only in the mind" (Book Two, p. 98). They can become educated in the self-knowledge that makes all other forms of knowledge meaningful.

Notes

1. Parental figures include at times teachers, relations, or friends of the family, etc. They are those with whom the child may form a "trans-ference relationship" that can strengthen their internal parenting. The concept of "parents" thus covers single-parent families and stepfami-

lies. The idea of the parental couple, or of parents and teachers, "pulling together" relates to the establishment of an ethical system internally within the child's mind. Ultimately, it is the internal family, with its male and female components, that must guide the adolescent in his future life. At the same time, relationships with guiding figures that are less emotionally charged have another type of usefulness; e.g., family friends may be able to offer advice that would be rejected if it came from the actual parents, whose function then becomes one of "taking the heat off the advice". (Book Three, p. 166).

2. Martha Harris changed the title of her book on infants from *Understanding Infants and Young Children* to *Thinking about Infants and Young Children*, in order to make a connection with the work of W. R. Bion, where "thinking" is a term of precise psychological significance, rather than being synonymous with such terms as "suppose", "belief", "assume", "wish", etc., as it frequently is in everyday usage.

3. This paper is based also on work carried out in schools in collaboration with Roland Harris. It was written in 1976 at the request of Beresford and Ruth Hayward for the Organization of Economic and Cultural Development of the United Nations, and published in English for the first time in Meltzer's collected papers (*Sincerity and Other Works: Collected Papers of Donald Meltzer*, ed. A, Hahn [Karnac, 1994]), though it had been published earlier in Italian, French, and Spanish. The paper, like these Teenager books, is essentially psychoanalytical rather than sociological in its approach, while dealing with the growth of the individual in society and with the evolution of ethics. The "six forms of learning" are described on pp. 393–394 (see Appendix II of this book, pp. 253–254).

4. Martha Harris, "The Tavistock training and philosophy". In: M. Harris Williams (Ed.), *Collected Papers of Martha Harris and Esther Bick* (p. 277), Clunie Press, 1987.

5. In the "Dolls House" type family, according to the Model, "dislocation may occur if, as the children grow older, their educational and social skills begin to exceed those of the parents" (Meltzer & Harris, 1994, p. 442). The same possibility is discussed in the Teenager books under the heading "When a child does better than his parents", (Book Three, p. 156). This kind of dislocation, which means the family is insufficiently flexible to accommodate new ideas, is to be distinguished from the egocentric "idealism" (standard in adolescence) that fails to adapt to "reality" (see, for example, Jane, Book One, p. 37; Julia, Book Three, pp. 194–197; Richard, Book Three, p. 199–201; Matthew, Book Three,

p. 215, etc.). Such a distinction—in family life—has its parallel in social life, in terms of "the problem of distinguishing the revolutionary expression of a new idea from the rebellion of the disgruntled who cannot master the old idea" (Meltzer & Harris, 1994, p. 453; below, p. 265).

6. The "adult" mental structure is defined by its "aspirational" identification with teachers and mentors; "identification with the combined object being a precondition for creative mental functioning" (Meltzer & Harris, 1994, p. 398).

7. Bion's term for our unthinking obedience to given creeds, or "myths", as they are called in the model (Meltzer & Harris, 1994, p. 403).

8. Referring, of course, to psychological harm, rather than physical harm, which is quantity-related.

9. An example of the book's teaching method of packing its punches slantwise, in brackets or subordinate clauses.

10. See *Hamlet* I, iii: 84. Hamlet is the archetypal adolescent, and there are many implied references to the play in these books.

11. The Model states:

> One task of the analyst is to find his way into the world inhabited by his patient, but this is just as true of parent or teacher. A person or part of the personality trapped inside an object can usually be helped and enticed out . . . given at least one person interested enough to seek him out in his claustrum. [Meltzer & Harris, 1994, p. 408]

12. "For that matter, there has always been plenty of unhealthy and sadistic material in children's . . . entertainment" (Book One, p. 22).

13. Of course, this book was written before our current conceptions of social correctness regarding corporal punishment. But in terms of the principles involved, we should note that reward and punishment ("whether corporal or otherwise", as Harris states) are described not as wrong but as "not useful" (Book One, p. 35). The Model points out that any educational system will, to some extent, be, and will certainly be *experienced* as, "bestowing and withholding" and thereby rewarding and punishing (Meltzer & Harris, 1994, p. 453; below, p. 265). In so far as the family is an "educational institution" it falls into this category; but not in so far as it develops reliance on internal parental objects for the benefit of *all* the mind's children.

14. Another example of the author's "slantwise" penetration.

15. This does not mean that manners should not, additionally, be straight-

forwardly taught—simply that if they are only a carapace, it is not ultimately enough: "There is a sort of mirror in society, wherein 'please' and 'thank you' reflect 'thank you' and 'please'" (Book Two, p. 120).

16. As in the case of Christopher, whose mother's sympathy took the form of "identifying with him some inadequate side of herself that she did not know how to help along" (Book One, p. 68).

17. The confusing influence of parents' or teachers' own hidden infantile sexual anxieties is frequently discussed; for example, in Book One, p. 50; Book Two, p. 125.

18. Martha Harris writes that the "educational system" is responsible for many teenagers having a "poor opinion of themselves" by the time they leave school (Book Three, p. 162). This is the result of a quantitative definition of success: a failure to harness natural competitive energies into the service of "competing with oneself".

19. See, for example, Book One, p. 31; Book Three, pp. 162–163, 179.

20. In order to define an object of hostility, without taking responsibility for exclusion, the group merely "alters the definition of member" (Meltzer & Harris, 1994, p. 416).

21. See, for example, Book One, p. 43; Book Three, pp. 195–199.

22. "Catastrophic change" being Bion's term for both major and minor growth points in the developing personality. The model summarizes: "The view taken here is that 'learning from experience' occurs where a new idea is assimilated by the internal combined object, which then helps the self to master it and the emotional upheaval that attends its advent" (Meltzer & Harris, 1994, p. 398).

23. A reference to Shakespeare's *Venus and Adonis* ("The snail . . . Shrinks back into his shelly cave with pain") and Keats's comment on it: "He has left nothing to say about nothing or anything . . . you know what he says about snails" (letter to Reynolds, 22 November 1817).

24. As in my interpretation "The undiscovered country: the shape of the aesthetic conflict in *Hamlet*", in Donald Meltzer and Meg Harris Williams, *The Apprehension of Beauty*, Clunie Press, 1988, pp. 84–133.

25. The model mentions only the "masculine infantile" aspect of machines as an extension of the body (Meltzer & Harris, 1994, p. 443); Harris here suggests another possibility that would need to be differentiated in the individual case.

26. As in the case of Rosalind (Book Three, p. 187).

27. This applies, of course, not necessarily to literal "couples" but to the dominant ethical aegis of the family. The "benevolent community of the combined object", on the other hand, maintains its attitude of

benevolence only by excluding bad or destructive members "as if they were in fact members of some paranoid community who had wandered or slipped across its borders" (Meltzer & Harris, 1994, p. 416). The Model then distinguishes between this "mythic area" of cosy basic assumptions, and the "work-group" area that regards itself as comprised of a collection of distinct individuals.

28. See the Model's distinction between "status" and "self-respect" that exists in relation to the "family name" of the couple-family (Meltzer & Harris, 1994, p. 427: below, p. 258). Loss of self-respect results in loss of respect for the school (Book Three, p. 153).

29. What Milton called being "competently wise in one's Mother Dialect", as distinct from being either tongue-tied or a Babel-tongued linguist (*Of Education*, 1644). In the same context, it is interesting to remember the description by Donald Meltzer of Martha Harris's own way of speaking: "She had a particular way of talking that often seemed at first a stutter but was in fact a complicated process of accommodation between the complexity of her thought and the minute responses of her audience" (Harris & Bick, 1987, p. vii).

30. As in the "honest basis" for life that became promising in the case of Elizabeth (Book Three, p. 217).

31. See also Book Three, pp. 210, 229.

Extracts from *A Psychoanalytic Model of the Child-in-the-Family-in-the-Community*[1]

Donald Meltzer and Martha Harris

The six forms of learning[2]

Six categories of learning are distinguished, each with a partic-ular mental state underlying them and with particular conse-quences for personality development.

Learning from experience, as described by Bion (Heinemann, 1965), involves participation in an emotional experience in such a way that a modification of the personality takes place. The person "becomes" something that he was not before, say a "walker" in the case of a small child, or a "doctor" in the case of an adult. Internal qualification of this sort may be contrasted with the varieties of external qualification bestowed by social structures.

In contrast, *learning by projective identification* involves an omnipotent phantasy of entry into, and taking over, the mental qualities and capabilities of another person. Because the conception of the other person is limited, and since the projection imbues him with qualities of the subject, the result is something of a caricature. Where the projective identification is with an internal object, quali-ties of omniscience and judgemental attitudes predominate.

On the other hand, in *learning by adhesive identification*, which involves a deeply unconscious phantasy of sticking on to the surface of the object, the resulting identification picks out only the social appearance and thus takes on the attributes of a somewhat mindless imitation of appearance and behaviour. It is characterized by instability, tending to collapse easily under stress, and fickleness, easily shifting to new objects of immediate interest or attachment.

Learning by scavenging typifies the envious part of the personality that cannot ask for help or accept it with gratitude. It tends to view all skill and knowledge as essentially secret and magical in its control of nature and people. It watches and listens for items "thrown away", as it were, where no "please" or "thank you" need enter in, and therefore tends to feel triumphant over the stupidity of others for giving away the formula.

Delusional learning is of an entirely different order, believing that whatever is revealed in nature or by man is essentially worthless and that only the hidden, and therefore occult, is of value. It sees evidence in the nuances while neglecting the apparent, and constructs a world that is essentially anti-nature.

All five of these forms of learning are essentially autonomous in their inception and express either the thirst for knowledge and understanding, or its converse, intrusive curiosity. By contrast, *learning about the world* has its source in the motives of the teacher. Its methods are essentially those of animal training, stick-and-carrot, dependent for their success on co-opting greed, timidity, docility, or competitiveness of the subject. Its achievements effect no deep modification of the person, but rather decorate his social persona for purposes of adaptation to the demands of the environment and have little connection with ultimate goals or ethical principles.

Of these six forms of learning only the first, learning from experience, requires a shift in values in keeping with the move from the paranoid–schizoid to the depressive position. It is heavily dependent on the assistance and guidance of benevolent objects (either internal or external) with whom it can share the burden of the anxiety (confusional or persecutory), attending the impact of a new idea. The advent of the depressive feeling resulting from the changed view of self and world inherent in such learning is accompanied by feelings of gratitude and privileged indebtedness to the mentor.

The epistemological dilemma of the individual[3]

In keeping with the general point of view of psychoanalysis, with its emphasis on the primary position of psychic reality for the generating of meaning and the overriding importance of intentionality in generating value, a concept of knowledge would need to be divided into two great categories: knowledge directed towards understanding the world, and knowledge directed towards controlling the world. It would be amiss to equate these with art and science for we would then have to talk about the art of science and the science of art. Nor can we distinguish them as contemplative and active, for action follows from the one as surely as planning characterizes the other. We will adhere to a motivational definition, recognizing that this is only observable to the person himself, never directly to another.

The second stone in our philosophical foundation is the idea that all knowledge must derive from thinking, and cannot be given, as, for instance, items of a dream may be given, without being represented in the dream content. Further, thinking can only operate upon observations of fact, be they facts of the external or internal world.

As the facts of the external world are knowable only by their secondary qualities as they impinge upon our senses in the context of an emotional experience, the ability to think about these facts of an emotional experience requires that the emotionality, especially the pain, be contained. This pain is essentially the "cloud of unknowing", the "negative capability", related to uncertainty.

We will take the position that few people are thinkers but that many are learners capable of teaching. Our theory of knowledge is therefore a trickle-down theory starting with the rare genius or prophet. But as there are good geniuses there are also evil ones, the inventors of the great lies and the technologists of misrepresentation (*Dulce et decorum est pro patria mori*, for instance, as promulgated by a Hitler).

We have therefore ranged the epistemological dimension alongside the economic one to emphasize the parallelism between introjection, depressive position and learning from experience (truth) as against projection, paranoid–schizoid position and propaganda (lies).

The other forms of learning and training we have mentioned may take place outside the emotional context of an intimate relationship and therefore outside the dominance of the paranoid–schizoid and depressive positions, essentially hedonistic or conditioned.

But the influence of Ps–D may be felt as a subsidiary force,[4] as with children at school who do not form a transference relation to their teachers, yet their performance at school may be heavily influenced by their relationship to parents at home as well as to their internal objects. For this to be so, they must carry some identification with the family, internal or external, with them into the community to function as representatives of the family group. One might think this was always the case, but the study of children so often indicates a gross disparity between their states of mind in and out of the home, and in fact experience in schools and child guidance clinics seems to reveal how often the child in the community is a stranger to the parents.

The family organization[5]

At any given moment an individual family member may have any of the following functions: generating love, promulgating hate, promoting hope, sowing despair, containing depressive pain, emanating persecutory anxiety, creating confusion, thinking. The following descriptions of six types of family organization pertain to a dynamic model in which the functions of individual members may be in flux, and the family as a whole may be generally, or just momentarily, in this particular state of organization.

The couple family

At the moment when the family is presided over by a couple (not necessarily the actual parents) this combination will be seen to carry between them the functions of generating love, promoting hope, containing depressive pain, and thinking. The other members will be dependent upon them for these functions and thus for the modulation of their mental pain to a level consonant with growth. This will place them in conflict with any member promulgating hate, sowing despair, emanating persecution or creating confusion; in the interest of protecting the members who are dependent upon them for their modulating functions.

The capacity of the couple to perform these functions will be felt to require their periodic withdrawal into privacy, supposed to be sexual and mysterious. The times when they are obliged to be apart produces a hovering Sword of Damocles atmosphere while their conjunction arouses a constant expectation of the new baby members of the family. The history of their courtship is of mythological interest to the dependent members, giving form to their hopes for the future.

The four introjective functions of the couple—generating love, promoting hope, containing pain and thinking—are not felt to subdivide into masculine and feminine aspects but rather to be arranged in a more linear way, with the maternal person taking the brunt of the children's projections and the father being the end of the line for these mental waste products (Harry Truman's "the buck stops here").

All the catastrophic anxiety of the dependent members tends to centre on the mother, regardless of the intensity of love that may be felt for the father and the depressive anxieties that may accompany it. Therefore any evidence of debility in the mother tends to be blamed on the father's possible or suspected inadequacies. On the other hand debility in the father is taken as evidence that the system is being overloaded with hate and projected persecution, and encourages polarization among the dependent members with scape-goating tendency.

The growth of all members of the family, as evidenced by carefully monitored and frequently discussed indicators of physical, social, intellectual and emotional development, is necessary to maintain the sense of security, which is intrinsic to the family and is felt to be utterly independent of the community, despite the overall optimistic and benevolent view taken of the natural and social milieu. Thus the family is felt to be mobile potentially, even though it may be tenderly attached to the home or landscape or community of friends and neighbours. If opportunity glows on the horizon, a pioneer atmosphere begins to scintillate, akin in feeling to the times when the mother is pregnant.

The overall relation to the community is felt to proceed through the individual members moving about: at school or at work or shopping, etc., as representatives of the family. Their individual identities (Christian name) are secondary in significance to their family identity (surname), not as an indicator of status but as a burden of responsibility. It is not so much a matter of, "what will the neighbours think?" as of "letting the side down", in the matter of contributing to the general ethos of the community.

The great vulnerability of the couple family resides in the unique identity of each individual, for the death of a child seems to be the one unbearable stress (Wordsworth's "We are seven"). Even a miscarriage or a stillbirth can have a shattering effect upon the joyousness and commence a deterioration in ethos, relationships, cohesiveness, from which recovery may seem impossible. It has a more devastating effect than, say, the impact of a defective child, the development of a schizophrenic illness in a child, or the delinquency or defection of a member.

The matriarchal family

Where the mothering person (generally a woman but not necessarily) seems to arrogate to herself all the introjective functions, the difficulty may lie in the inadequacy, absence or debility of the fathering one, or it may reflect the force and vitality of the woman. Where this force has a hostile anti-masculine flavour the matriarchal shades into the girl-gang family or delinquent type. But in some cases the mothering person combines in herself such bisexual attributes of character and outlook, skills and strength, that the matriarchy shades into the Couple family in its ethos.

In the aspects of the community where the matriarchal family is traditional (the Jamaican immigrant population, for instance), the paternal function is fulfilled in a split way, by a combination of avuncular and grandfatherly figures. Where the father is absent through death or from necessity for some period, his presence as an absent object may fulfil the necessary function in spirit, while the actual psychological services are distributed among intrinsic or extrinsic male figures.

But often the community is looked to for this function and these services. This is particularly true of the matriarchal family which has been constructed around the strength and anti-masculine aspects of the mothering person.

It is this configuration in particular which most easily slips into the Basic Assumption dependent relation to the community, not in a hostile parasitic way but taking for granted the benevolence and generosity of the community, particularly of male figures in authority. Bank managers, social workers, ministers, doctors and solicitors are naturally looked to for services and are preferably brought into some degree of avuncular intimacy with the family group. The education of the children and their health supplies the motivation and justification for any degree of financial, moral or intellectual support, and since the mothering person often, in her vitality and optimism, makes an attractive figure, this support is readily proffered. The possibility of sexual entanglements is never far off but is generally denied unless marriage seems feasible, even if unlikely.

The atmosphere in the home tends to rest upon discipline through guilt, and the standards are different from the growth-indicator one of the couple family. In the matriarchal family the standards are more likely to be moralistic, aiming at adaptation to the supposed standards of the community. "What will the neighbours think?" is therefore more important, and in a persecutory way, as if the moral status of the mother were in question for unaccountable reasons. This is most pressing where the mother is divorced or the children are illegitimate.

Unlike the outcome one would expect in the couple family, serious maladjustment of an anti-social, psychotic or defective sort cannot be easily contained by a matriarchal family structure. Children who come into these categories tend more easily to be farmed out to childless relatives, grandparents or placed in care in the community.

It is unusual for the matriarchal figure to be able to carry all four of the introjective functions of generating love, promoting hope, containing depression and thinking. One or more of these tend to be placed out, as it were. For instance, a good baby may be treated as the generator of love; a particularly clever child may be the thinker; a cheerful one as the generator of hope; or an obsessional one the reservoir of depressive feelings. Since these surrogates for parental part-functions are more able to represent, than actually to perform, the function, the basic instability of the situation declares itself whenever these functions are strained. The move into BA dependence or regression to a more narcissistic pseudo-family organization ensues.

The patriarchal family

A very different atmosphere is found where the paternal figure is very dominant, in particular if the mother has become incapacitated for psychological reasons, for example, alcoholic or depressed; or because of diagnosed physical illness, generally presumed to be post-partum in origin.

A soft type of paternalism may resemble the matriarchal family, and again where strong bisexuality in character exists may approximate to the couple family even when the mother is one of the dependent figures. But where the patriarchy is imposed by the father's aggressive and often somewhat grandiose character, and particularly where the mother has defected, a stern discipline rules both boys and girls, often supplemented by father's unmarried sister or ageing mother. A bullying and punitively scathing type of tongue-lashing may follow upon the actual beating of younger children and the relics of religiosity are brought in to shore up the authority of the father.

A feudal system arises with economic control at its centre, from which the adolescents are quick to escape, being "ungrateful" to their father. But girls may be held in masochistic quasi-sexual submission well into their twenties; partly to protect younger children from the father's harshness, and partly for unconscious erotic attachment to the father, characteristically followed by equally unsuitable marriages.

The relation of the patriarchal family to the community is one of proud independence and of unacknowledged dependence, for the father is unlikely to notice how much nurturing his children seek and get from neighbours, teachers, club leaders, etc. Denigration of the female is unmistakeable, tenderness is held to be soft or weak, and lying is the worst crime, for it threatens to plunge the family into a paranoid atmosphere. But the goodness of the father in terms of dependability, selflessness and unequivocal devotion to the children may save the atmosphere from dourness.

The father may be able to carry some of the introjective functions, particularly those of promoting hope, of containing depression or of thinking, if he is an educated man. But the more common pattern would seem to be that the generating of love becomes a grandparental function and binds the children very closely to these figures, the maternal ones in particular when the mother has died. The function of thinking may pass at an early age to the most forward child at school when the father is of low educational level.

The containment of delinquent or even of psychotic or defective children is much better than in the matriarchal family, aid being sought from relatives or the community only when the best interest of the child seem to demand it.

The prospect of the father's remarrying, where this is a possibility, is held to be remote on the basis of his presumed "seriousness", implying a desexualized state based on disillusionment. Only if the children are numerous or still very young does the figure of a housekeeper appear, gradually metamorphosing into wife in name, but not really in acknowledged function.

The patriarchal family is far more unstable in certain respects than the matriarchal one because of the ease with which the tyrannical aspect can escalate into gang-formation on the one hand, or the quasi-religious aspect slip into BA dependent organization of a particularly delicately balanced sort. Illness in the father can bring sudden disorganization, at which point the unacknowledged dependence on the benevolence of the community becomes apparent. If the father's wage -earning capacity is thereby threatened, disintegration and dispersal may result, the children going to relatives or into care. Family reorganization after such a breakdown is far more difficult than in the matriarchy because once the authority behind the discipline is broken it is difficult to reconstitute.

The gang-family

Both matriarchy and patriarchy tend easily to slip into the more narcissistic state of gang-formation when the dominant person's character is delicately balanced between maturity and pseudo-maturity. But the more characteristic configuration arises when either one or both parental figures are strongly impelled by negative identifications. This is to be found in people who have established an early independence from parents whom they considered inadequate, bad or misguided in their methods of child-rearing.

Since policies built upon the foundation of criticism of the grandparents have largely negative implications, positive policies tend to be constructed intellectually rather than on the basis of feeling for the children or understanding and sensitivity to their feelings or anxieties. An underlying determination to be right, to demonstrate their superiority and thereby justify their earlier rebellion promulgates a certain urgency to make the children conform to expectations, whether these be of "goodness", or "independence", or accomplishment.

In this atmosphere the introjective functions tend to be simulated rather than performed, so that the titular roles [mother, baby, etc.] and their dramatization replace the genuine functions. Feelings of love are replaced by seductiveness, cuddling and indulgence. Hopefulness is simulated by manic cheerfulness, thereby denying the quantities of depressive feeling; while thinking is replaced by slogans, cliché, dogma, catechism, often at a shallow level dealing with posture, dress, deportment, cleanliness, accent, the status of friends' families and other forms of snobbery.

Rebellion or failure to meet the requirements tends to bring sharp rejection and recourse to punishment or exclusion. Since the gang-family is matriarchal or patriarchal (Amazonian and Titan might be better terms), it is not inclined to acknowledge its dependence on the community, but adopts a delinquent and scavenging attitude towards the facilities and services that are potentially available.

Its tendency to metamorphose at a moment's notice into a Basic Assumption fight–flight group is forestalled by the excitement of the delinquent system. The evasion of feelings of guilt by projecting all responsibility for exercising ethical judgement places the gang in a field of high tension and attention. Bold and clever exploitation of the loopholes of either the benevolent social services or the potentially punitive legal system places a premium on the capacity to lie.

Since this in turn depends on some considerable recognition of the truth, leadership of the family gang can easily pass from parental hands to those of the clever child who functions as prime minister to the ruling parent. Thus a high premium can be placed on gift-of-the-gab, especially in so far as it includes a facility for misrepresenting the truth, either in terms of historical facts or logical operations.

The aggressive attitude towards the community tends to find its most unassailable position in defence of debilitated members of the family, particularly if this is due to physical illness, accidental injury or mental deficiency. Righteous indignation in defence of the weak against the strong serves as a banner for endless raids on community resources.

The gang-family, by virtue of its ambiguous relation to the community, at once defiant and yet seeking acceptance, greedy and at the same time scornfully proud, imposes a very confusing task on its members *vis-à-vis* the educational facilities available. Its members are forestalled from forming a dependent and trusting relation to teachers and yet are expected to make sufficient progress to substantiate the ethos of the home environment and its avowed principles of child-rearing and social organization. Defiance of authority and scholastic accomplishment are unlikely partners until a firm foundation of learning skills has been established. This can seldom be expected before late adolescence, because of lack of skill early on and lack of discipline later. Consequently low accomplishment or very unbalanced school achievement seems to be the rule.

Where it is possible to rationalize away the responsibility, the situation is then used as a further pretext for raids on the community's facilities for special schooling. The strong tendency to *folie-à-deux* relationships of parents and children predisposes to school refusal and school phobia.

The reversed family.

A hostile caricature of family life may arise when one or both parental figures are either psychotic or are dominated by sexual perversity or criminal tendencies. The reversal of values sets the family group in a defiant relationship to the community and its values, in an isolating way which tends to be obscured by its mobility.

Since its members are seldom skilled, their economy is precarious with a clear tendency to be illegal. The relation to neighbours is therefore clearly predatory and provocative, where it is not frankly collusive with similar families. It tends easily to accrue new members from migratory figures and gravitates towards gainful activities in the entertainment, second-hand goods, criminal, prostitute or corrupt political areas. Gambling, drinking, promiscuity, drug-taking, sexual perversions, incest and assault are part of the atmosphere of family life.

The introjective functions, and therefore thinking and planning, are almost absent. Consequently action tends to be unrestrained, with the result that the mental pain (almost entirely persecutory) tends to circulate in the intra-familial pecking order and eventually to be evacuated into the community by predatory actions.

The tyrannical order strongly promotes projective forms of identification with the stronger figures, although the measure of strength is not always physical. It may reside in intelligence operating to promote confusion, aggravate rivalries, promulgate distrust or foster irrational persecutory anxieties. In consequence the titular roles in the family tend to be a travesty while the functions migrate in a haphazard way. The tendency to chaos plays an important role in the reversed family's strong tendency to move into Basic Assumption pairing, especially if the community reacts against its predatory or defiant attitude or actions. It can quickly tighten, become a kind of guerrilla band and take to the road. This, added to its general peregrinating tendency, adds to the likelihood of the children being maladjusted at school and unintegrated into any community or organization of neighbourhood children.

Such a description may seem to suggest a class implication, and in a sociological sense this may be true, but ethnically it is not. The characteristics of speech, mannerism, attitudes, interests and habits; the educational level of the parents; existence of private wealth and property; all these are extremely variable and might place such families in any class from decayed aristocracy to non-traditional gypsy.

We think it correct to say that bizarre beliefs, superstitions and delusions, along with the tendency to sexual perversity, arson and semi-accidental suicide are always close at hand. The flirtation with satanic religious sects and practices may be constant and can suddenly gel into a Basic Assumption with religious pretensions, caricaturing hopefulness that relieves the atmosphere of general despair hidden behind paranoid anger.

The educational function of the family[6]

Although this is intended to be a model and not a theory, it has a theoretical background—one which is intended to be descriptive rather than explanatory, based on experiences of living in general, and of the psychoanalytical consulting room in particular. While it makes room, as it were, for all possible philosophies, it can not hide the value system and view-of-the-world that it favours, if only by virtue of the twelve-o'clock position of this cross section.

But of course life is not simply occupied solely with the climb towards perfection—mystical union with the god-head, or experience of the pure Platonic forms. Education cannot concern itself only with the character but must also transmit skills, information, social habits, attitudes, values. It cannot content itself with facilitating the acquisition of internal qualifications: it must also bestow, or withhold, external ones.

No system of education can avoid entirely being, as well as being experienced as, tyrannical. By bestowing and with-holding it must seem to reward and punish, to create an elite and disinherited classes, to perpetuate whatever degree of exploitation already exists. Above all, the accumulation and institutionalization of knowledge creates a conservative bulwark which resists, if not from hostility, then from sheer inertia, any really new idea.

Since new ideas are easily confused with experimental actions, the latter may thrive as a stimulation of radical movement. An area for fraudulence and corruption then increases when the official system's rigidity has created a considerable class of refuses. Thus the problem of distinguishing the revolutionary expression of a new idea from the rebellion of the disgruntled who cannot master the old idea, is all a part of the educational system, which like any organism, must either grow or wither.

To employ this model with regard to the special problem of the educational functions of the family is, we suggest, to use it to view the family as an educational institution.

The model embraces seven [six] types of learning, six types of families, six plus one (the schizophrenic) states of mind in the individual, the three types of the Basic Assumption groups where learning is replaced by action, and six types of orientation which the community may seem to manifest towards families and their members. It represents the six dimensions of mental functioning from which these different levels of interaction and structure are fashioned, all in dynamic flux.

The benevolent community of the combined object[7]

We will take it that every community organizes itself around a myth of itself which in one form or another expresses the idea that a happy combination of a mother and father are presiding benevolently over the welfare of its children: king and queen; executive and legislature; capitalist and entrepreneur; the party and the politburo; owner and manager; church and Pope, etc.

While it is a caricature and in a sense a travesty of the family, for the emotionality is sentimental when not frankly hypocritical, the community under this myth is certainly able to behave in a parental fashion with regard to such descriptive qualities as generosity, forgiveness, tolerance, patience, wisdom, justice.

But it is all *as if* and therefore has very little perseverance under stress or disappointment. The myth of benevolence fades and the community shifts its attitude and behaviour. This shift does not require any change in the contract but merely a change in the interpretation of the contract. And this need not, perhaps, must not be acknowledged.

Certainly the community must not acknowledge that any of its members reside outside the sphere of its benevolence. But this is easily done by altering the definition of member (for instance "Jew"="vermin"), implemented by liquidation, exile, sequestration, ghetto formation or denial of existence (the tramp, for instance).

The benevolent community treats the destructive and schizophrenic aspects of the personality of its members as if they were in fact members of some paranoid community who had wandered or slipped across its borders. The obstinate obtrusiveness of such a part of a member's personality can have a paralysing and schismatic effect: (see for instance Melville's wonderful story "Bartleby" or the impact of James Wait in Conrad's *Nigger of the Narcissus*), or may seize the leadership and alter the community itself into a paranoid one (see Bion's *Experiences in Groups*).

In keeping with its central historical myth, the benevolent community behaves as if it were the fountain-head of all order and creativity, the powers for which it delegates down the line to its subsidiary levels of organization and ultimately to the individuals it has invested as its surrogates. Whether it is the humblest worker or the most celebrated artist or scientist, the community presumes to take the credit for any accomplishment of value; enabling all members to participate in the central myth that progress is always being made although everything is already perfect, if only the ungrateful and naughty children would behave themselves (see Bion's myth of the scientists and the liars in *Attention and Interpretation*).

We wish to stress that we are discussing the mythic organization of the community corresponding to the principles of Basic Assumption Group formation, which we will discuss at greater length in the next section.

Outside this mythic area, which embraces generally the political organization of the community, there exists of course an entirely different area: the housekeeping, work-group area, in which individuals do their assigned and accepted tasks with their learned skills as individuals *vis-à-vis* other individuals, as adult to adult, taking their own decisions, carrying their own responsibilities, making their own mistakes. But the two co-exist. You get oil or vinegar depending on which cork you pull, the individual or group psychology cork.

Notes

1. This paper was first published in English in Donald Meltzer's collected papers (*Sincerity and Other Works: Collected Papers of Donald Meltzer*, ed. A, Hahn, Karnac, 1994, pp. 387–454)

2. Extract from the Introduction (pp. 393–394), delineating the "epistemological dimension" of the six dimensions of this branch of metapsychology—"the structural, dynamic, economic, genetic, geographic, and epistemologic" (p. 388).

3. This extract is taken from "the epistemological dimension" of the model (pp. 411–413). Its philosophical position is described as "implicit in all that has gone before": the "structural dimension" (the relation of innate qualities to life-experience, internal object organization, both adult and infantile, and family and community organization); the "genetic dimension" (relation to time and change); the "dynamic dimension" (ways of modulating or defending against mental pain); the "geographic dimension" (the different "worlds" inhabited by the self), and the "economic dimension" (repetitive training, pleasure-principle training; containment of psychic pain in the oscillation between paranoid–schizoid and depressive mental positions.

4. Ps–D is Bion's shorthand for the oscillation between the two mental value-systems or "positions" of paranoid–schizoid and depressive. "The persecutory pains of the one (persecution, dread, terror, paranoid fear, confusion, etc.) overlap the pains of the other (sympathy, remorse, regret, loneliness, grief etc.)" (p. 410).

5. This section is described as "the heart of the model" and is given here complete (pp. 424–434).

6. These paragraphs are taken from the final section of the paper, "The specific use of the model with regard to the educational functions of the family" (pp. 452–453).

7. This extract is taken from the section on "The community" (pp. 415–417). The other classes of community are: the supportive maternal and paternal communities; the parasitic maternal and paternal communities; the paranoid community. The types of community correspond in psychological orientation to the types of family (couple, matriarchal–patriarchal, gang and reversed). They all bear a grid-like parallel to the different states of mind of the individual (adult, bisexual infantile, masculine–feminine infantile, boy- or girl-gang and perverse), and all states are considered to be in flux, but there is a significant difference between the "adult" or highest state of mind and the highest or "benevolent" community, where the myth of a presiding "couple" is a kind of pretence or basic assumption.

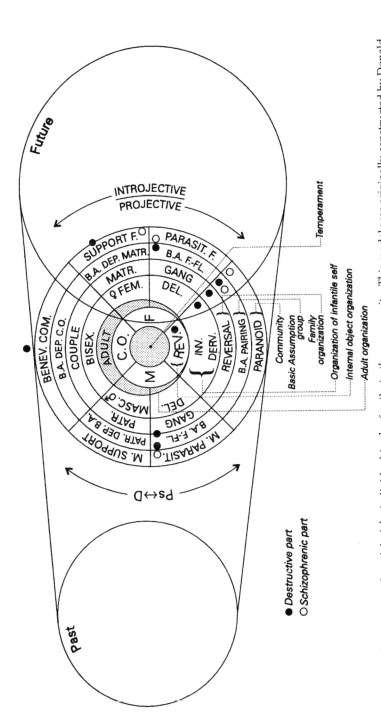

Figure 1. Cross-sectional model of the individual-in-the-family-in-the-community. This model was originally constructed by Donald Meltzer in three dimensions with cardboard intervolving wheels.

Mattie as educator

by Donald Meltzer[1]

B y both background and inclination, Mattie was a scholar of English literature and a teacher. Nothing was more foreign to her nature than the administrative requirements that eventually devolved upon her at the Tavistock. If ever anyone had "greatness thrust upon them", it was the reluctant Mattie at the time when Mrs Bick left the Clinic and it was either up to Mattie to take over or let the infant Child Psychotherapy Course fade away.

The way in which she came to terms with this crisis in her life—and here Roland's encouragement and help was essential—was by framing a radical pedagogical method. Many of the central ideas came from Roland, who was at that time deputy headmaster of a large comprehensive school in London, prior to his going to the Ministry of Education and later to Brunel University. The central conviction, later hallowed in Bion's concepts of "learning from experience", was that the kind of learning which transformed a person into a professional worker had to be rooted in the intimate relations with inspired teachers, living and dead, present and in books. Roland himself, as poet and scholar, was an inspired teacher and the many textbooks he wrote concentrated on the development in the student of the capacity to read in both a comprehensive and a penetrating way.

The second central thesis was that learning takes place in a group context and that the management of the atmosphere was an essential task of the teachers. The prevention of elitism, the avoidance of competitiveness, and the replacement of selection by self-selection through hard work-tasks were the essential components of this task. But Mattie's experience as a teacher, during the war years and after, before she trained as a child psychotherapist and psychoanalyst, had taught her the importance of meeting the formal requirements of the Establishment if there was to be founded a profession of Child Psychotherapy with positions in clinics and schools for the graduates of the Course. Here again Roland's extensive administrative knowledge was an invaluable aid to Mattie, who was not naturally given to orderliness, let alone to giving orders. Eventually she became an impressive negotiator and even, some claimed, a politician in the interests of the Course and of the Association that was later formed in conjunction with the Hampstead Clinic and the Margaret Lowenfelt group.

Here again Bion's teaching about groups, and later about the structure of the personality, with its endoskeletal structure and its social exoskeletal carapace, played a central role in her thinking. In keeping with the differentiation between Christ and Caesar, Mattie worked out her method for meeting the requirements of the Establishment without sacrificing the ethos of the learning work-group. But it cost her a lot, which only the support of Roland made it possible for her to sustain. When he died suddenly in 1969 of a ruptured cerebral aneurism, she developed an acute aplastic anaemia from the potentially fatal consequences of which she was saved by timely diagnosis, medication with cortisone, and a dream in which Roland told her she still had work to do for the family and the Course.

Note

1. This was first published in *Quaderni di psicoterapia infantile* no. 18 (Borla, 1988), pp. 10–11. Donald Meltzer married Martha Harris after the death of her husband Roland and together they travelled abroad extensively, teaching child psychotherapists.